Bayou

volume two

FIc
T
Love

Jeremy Love & Patrick Morgan

Ron Perazza *Editorial Director – Zuda Comics* **Kwanza Johnson** *Editor*
Nika Vagner *Assistant Editor* **Jessica Numsuwankijkul** *Assistant Editor, Book Edition*

DC COMICS
Diane Nelson *President* **Dan DiDio** and **Jim Lee** *Co-Publishers* **Geoff Johns** *Chief Creative Officer*
Patrick Caldon *EVP – Finance and Administration* **John Rood** *EVP – Sales, Marketing and Business Development*
Amy Genkins *SVP – Business and Legal Affairs* **Steve Rotterdam** *SVP – Sales and Marketing*
John Cunningham *VP – Marketing* **Terri Cunningham** *VP – Managing Editor* **Alison Gill** *VP – Manufacturing*
David Hyde *VP – Publicity* **Sue Pohja** *VP – Book Trade Sales* **Alysse Soll** *VP – Advertising and Custom Publishing*
Bob Wayne *VP – Sales* **Mark Chiarello** *Art Director*

Cover by Jeremy Love

BAYOU

BAYOU 2 Published by DC Comics. Cover and compilation copyright © 2010 DC Comics. All rights reserved. Originally published online at ZUDACOMICS.COM.
Bayou © Gettosake. All rights reserved. All characters, their distinctive likenesses and related elements featured in this publication are trademarks of Gettosake.
Zuda Comics and the Zuda logo are trademarks of DC Comics. The stories, characters and incidents featured in this publication are entirely fictional.

DC Comics, 1700 Broadway, New York, NY 10019 - A Warner Bros. Entertainment Company. Printed by RR Donnelley, Willard, OH, 12/8/10. First Printing.
ISBN: 978-1-4012-2584-1

SUSTAINABLE
FORESTRY
INITIATIVE

Certified Fiber Sourcing
www.sfiprogram.org

Fiber used in this product line meets the
sourcing requirements of the SFI program.
www.sfiprogram.org SGS-SFI/COC-US10/81072

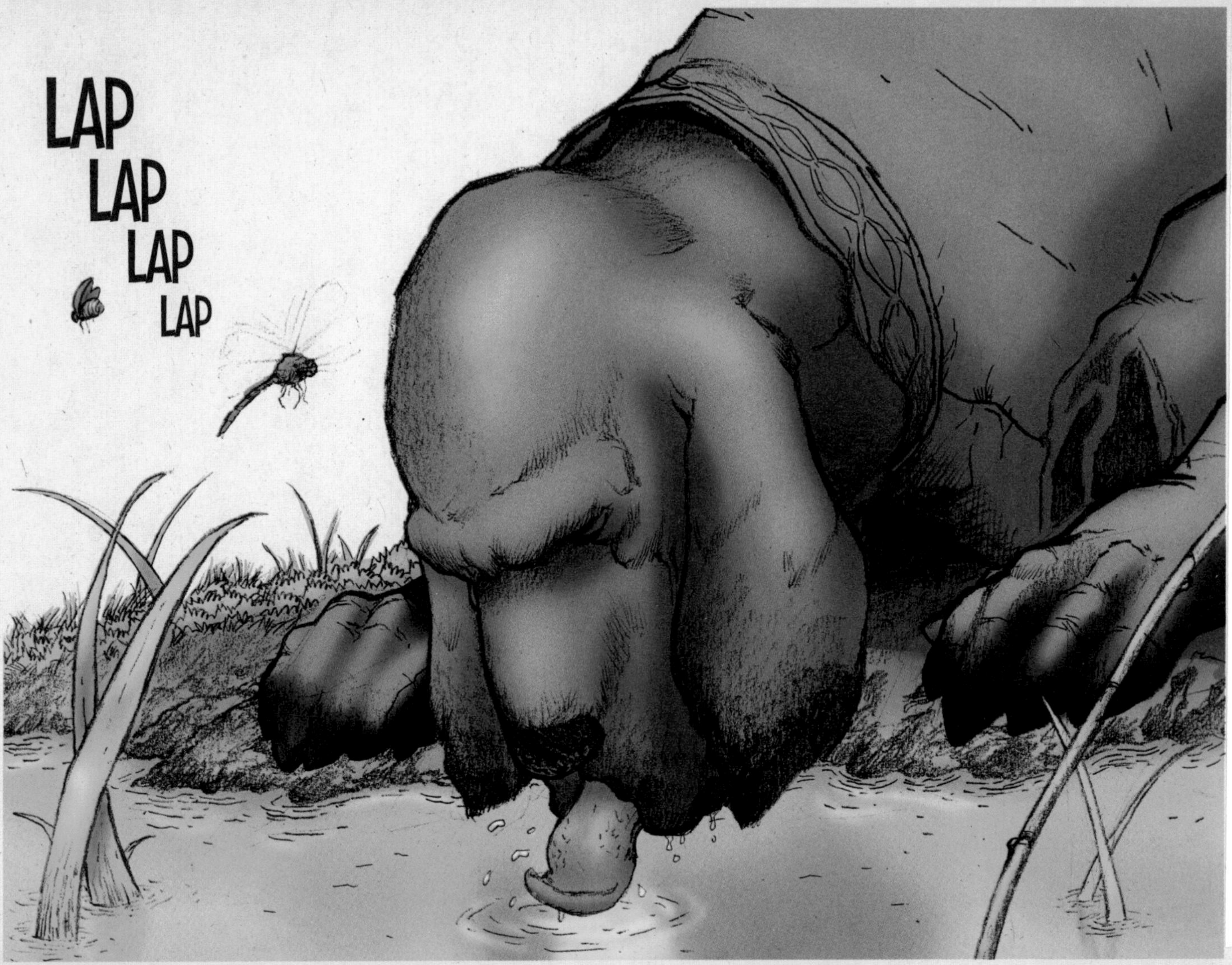
LAP
LAP
LAP
LAP

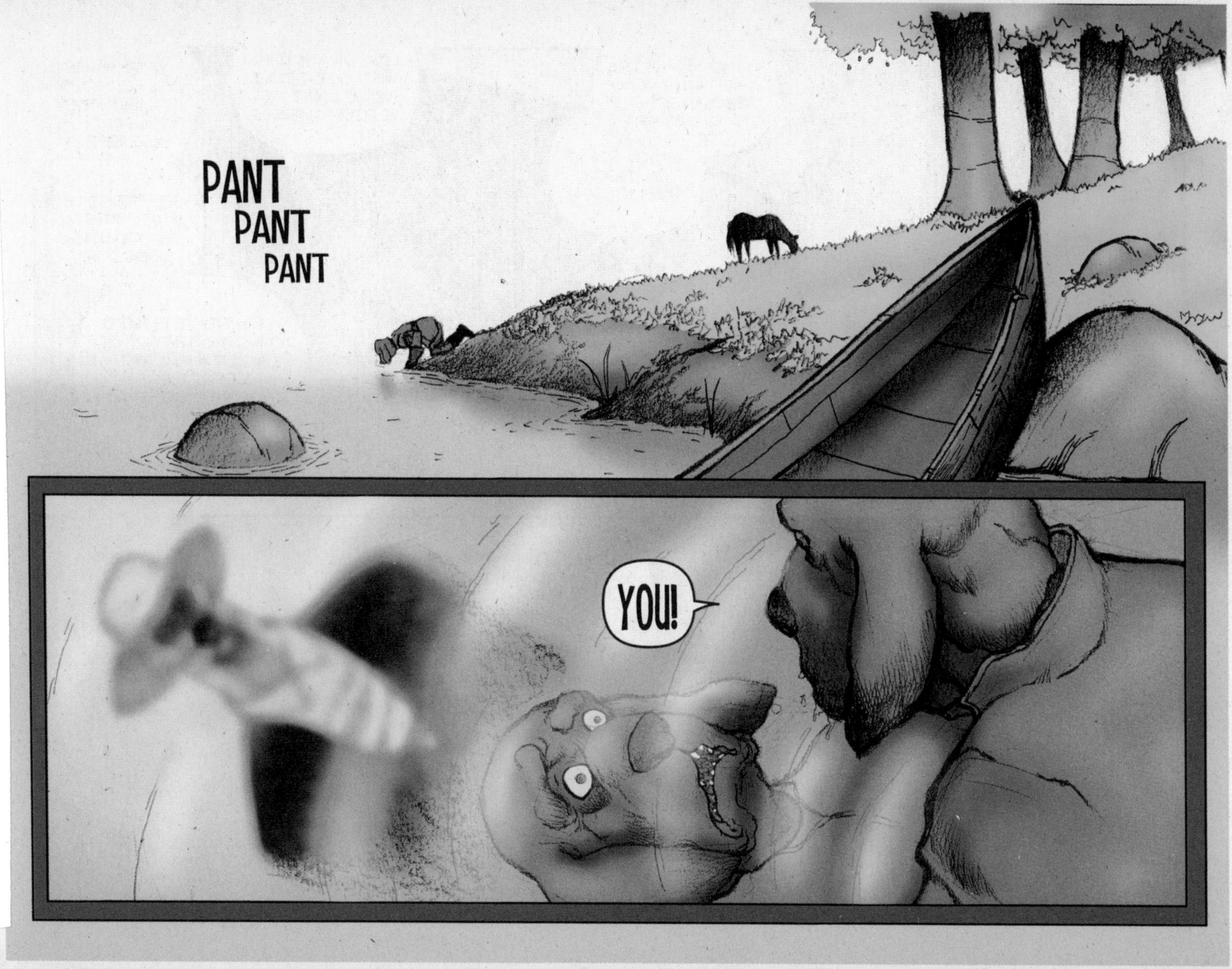
PANT
PANT
PANT
YOU!

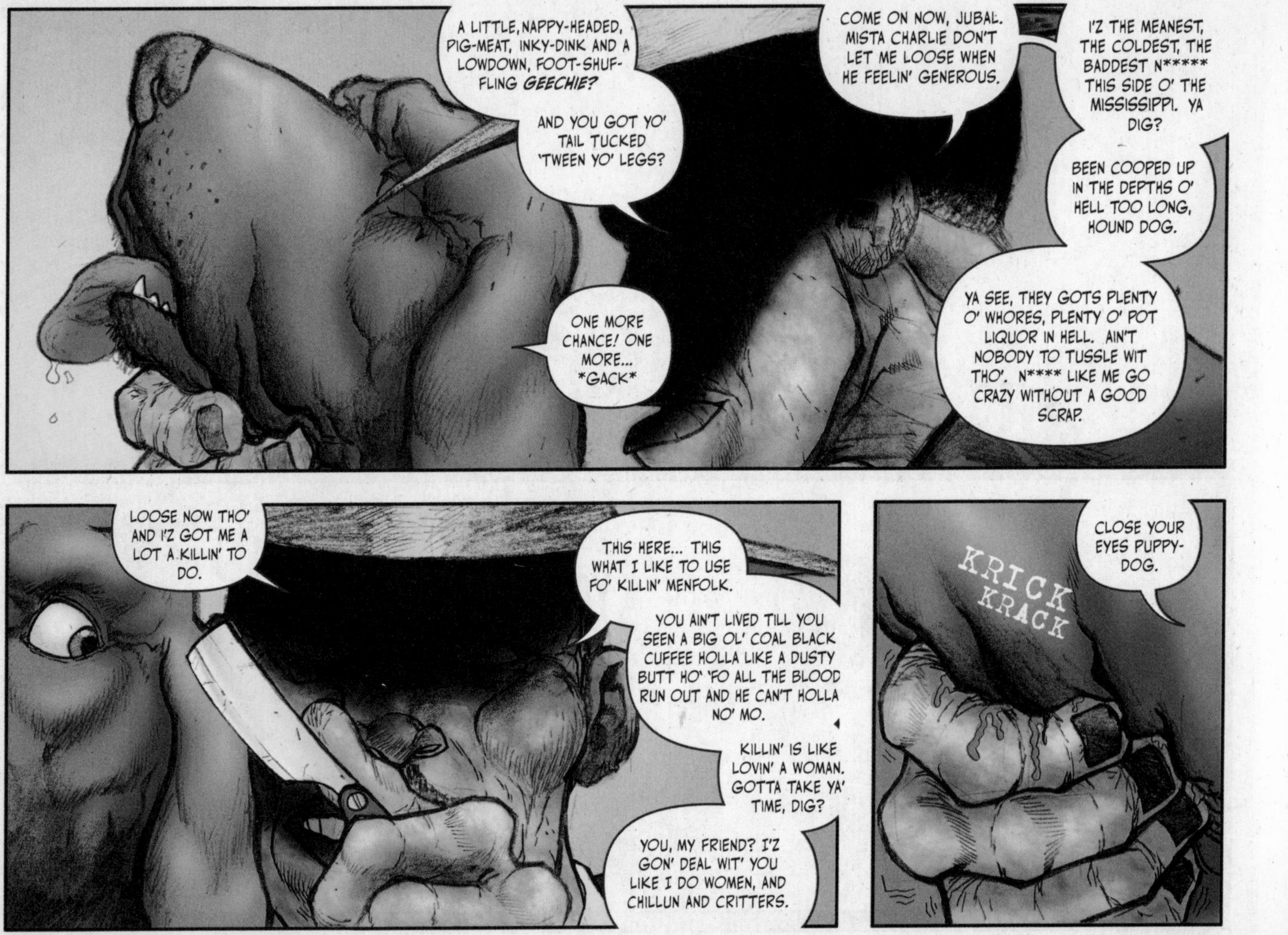
A LITTLE, NAPPY-HEADED, PIG-MEAT, INKY-DINK AND A LOWDOWN, FOOT-SHUFFLING *GEECHIE?*
AND YOU GOT YO' TAIL TUCKED 'TWEEN YO' LEGS?
COME ON NOW, JUBAL. MISTA CHARLIE DON'T LET ME LOOSE WHEN HE FEELIN' GENEROUS.
I'Z THE MEANEST, THE COLDEST, THE BADDEST N***** THIS SIDE O' THE MISSISSIPPI. YA DIG?
BEEN COOPED UP IN THE DEPTHS O' HELL TOO LONG, HOUND DOG.
ONE MORE CHANCE! ONE MORE... *GACK*
YA SEE, THEY GOTS PLENTY O' WHORES, PLENTY O' POT LIQUOR IN HELL. AIN'T NOBODY TO TUSSLE WIT THO'. N***** LIKE ME GO CRAZY WITHOUT A GOOD SCRAP.
LOOSE NOW THO' AND I'Z GOT ME A LOT A KILLIN' TO DO.
THIS HERE... THIS WHAT I LIKE TO USE FO' KILLIN' MENFOLK.
YOU AIN'T LIVED TILL YOU SEEN A BIG OL' COAL BLACK CUFFEE HOLLA LIKE A DUSTY BUTT HO' 'FO ALL THE BLOOD RUN OUT AND HE CAN'T HOLLA NO' MO.
KILLIN' IS LIKE LOVIN' A WOMAN. GOTTA TAKE YA' TIME, DIG?
YOU, MY FRIEND? I'Z GON' DEAL WIT' YOU LIKE I DO WOMEN, AND CHILLUN AND CRITTERS.
KRICK KRACK
CLOSE YOUR EYES PUPPY-DOG.

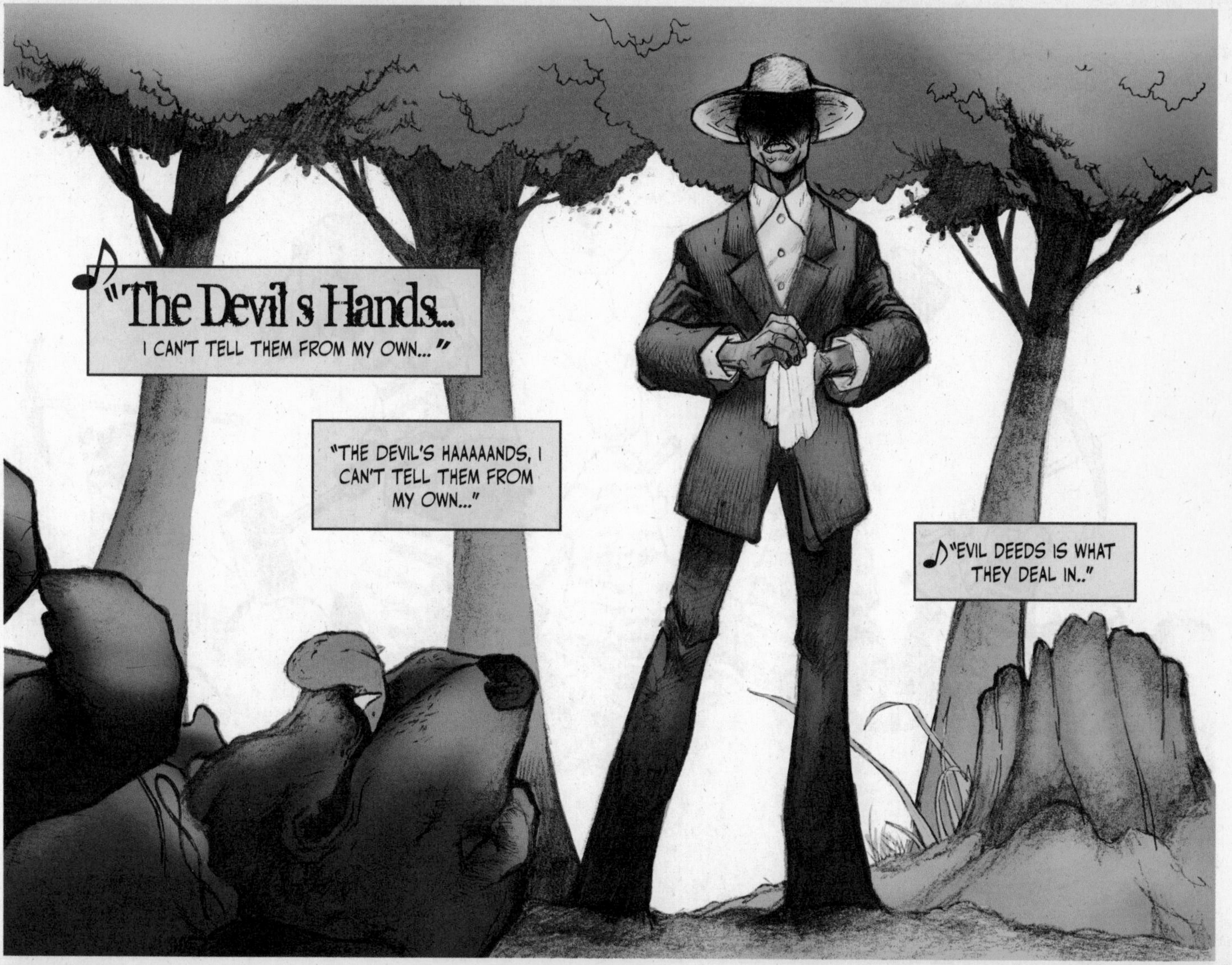
"The Devil s Hands...
I CAN'T TELL THEM FROM MY OWN..."
"THE DEVIL'S HAAAAANDS, I CAN'T TELL THEM FROM MY OWN..."
"EVIL DEEDS IS WHAT THEY DEAL IN.."

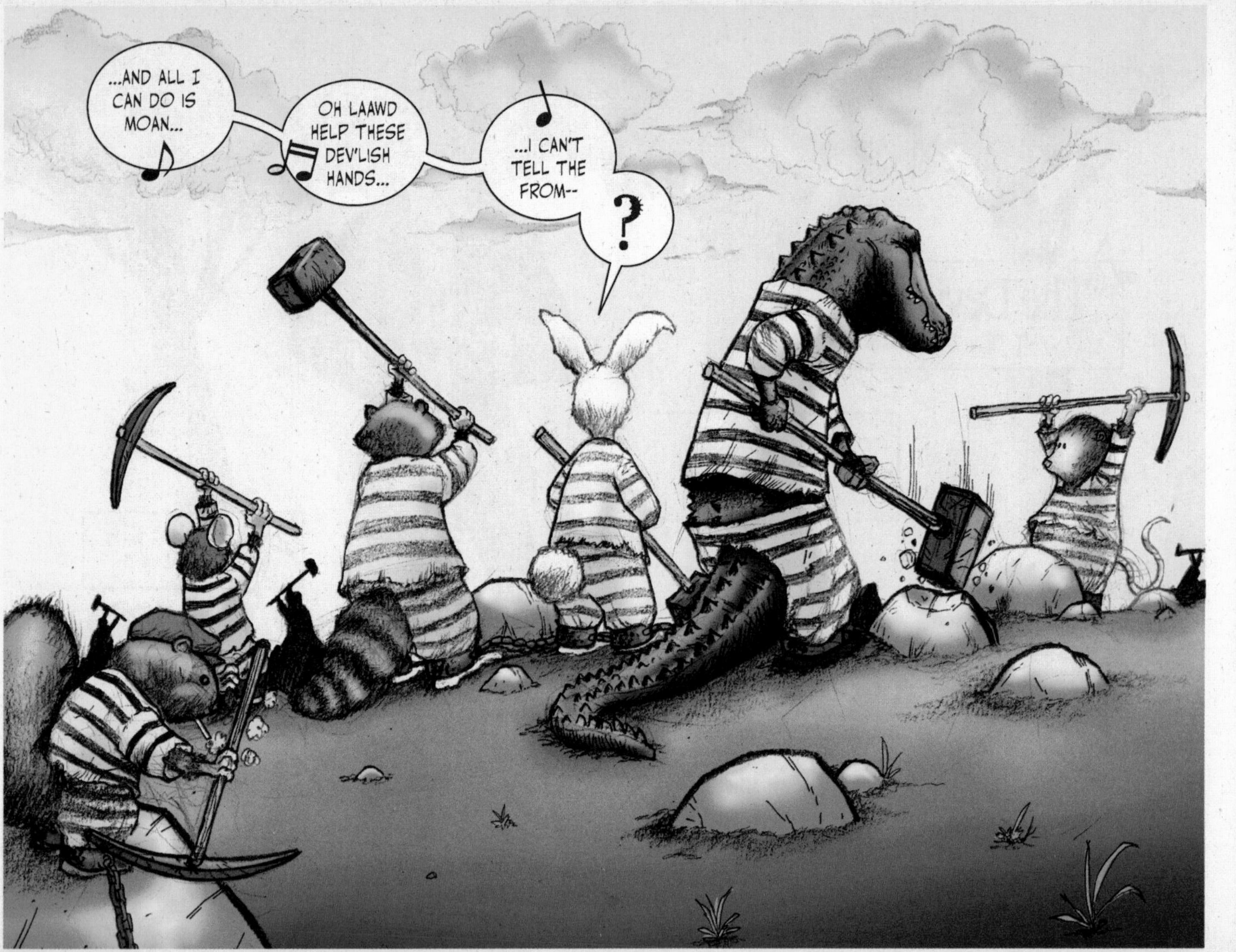
...AND ALL I CAN DO IS MOAN...
OH LAAWD HELP THESE DEV'LISH HANDS...
...I CAN'T TELL THE FROM--
?

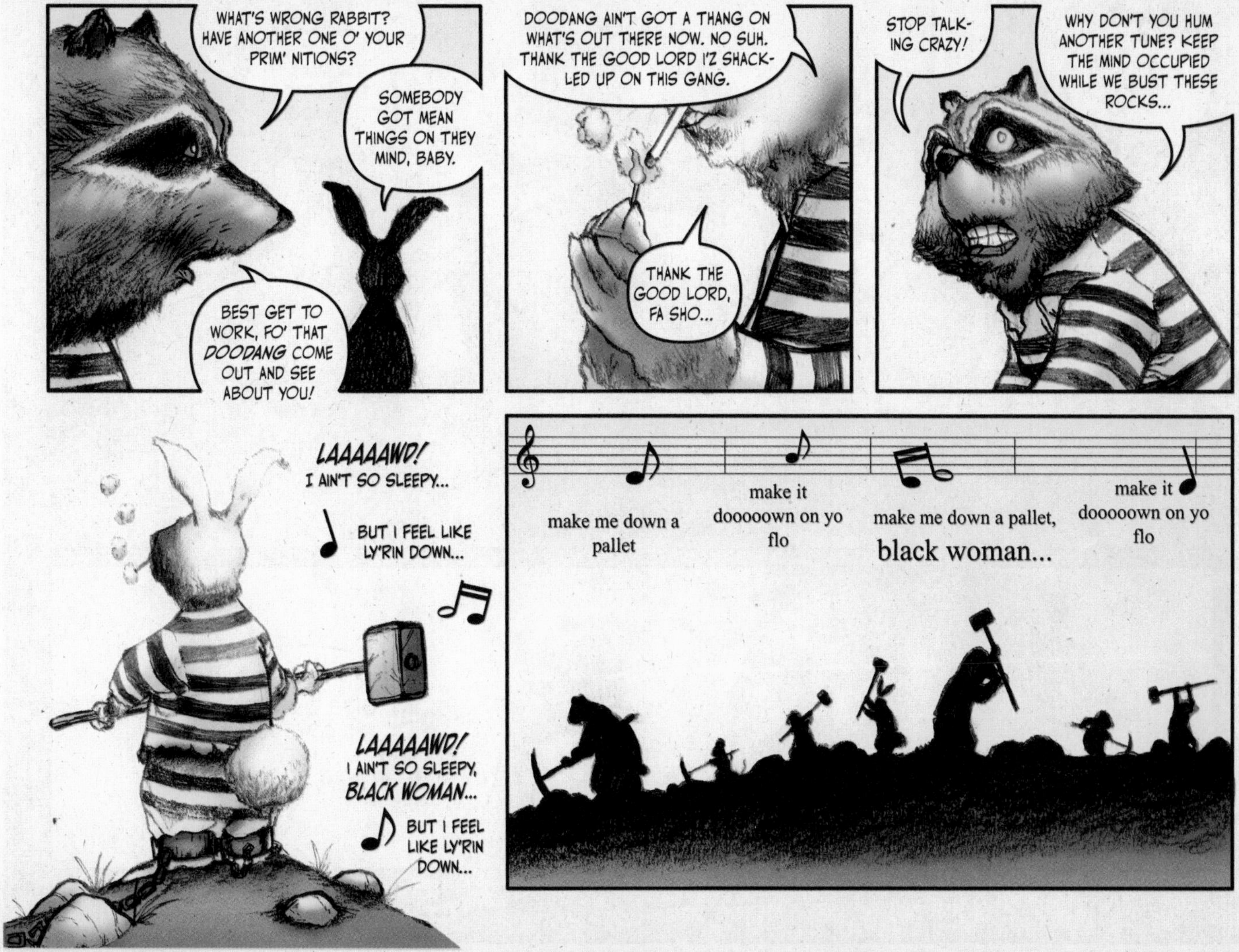
WHAT'S WRONG RABBIT? HAVE ANOTHER ONE O' YOUR PRIM' NITIONS?
SOMEBODY GOT MEAN THINGS ON THEY MIND, BABY.
BEST GET TO WORK, FO' THAT *DOODANG* COME OUT AND SEE ABOUT YOU!
DOODANG AIN'T GOT A THANG ON WHAT'S OUT THERE NOW. NO SUH. THANK THE GOOD LORD I'Z SHACK-LED UP ON THIS GANG.
THANK THE GOOD LORD, FA SHO...
STOP TALK-ING CRAZY!
WHY DON'T YOU HUM ANOTHER TUNE? KEEP THE MIND OCCUPIED WHILE WE BUST THESE ROCKS...
LAAAAAWD! I AIN'T SO SLEEPY...
BUT I FEEL LIKE LY'RIN DOWN...
LAAAAAWD! I AIN'T SO SLEEPY, *BLACK WOMAN...*
BUT I FEEL LIKE LY'RIN DOWN...
make me down a pallet
make it dooooown on yo flo
make me down a pallet, black woman...
make it dooooown on yo flo

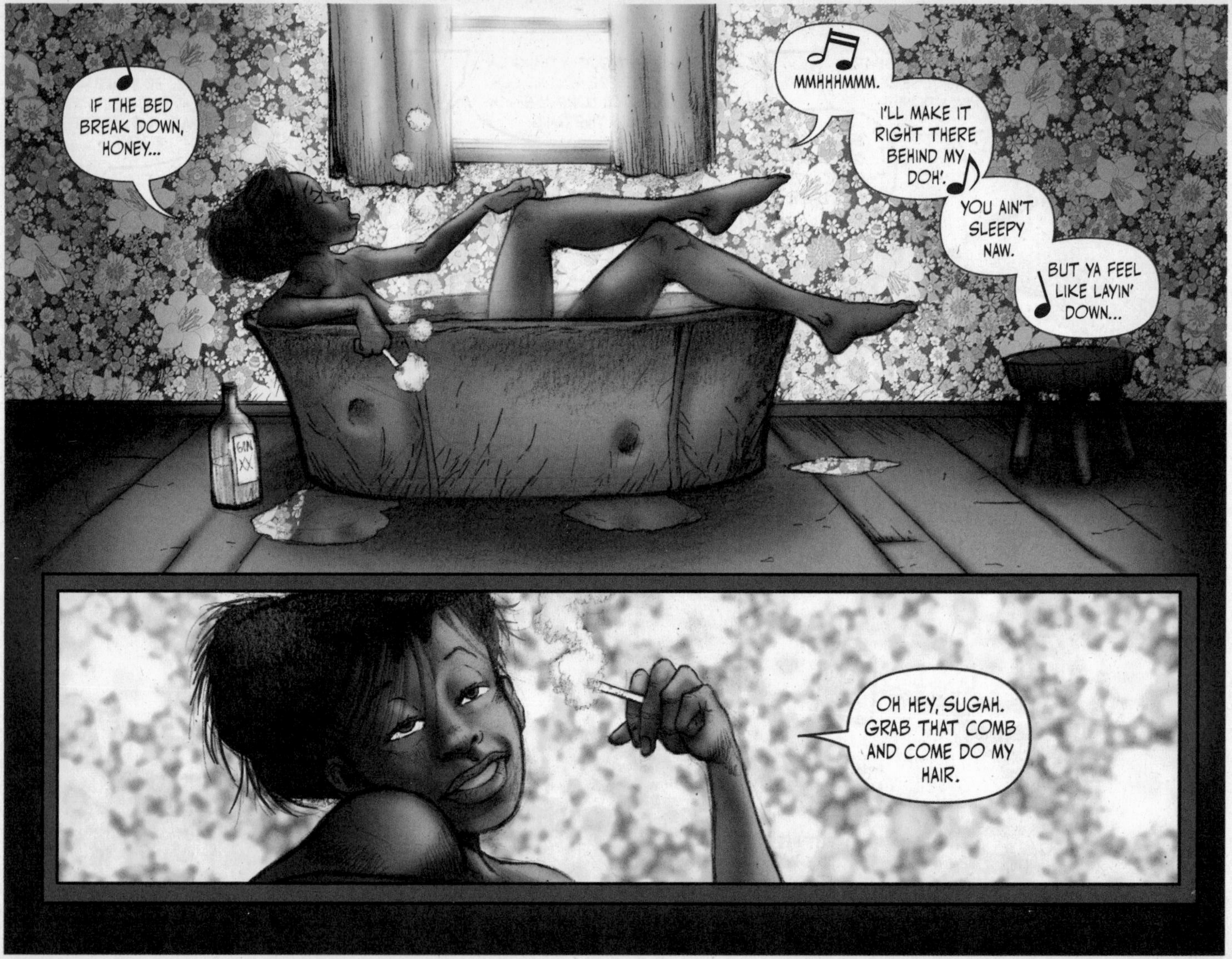
IF THE BED BREAK DOWN, HONEY...
MMHHHMMM.
I'LL MAKE IT RIGHT THERE BEHIND MY DOH'.
YOU AIN'T SLEEPY NAW.
BUT YA FEEL LIKE LAYIN' DOWN...
GIN XX
OH HEY, SUGAH. GRAB THAT COMB AND COME DO MY HAIR.

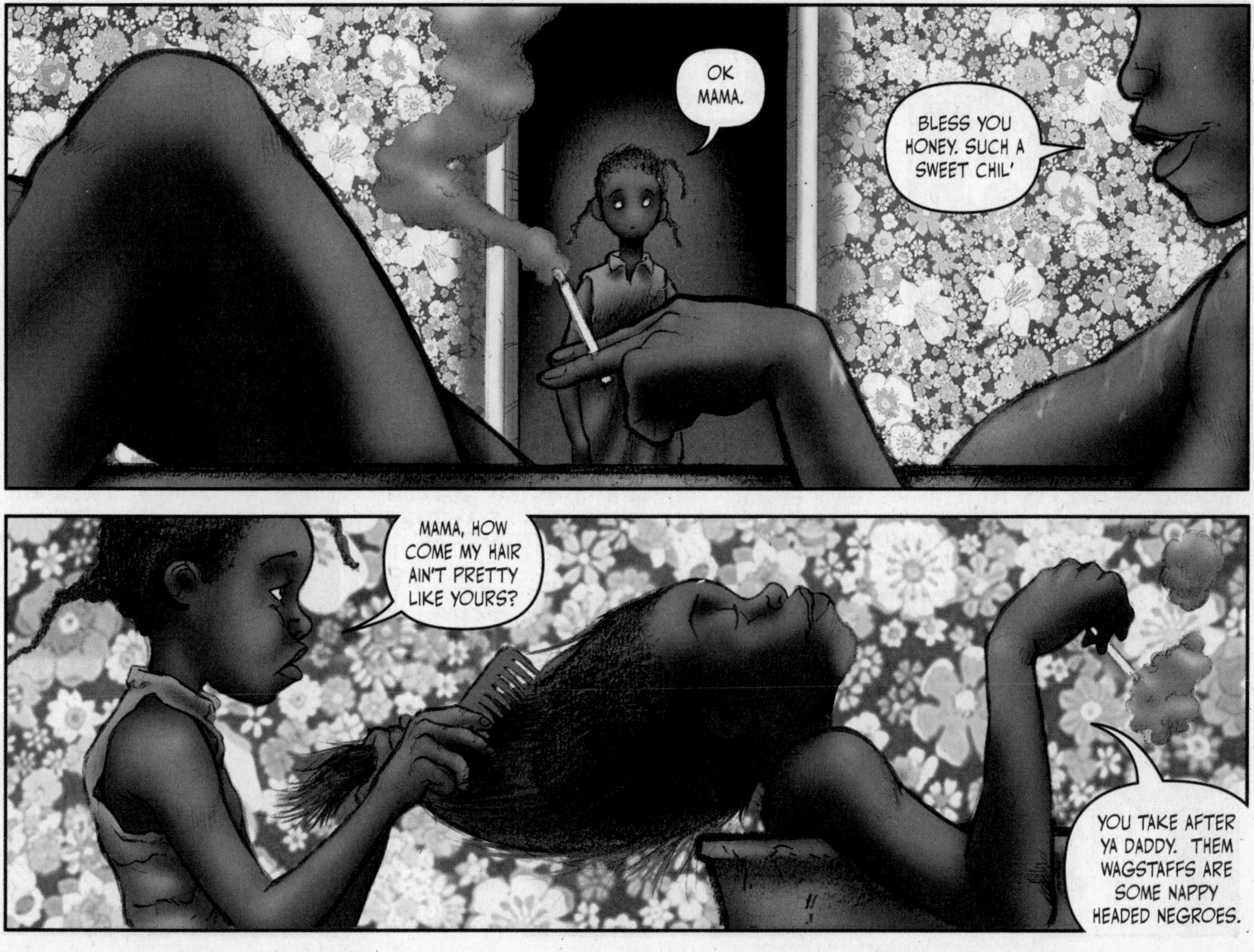
OK MAMA.
BLESS YOU HONEY. SUCH A SWEET CHIL'
MAMA, HOW COME MY HAIR AIN'T PRETTY LIKE YOURS?
YOU TAKE AFTER YA DADDY. THEM WAGSTAFFS ARE SOME NAPPY HEADED NEGROES.

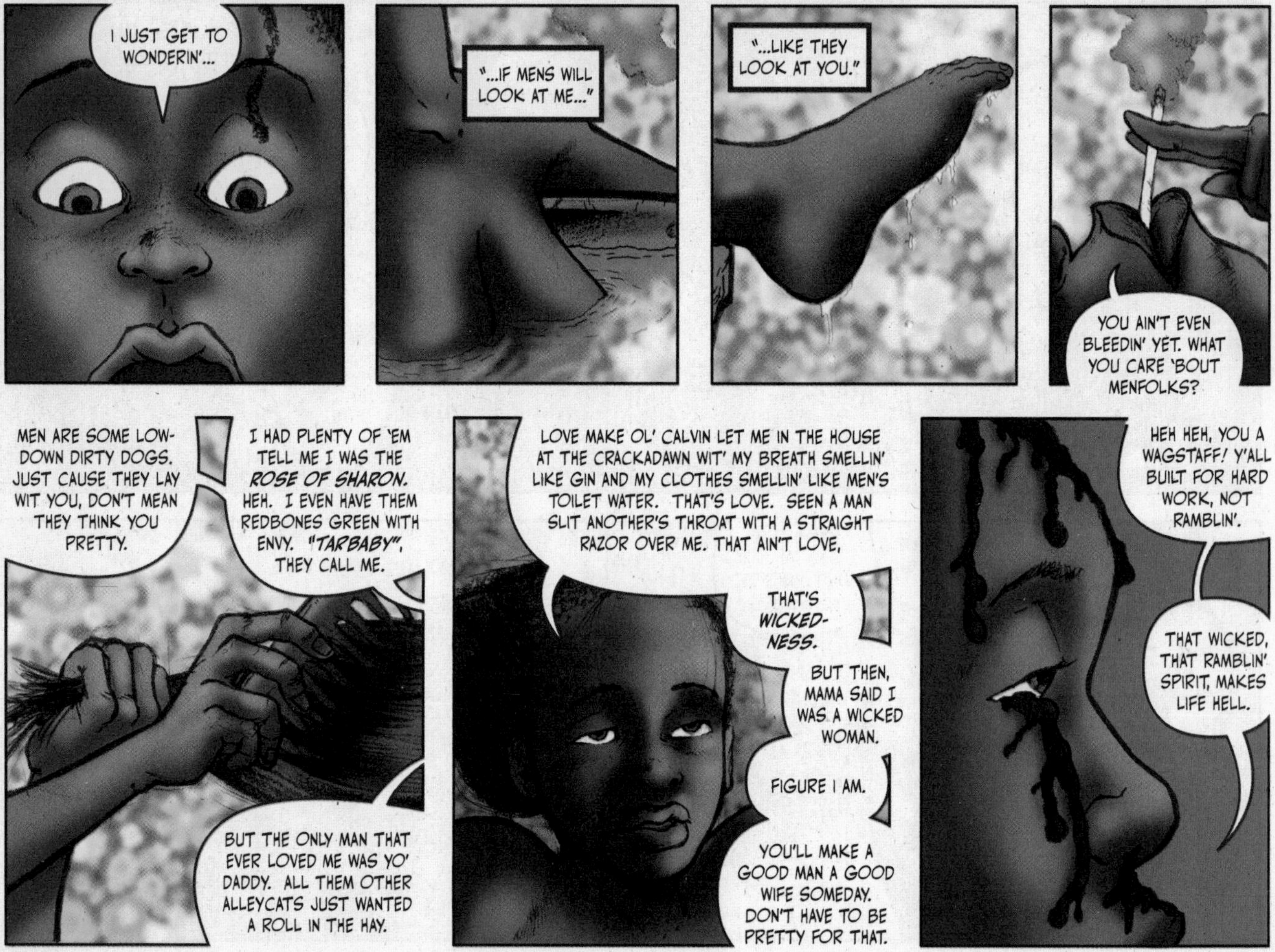
I JUST GET TO WONDERIN'...
"...IF MENS WILL LOOK AT ME..."
"...LIKE THEY LOOK AT YOU."
YOU AIN'T EVEN BLEEDIN' YET. WHAT YOU CARE 'BOUT MENFOLKS?
MEN ARE SOME LOW-DOWN DIRTY DOGS. JUST CAUSE THEY LAY WIT YOU, DON'T MEAN THEY THINK YOU PRETTY.
I HAD PLENTY OF 'EM TELL ME I WAS THE ROSE OF SHARON. HEH. I EVEN HAVE THEM REDBONES GREEN WITH ENVY. "TARBABY", THEY CALL ME.
BUT THE ONLY MAN THAT EVER LOVED ME WAS YO' DADDY. ALL THEM OTHER ALLEYCATS JUST WANTED A ROLL IN THE HAY.
LOVE MAKE OL' CALVIN LET ME IN THE HOUSE AT THE CRACKADAWN WIT' MY BREATH SMELLIN' LIKE GIN AND MY CLOTHES SMELLIN' LIKE MEN'S TOILET WATER. THAT'S LOVE. SEEN A MAN SLIT ANOTHER'S THROAT WITH A STRAIGHT RAZOR OVER ME. THAT AIN'T LOVE,
THAT'S WICKED-NESS.
BUT THEN, MAMA SAID I WAS A WICKED WOMAN.
FIGURE I AM.
YOU'LL MAKE A GOOD MAN A GOOD WIFE SOMEDAY. DON'T HAVE TO BE PRETTY FOR THAT.
HEH HEH, YOU A WAGSTAFF! Y'ALL BUILT FOR HARD WORK, NOT RAMBLIN'.
THAT WICKED, THAT RAMBLIN' SPIRIT, MAKES LIFE HELL.

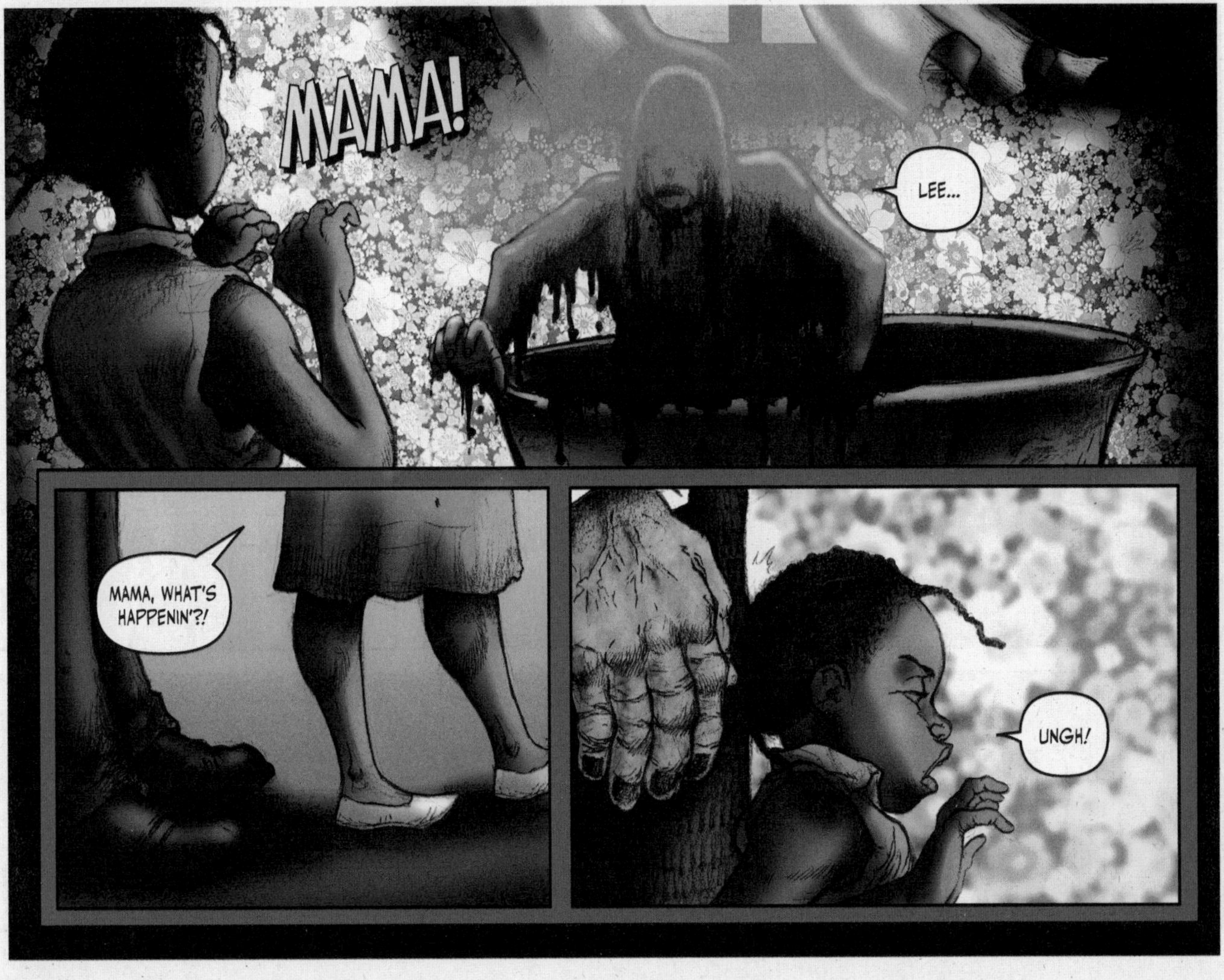
MAMA!
LEE...
MAMA, WHAT'S HAPPENIN'?!
UNGH!

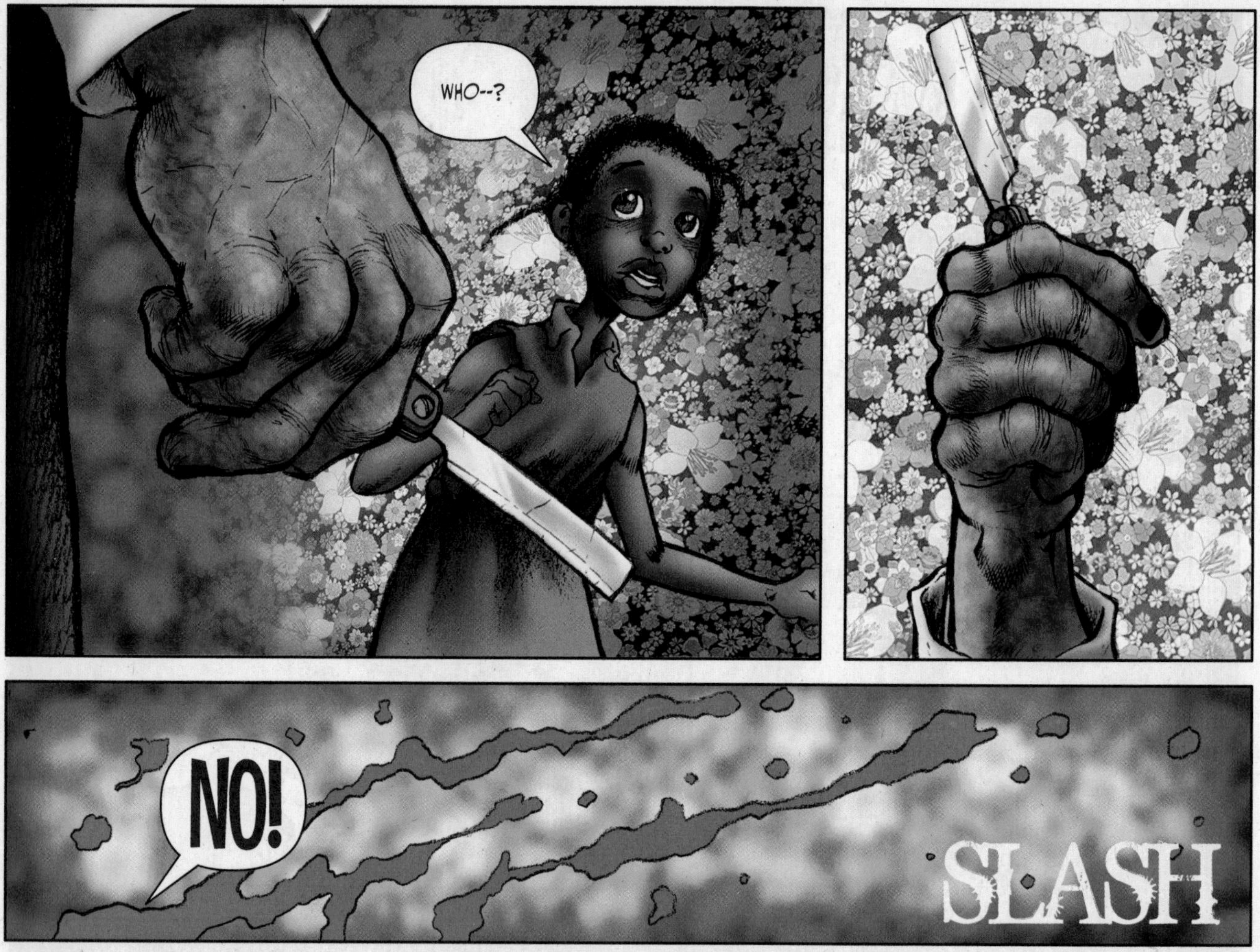

WHO--?
NO!
SLASH

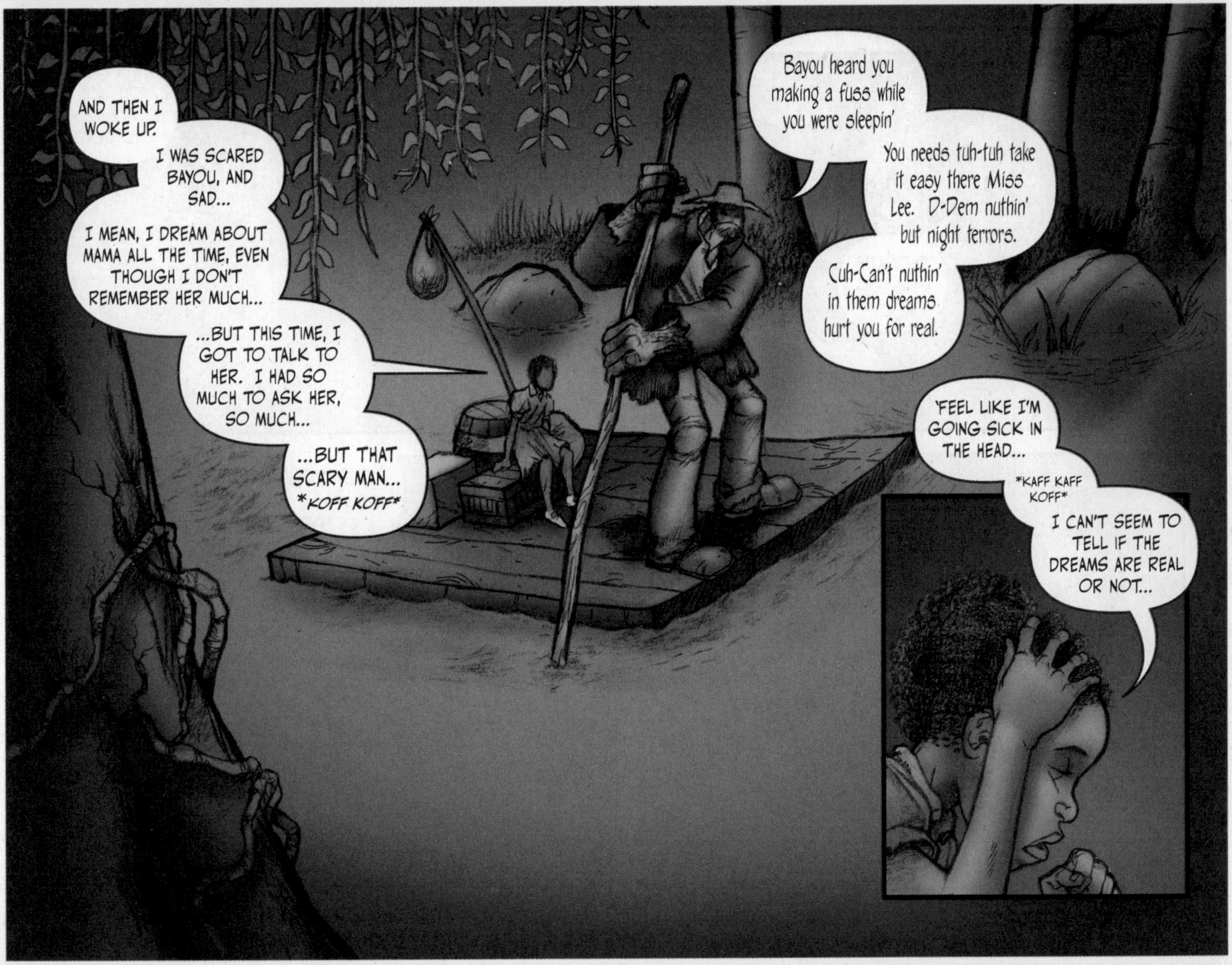
AND THEN I WOKE UP.
I WAS SCARED BAYOU, AND SAD...
I MEAN, I DREAM ABOUT MAMA ALL THE TIME, EVEN THOUGH I DON'T REMEMBER HER MUCH...
...BUT THIS TIME, I GOT TO TALK TO HER. I HAD SO MUCH TO ASK HER, SO MUCH...
...BUT THAT SCARY MAN... *KOFF KOFF*
Bayou heard you making a fuss while you were sleepin'
You needs tuh-tuh take it easy there Miss Lee. D-Dem nuthin' but night terrors.
Cuh-Can't nuthin' in them dreams hurt you for real.
'FEEL LIKE I'M GOING SICK IN THE HEAD...
KAFF KAFF KOFF
I CAN'T SEEM TO TELL IF THE DREAMS ARE REAL OR NOT...

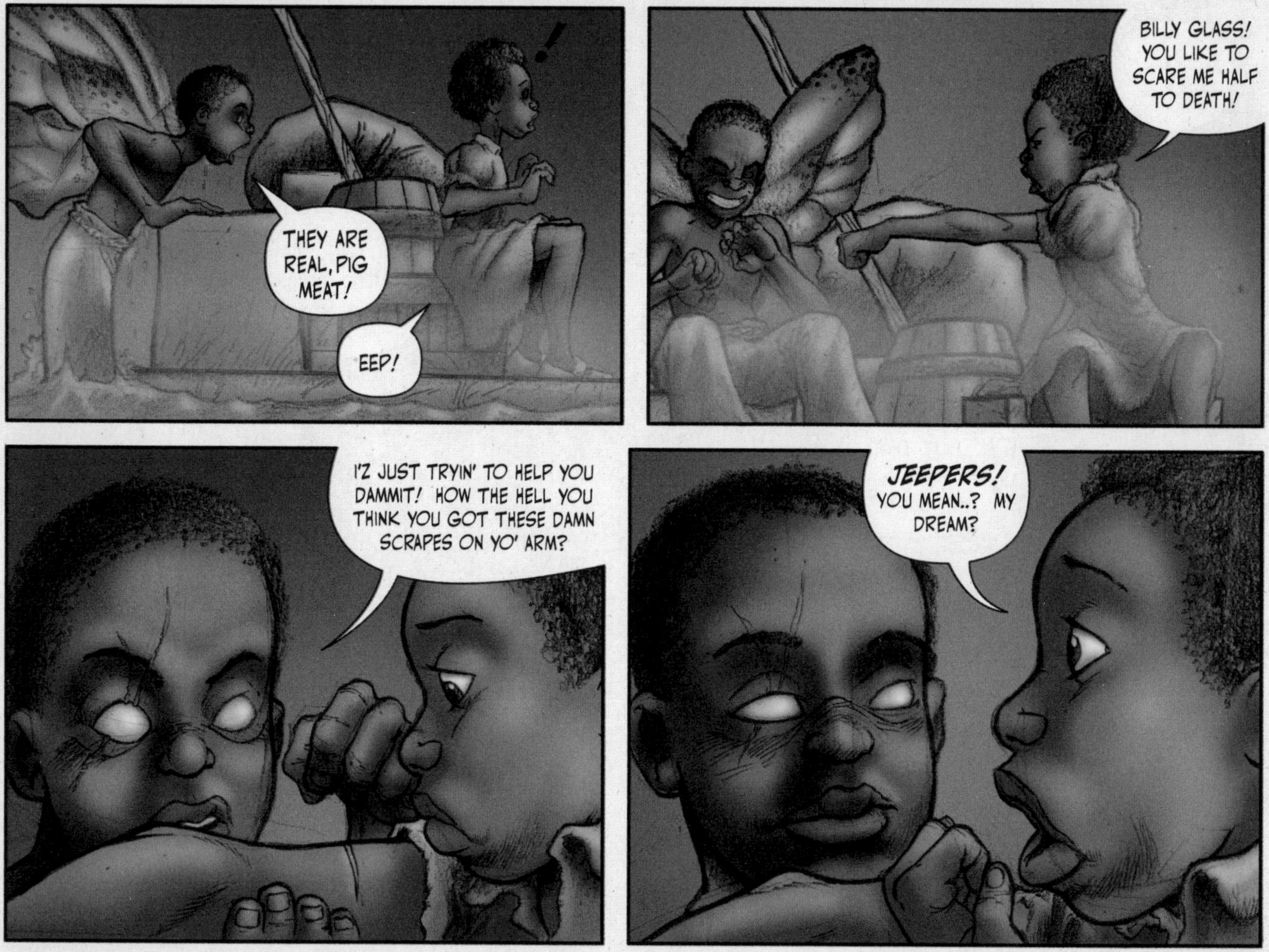
!
THEY ARE REAL, PIG MEAT!
EEP!
BILLY GLASS! YOU LIKE TO SCARE ME HALF TO DEATH!
I'Z JUST TRYIN' TO HELP YOU DAMMIT! HOW THE HELL YOU THINK YOU GOT THESE DAMN SCRAPES ON YO' ARM?
JEEPERS! YOU MEAN..? MY DREAM?

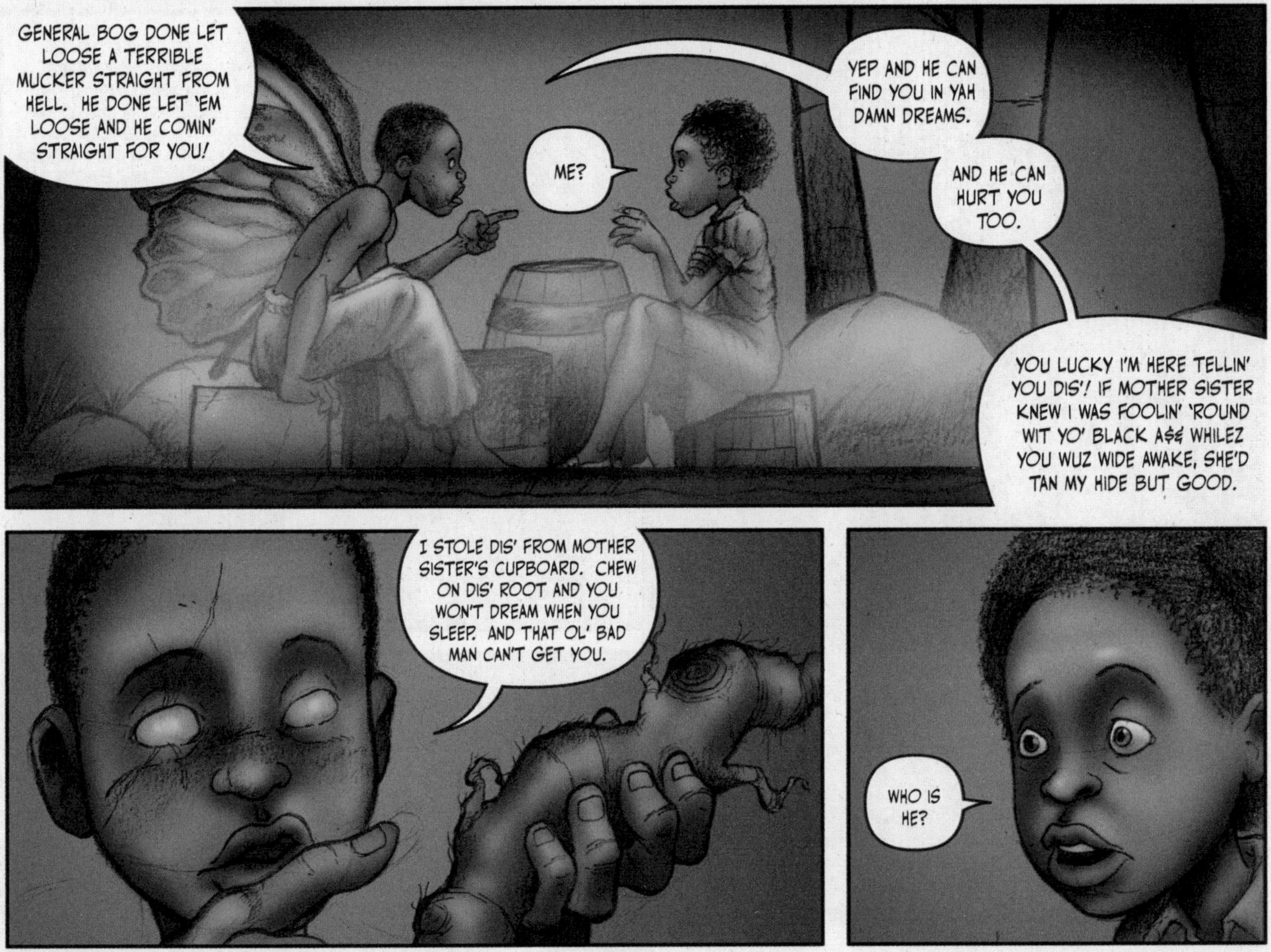
GENERAL BOG DONE LET LOOSE A TERRIBLE MUCKER STRAIGHT FROM HELL. HE DONE LET 'EM LOOSE AND HE COMIN' STRAIGHT FOR YOU!
ME?
YEP AND HE CAN FIND YOU IN YAH DAMN DREAMS.
AND HE CAN HURT YOU TOO.
YOU LUCKY I'M HERE TELLIN' YOU DIS'! IF MOTHER SISTER KNEW I WAS FOOLIN' 'ROUND WIT YO' BLACK A$$ WHILEZ YOU WUZ WIDE AWAKE, SHE'D TAN MY HIDE BUT GOOD.
I STOLE DIS' FROM MOTHER SISTER'S CUPBOARD. CHEW ON DIS' ROOT AND YOU WON'T DREAM WHEN YOU SLEEP. AND THAT OL' BAD MAN CAN'T GET YOU.
WHO IS HE?

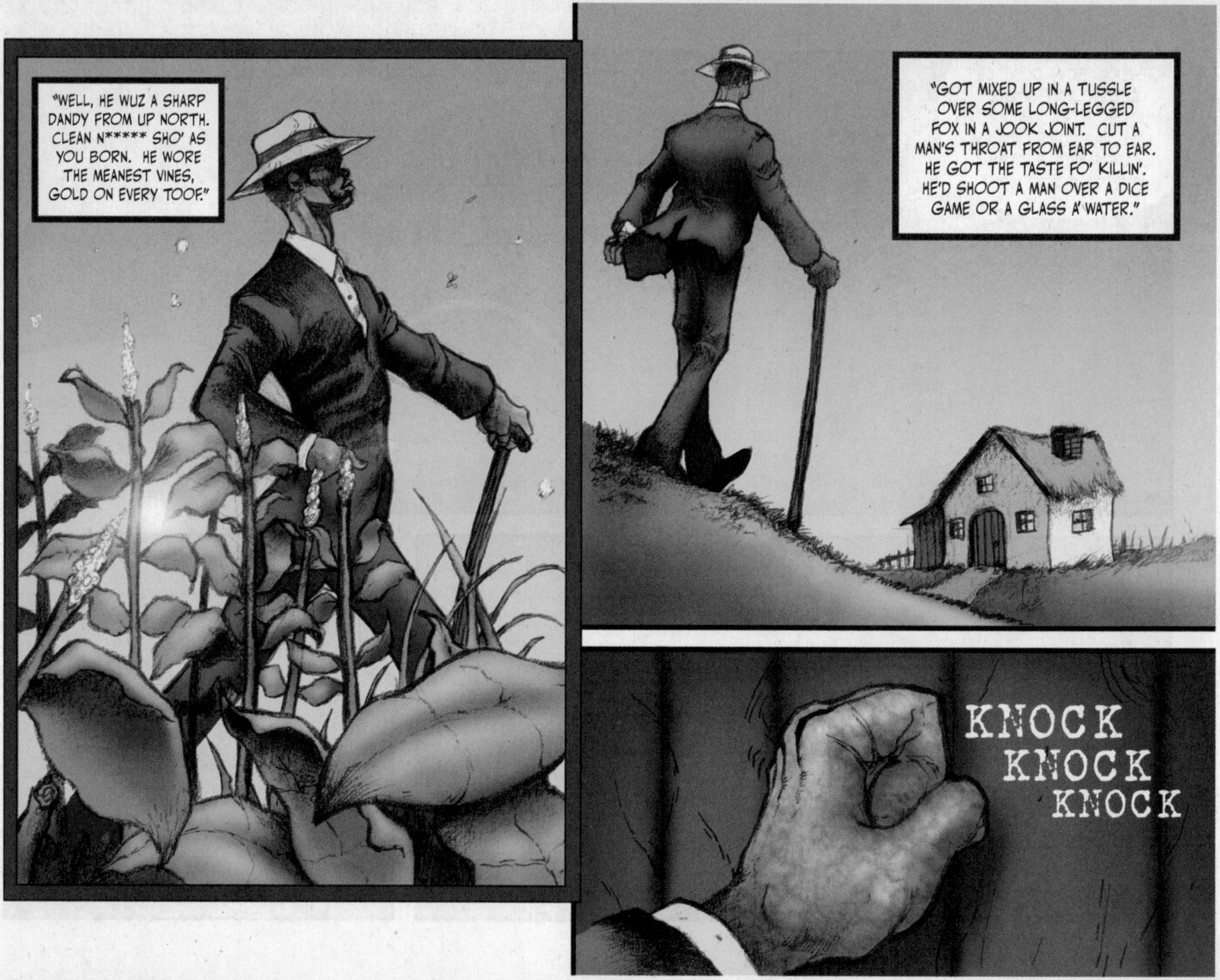
"WELL, HE WUZ A SHARP DANDY FROM UP NORTH. CLEAN N***** SHO' AS YOU BORN. HE WORE THE MEANEST VINES, GOLD ON EVERY TOOF."
"GOT MIXED UP IN A TUSSLE OVER SOME LONG-LEGGED FOX IN A JOOK JOINT. CUT A MAN'S THROAT FROM EAR TO EAR. HE GOT THE TASTE FO' KILLIN'. HE'D SHOOT A MAN OVER A DICE GAME OR A GLASS A' WATER."
KNOCK
KNOCK
KNOCK

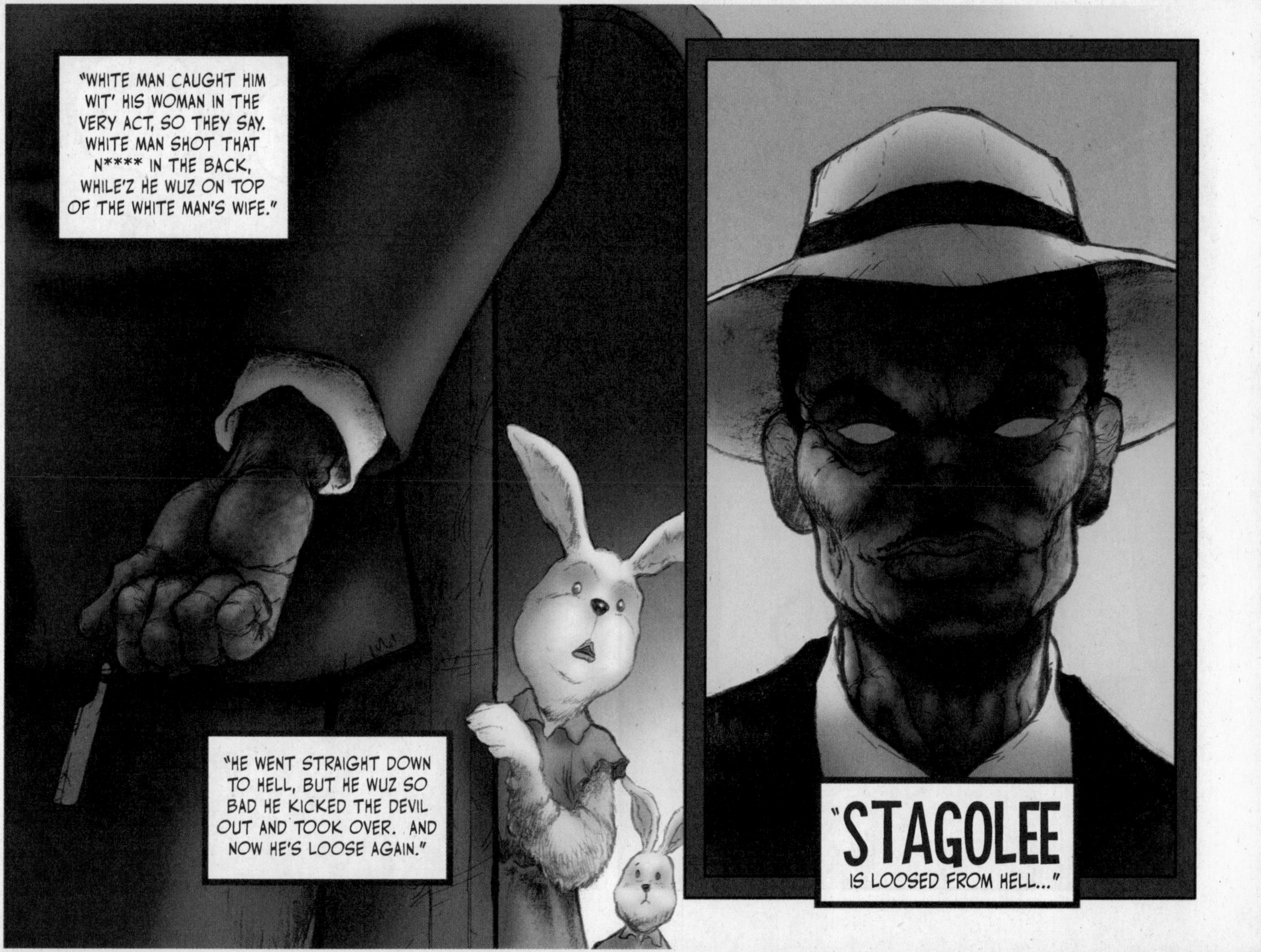
"WHITE MAN CAUGHT HIM WIT' HIS WOMAN IN THE VERY ACT, SO THEY SAY. WHITE MAN SHOT THAT N**** IN THE BACK, WHILE'Z HE WUZ ON TOP OF THE WHITE MAN'S WIFE."
"HE WENT STRAIGHT DOWN TO HELL, BUT HE WUZ SO BAD HE KICKED THE DEVIL OUT AND TOOK OVER. AND NOW HE'S LOOSE AGAIN."
"STAGOLEE IS LOOSED FROM HELL..."

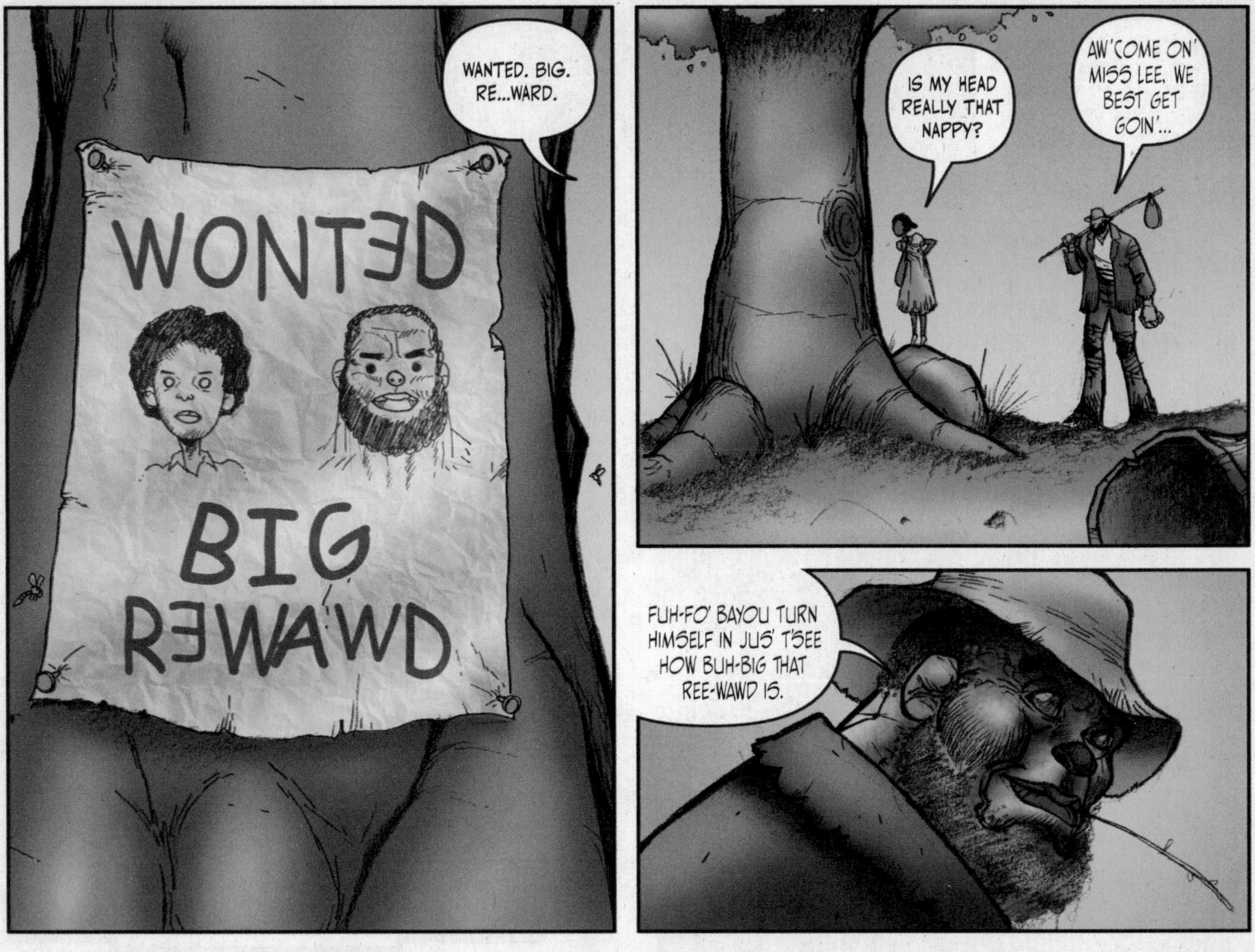
WANTED. BIG. RE...WARD.
WONT3D
BIG
R3WAWD
IS MY HEAD REALLY THAT NAPPY?
AW'COME ON' MISS LEE. WE BEST GET GOIN'...
FUH-FO' BAYOU TURN HIMSELF IN JUS' T'SEE HOW BUH-BIG THAT REE-WAWD IS.

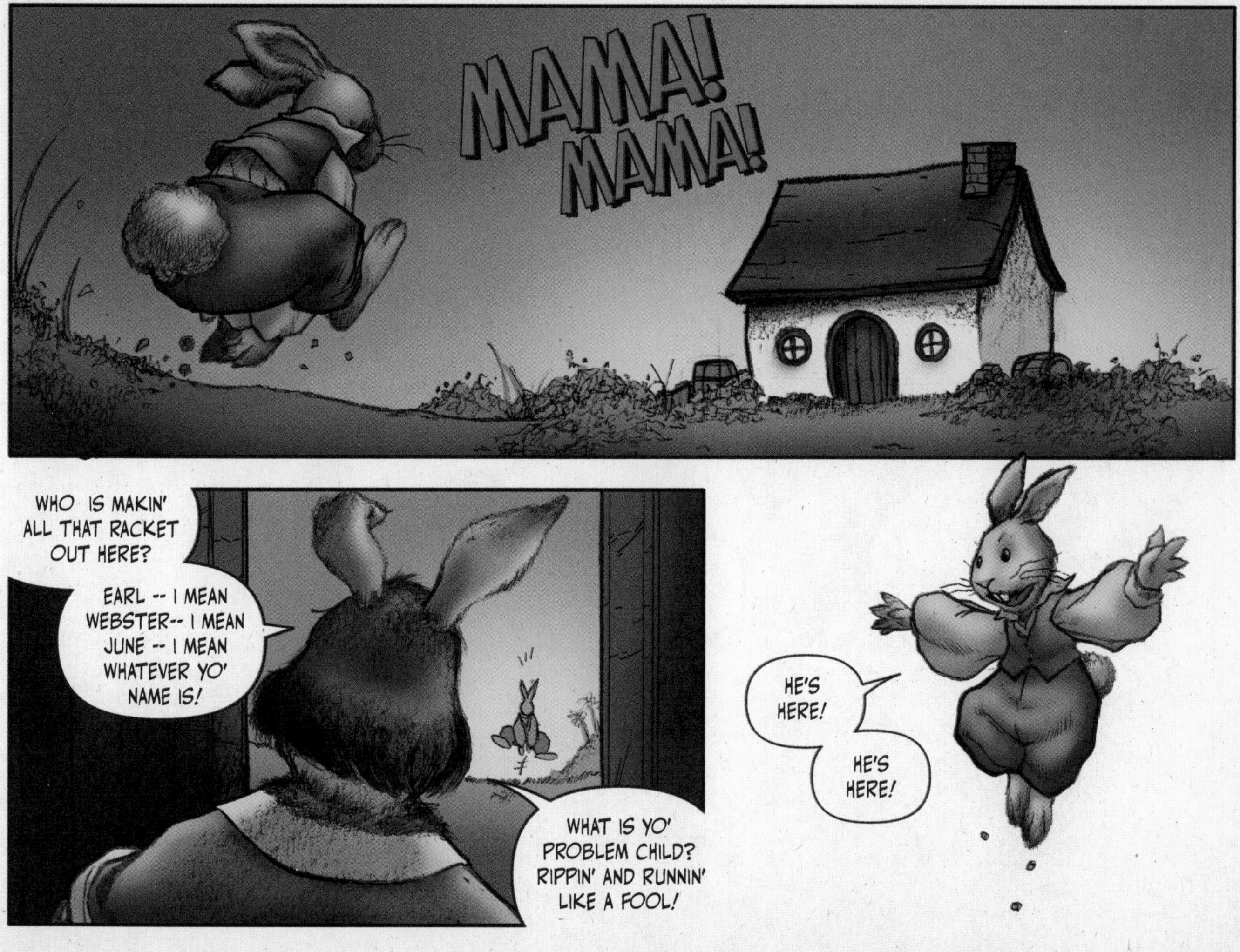
MAMA! MAMA!
WHO IS MAKIN' ALL THAT RACKET OUT HERE?
EARL -- I MEAN WEBSTER-- I MEAN JUNE -- I MEAN WHATEVER YO' NAME IS!
WHAT IS YO' PROBLEM CHILD? RIPPIN' AND RUNNIN' LIKE A FOOL!
HE'S HERE!
HE'S HERE!

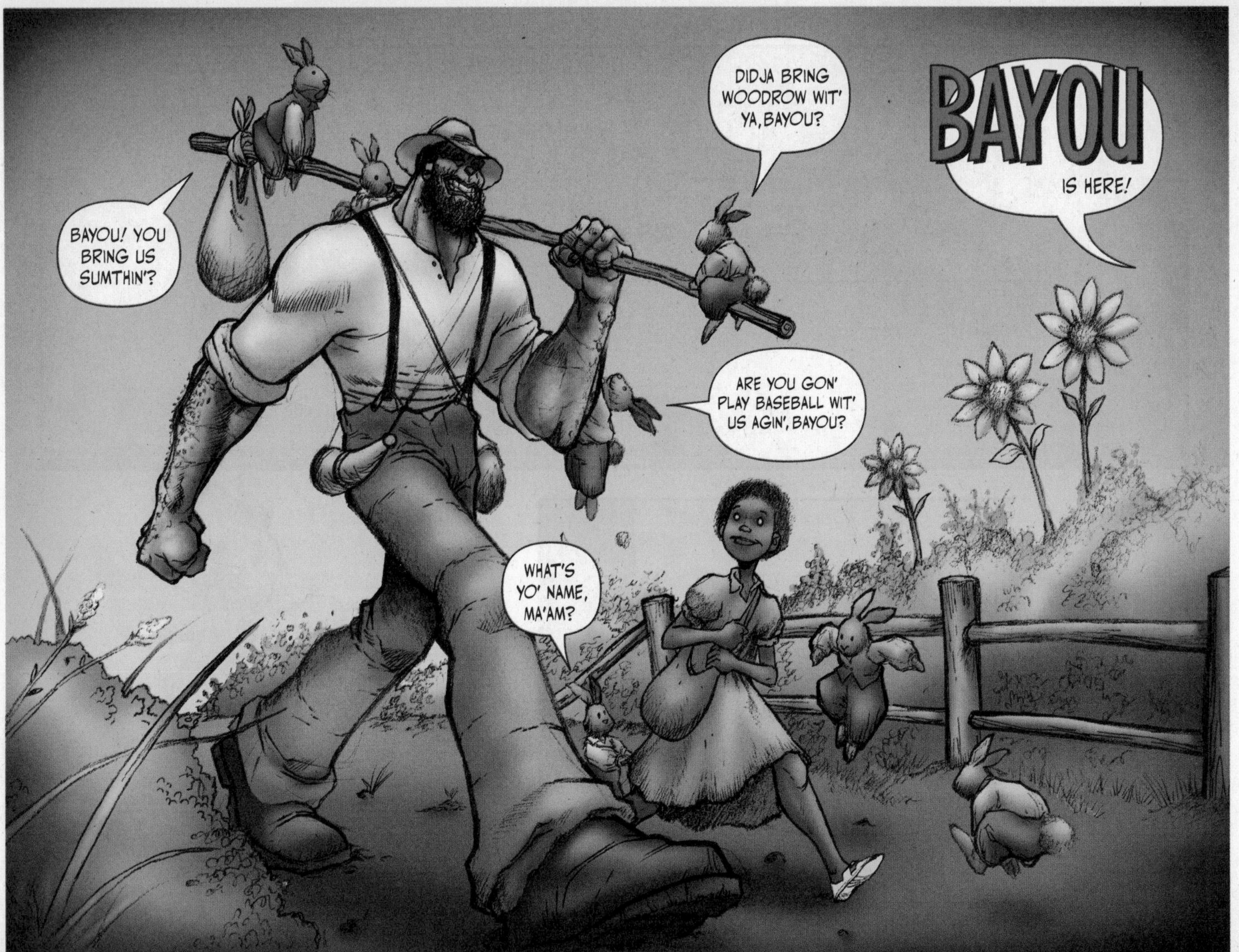
BAYOU! YOU BRING US SUMTHIN'?
DIDJA BRING WOODROW WIT' YA, BAYOU?
BAYOU IS HERE!
ARE YOU GON' PLAY BASEBALL WIT' US AGIN', BAYOU?
WHAT'S YO' NAME, MA'AM?

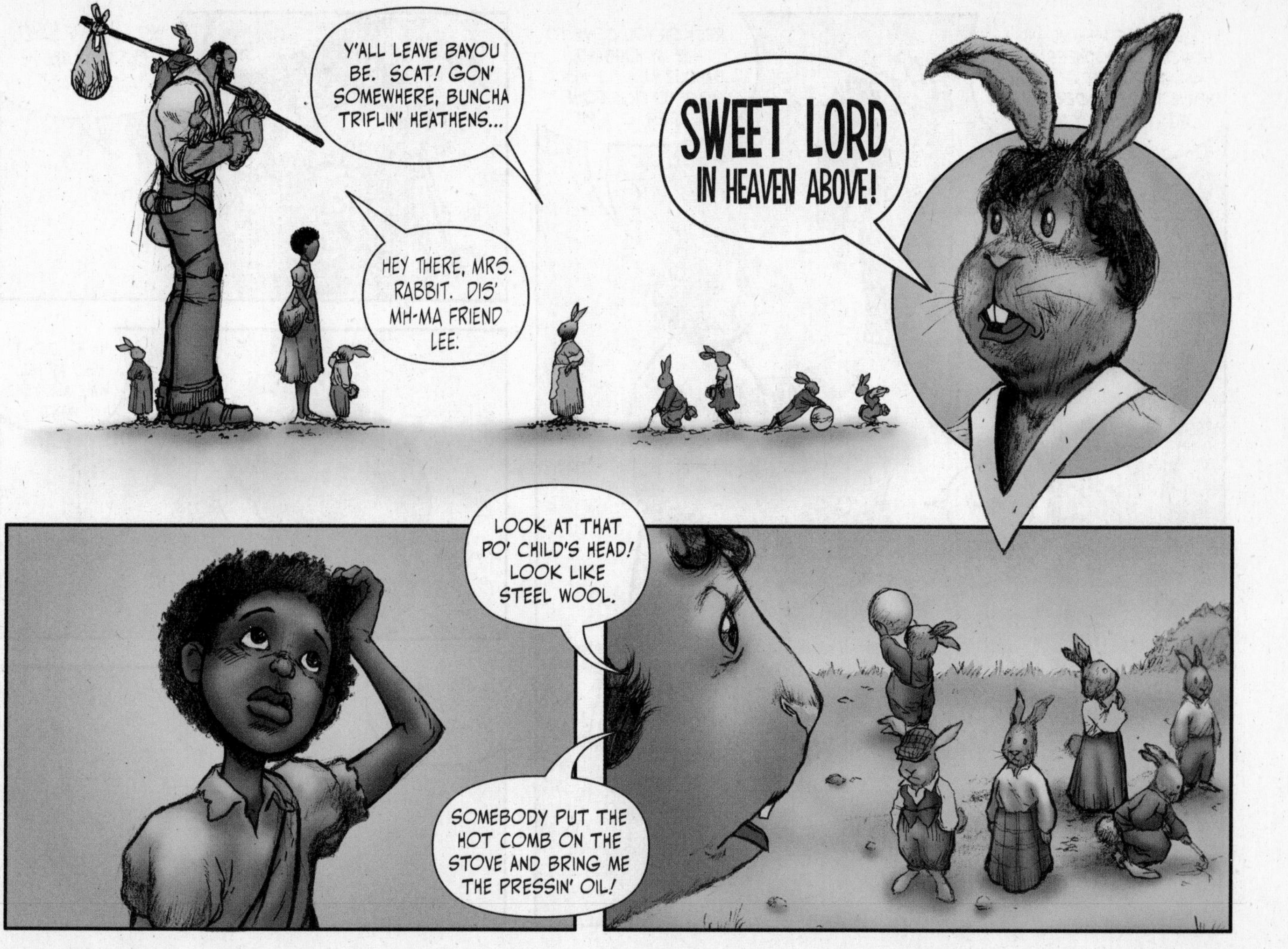
Y'ALL LEAVE BAYOU BE. SCAT! GON' SOMEWHERE, BUNCHA TRIFLIN' HEATHENS...
HEY THERE, MRS. RABBIT. DIS' MH-MA FRIEND LEE.
SWEET LORD IN HEAVEN ABOVE!
LOOK AT THAT PO' CHILD'S HEAD! LOOK LIKE STEEL WOOL.
SOMEBODY PUT THE HOT COMB ON THE STOVE AND BRING ME THE PRESSIN' OIL!

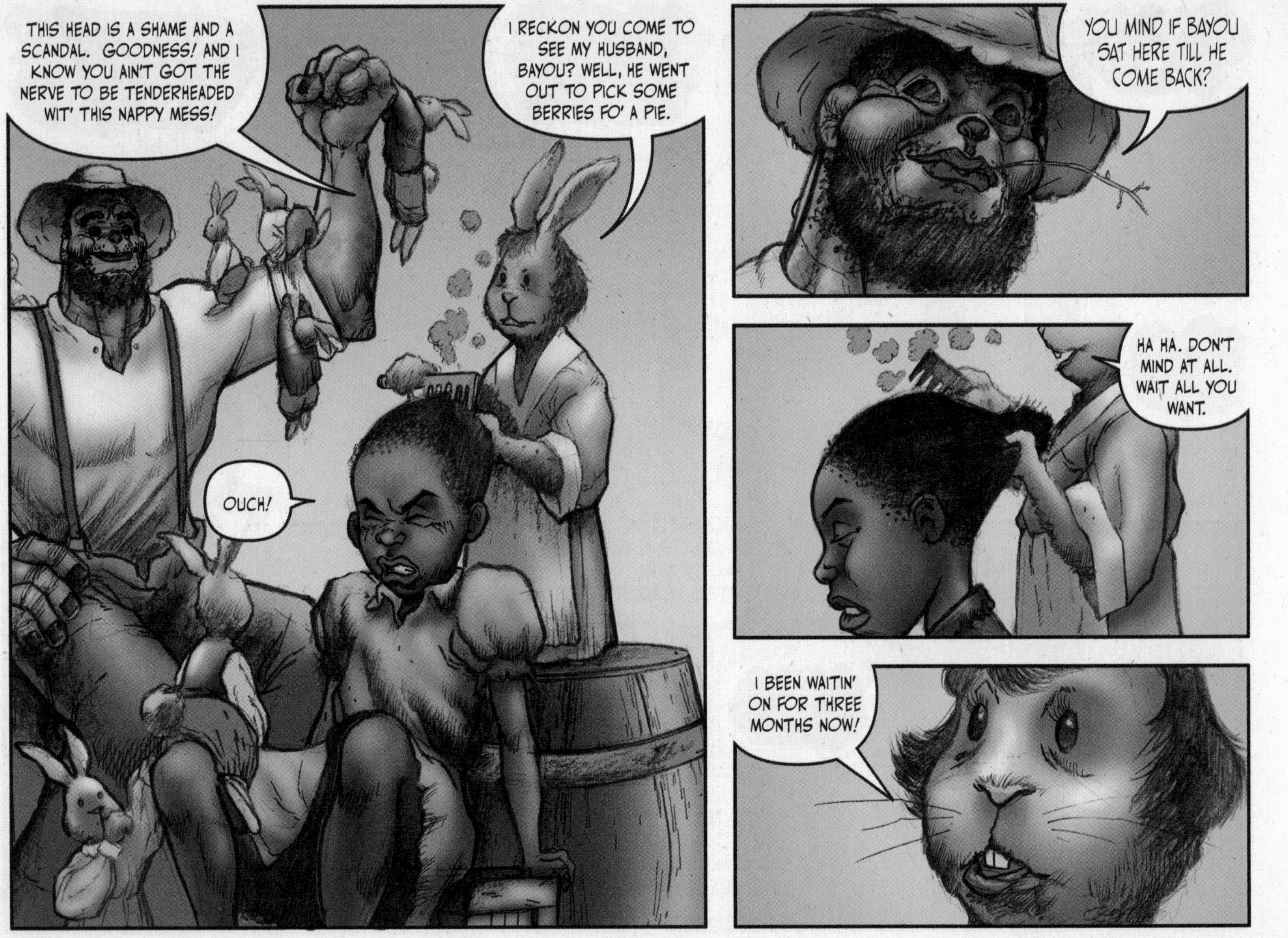
THIS HEAD IS A SHAME AND A SCANDAL. GOODNESS! AND I KNOW YOU AIN'T GOT THE NERVE TO BE TENDERHEADED WIT' THIS NAPPY MESS!
I RECKON YOU COME TO SEE MY HUSBAND, BAYOU? WELL, HE WENT OUT TO PICK SOME BERRIES FO' A PIE.
OUCH!
YOU MIND IF BAYOU SAT HERE TILL HE COME BACK?
HA HA. DON'T MIND AT ALL. WAIT ALL YOU WANT.
I BEEN WAITIN' ON FOR THREE MONTHS NOW!

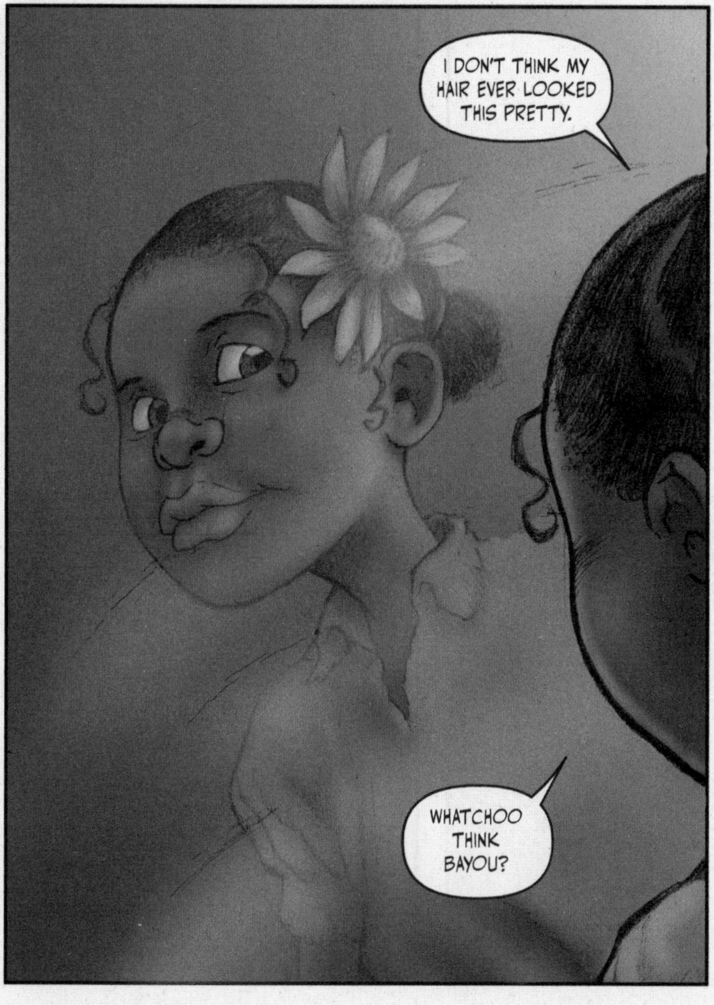
I DON'T THINK MY HAIR EVER LOOKED THIS PRETTY.
WHATCHOO THINK BAYOU?

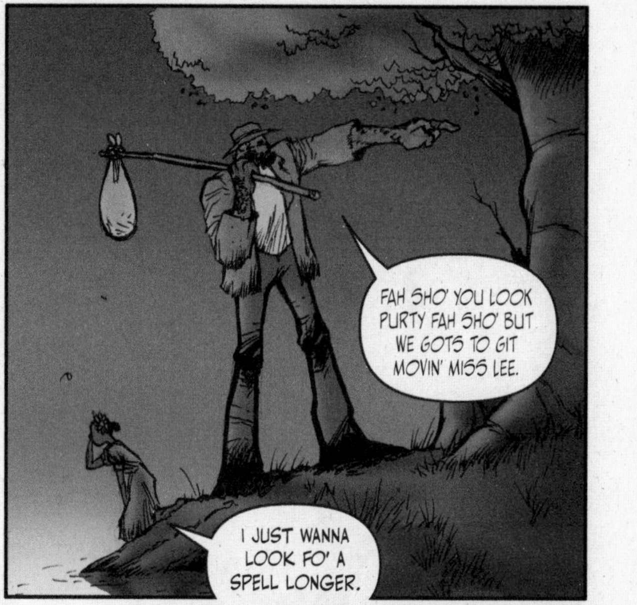
FAH SHO' YOU LOOK PURTY FAH SHO' BUT WE GOTS TO GIT MOVIN' MISS LEE.
I JUST WANNA LOOK FO' A SPELL LONGER.

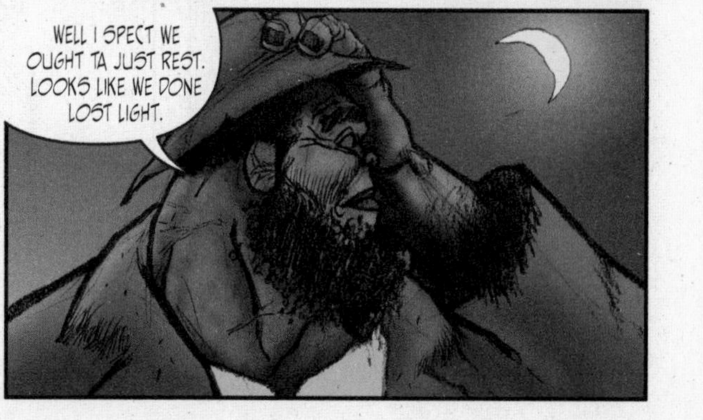
WELL I SPECT WE OUGHT TA JUST REST. LOOKS LIKE WE DONE LOST LIGHT.

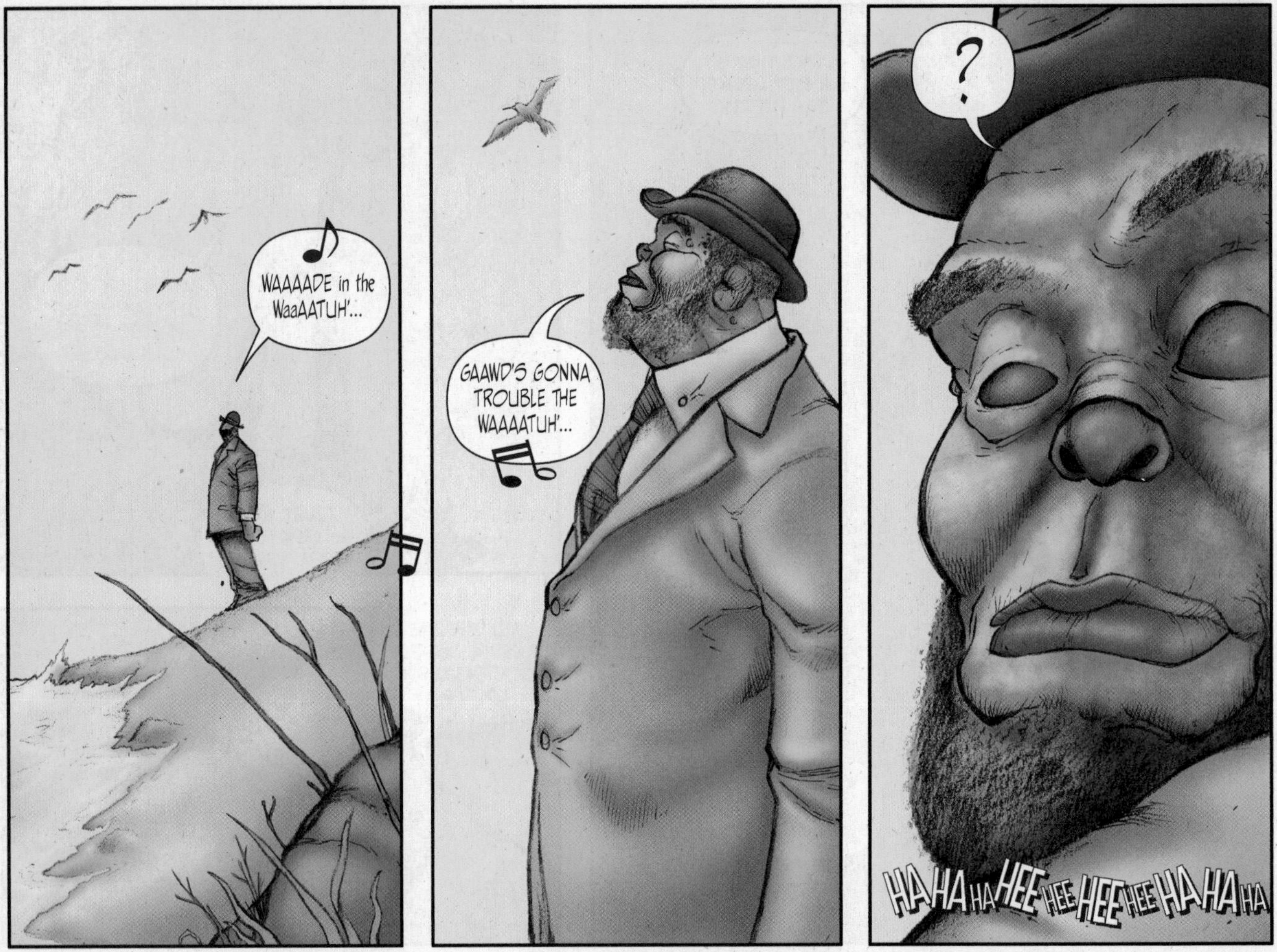
WAAAADE in the WaaAATUH'...
GAAWD'S GONNA TROUBLE THE WAAAATUH'...
?
HA HA HA HEE HEE HEE HEE HA HA HA

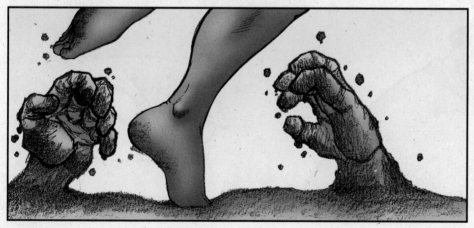

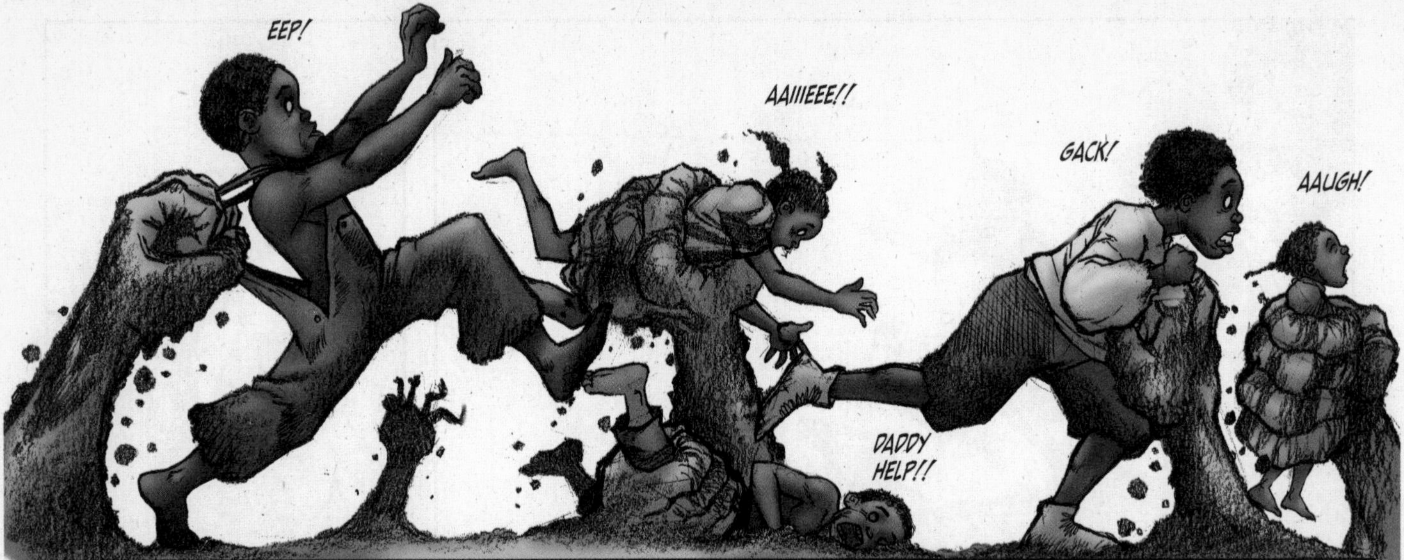
EEP!
AAIIIEEE!!
DADDY HELP!!
GACK!
AAUGH!

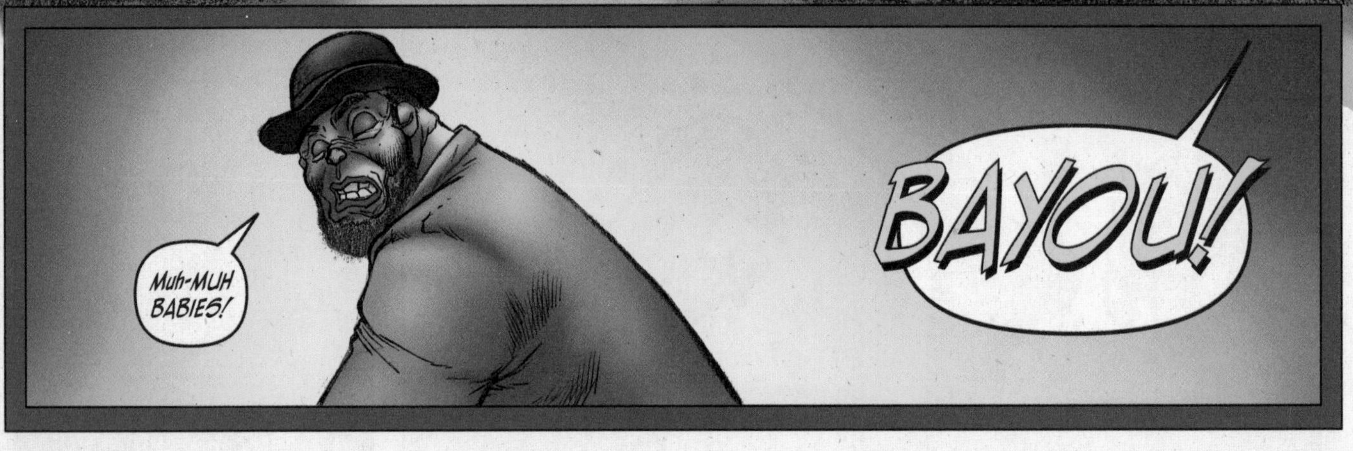
Muh-MUH BABIES!
BAYOU!

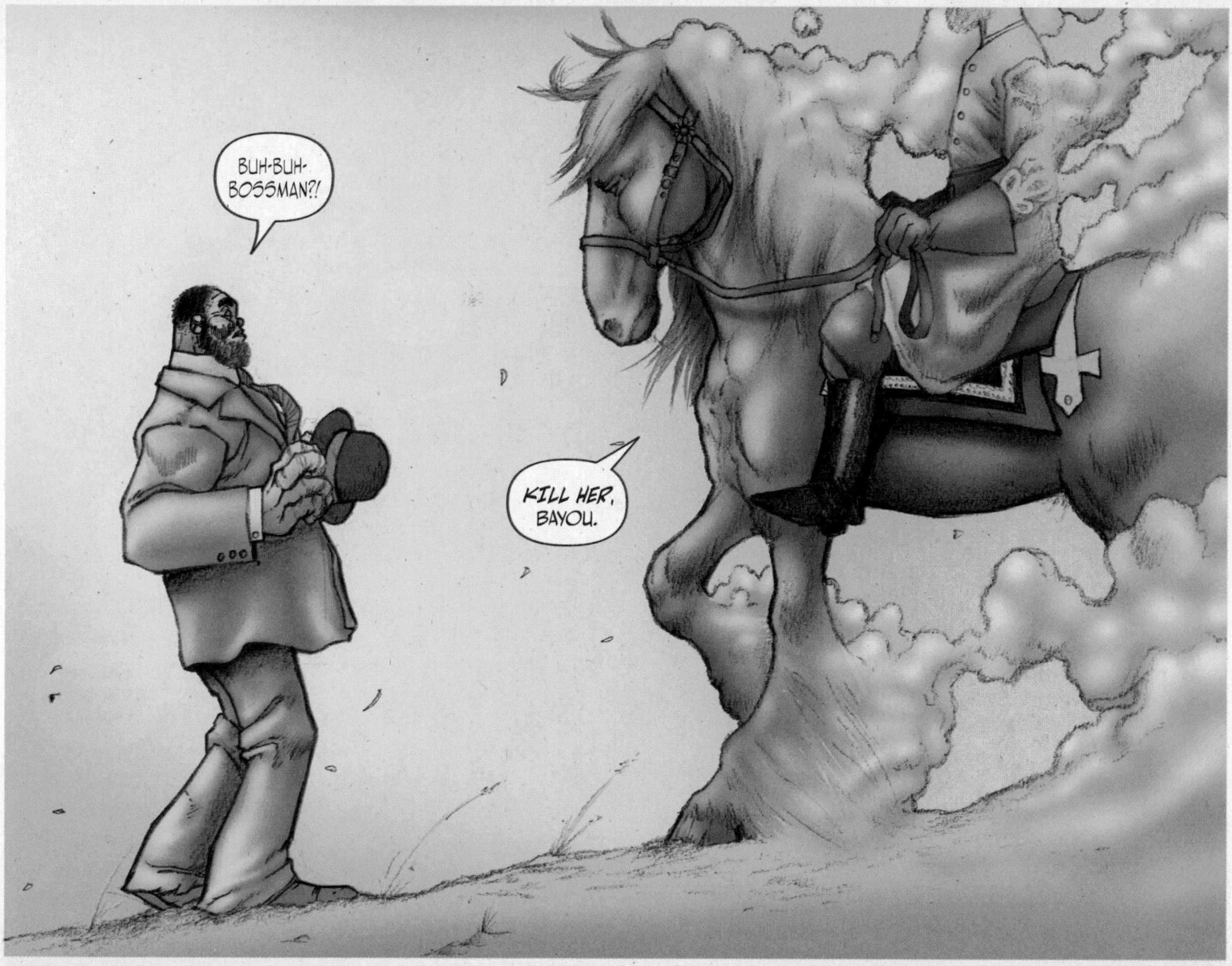
BUH-BUH-BOSSMAN?!
KILL HER, BAYOU.

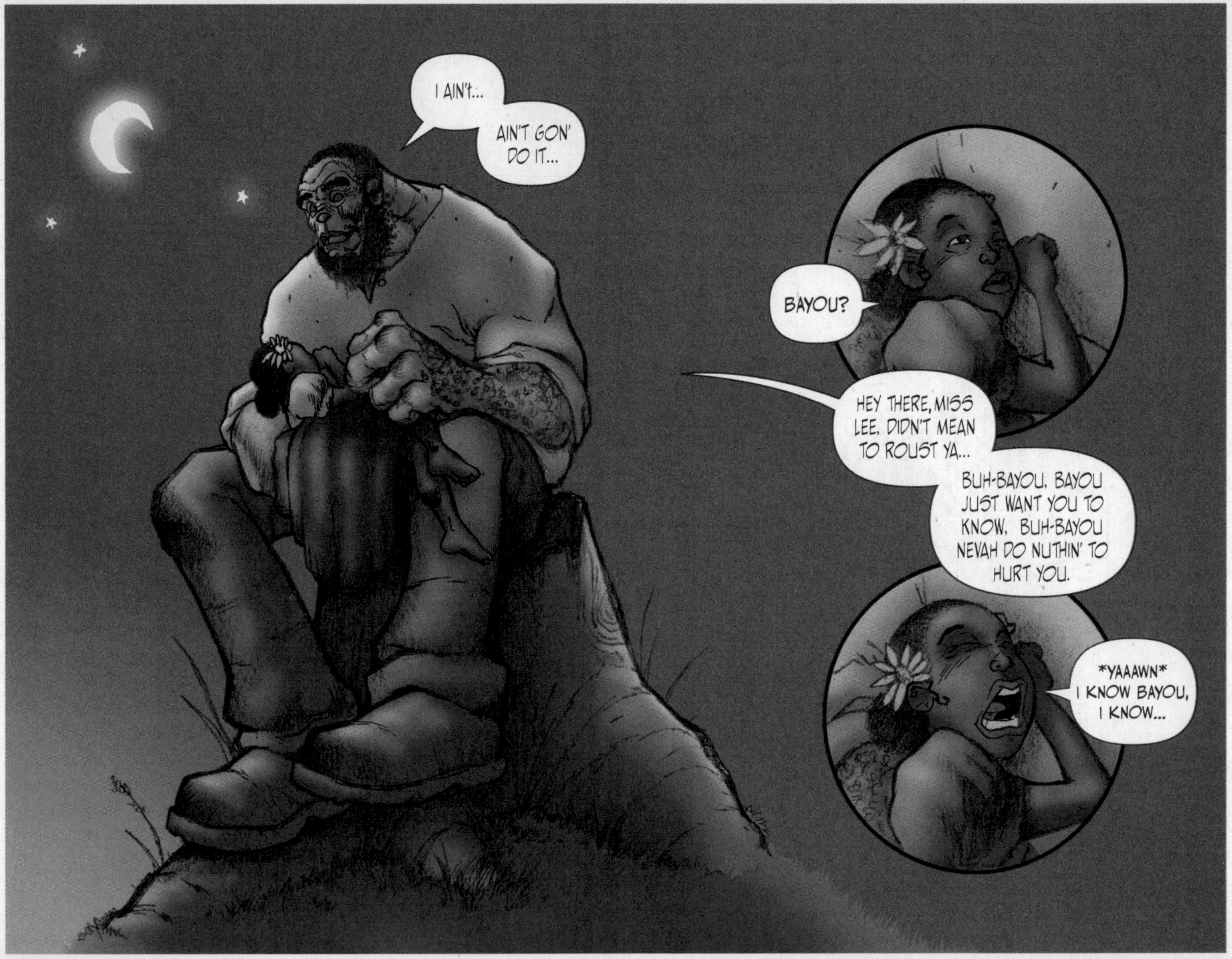
I AIN'T...
AIN'T GON' DO IT...
BAYOU?
HEY THERE, MISS LEE. DIDN'T MEAN TO ROUST YA...
BUH-BAYOU, BAYOU JUST WANT YOU TO KNOW. BUH-BAYOU NEVAH DO NUTHIN' TO HURT YOU.
YAAAWN I KNOW BAYOU, I KNOW...

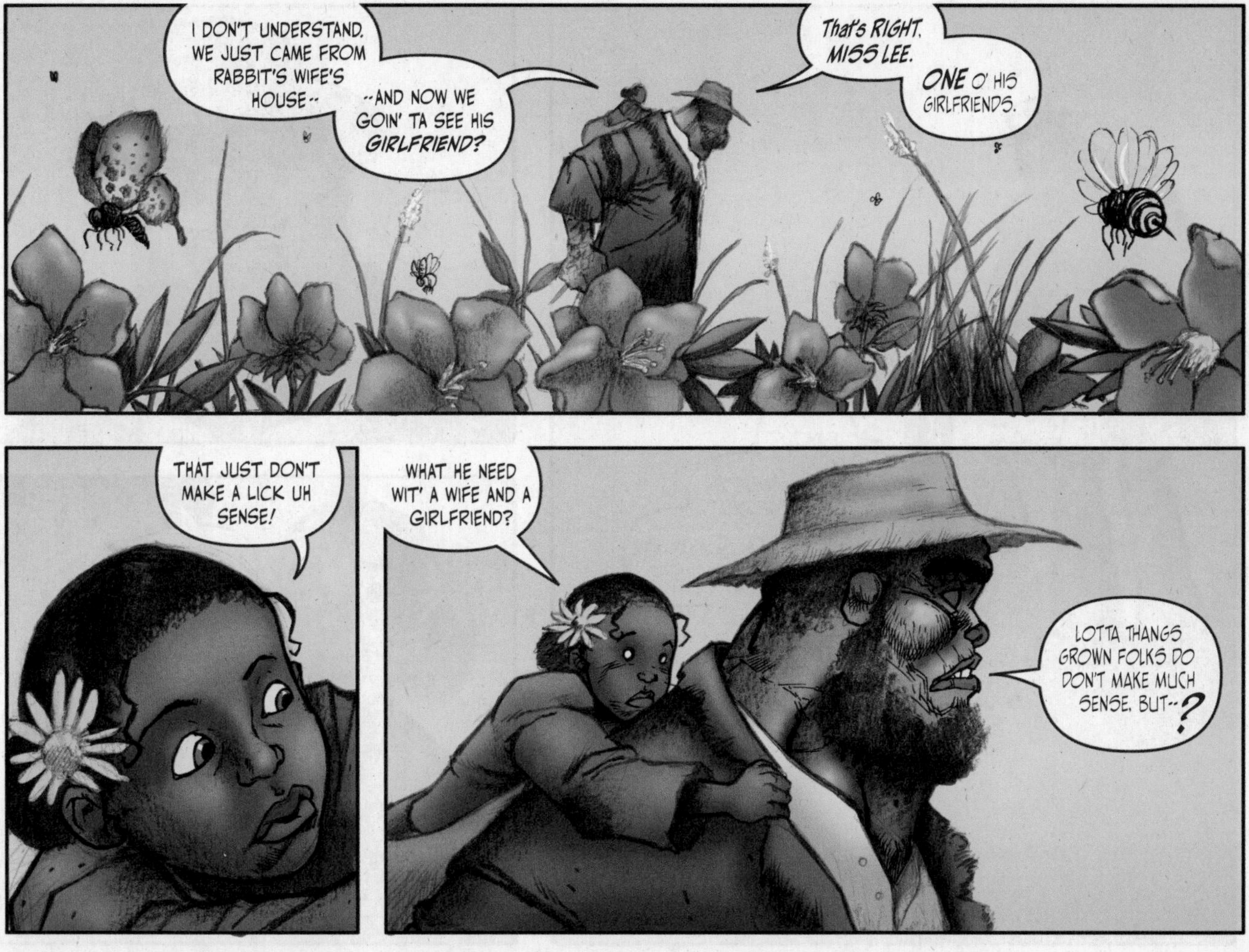
I DON'T UNDERSTAND. WE JUST CAME FROM RABBIT'S WIFE'S HOUSE--
--AND NOW WE GOIN' TA SEE HIS GIRLFRIEND?
That's RIGHT, MISS LEE.
ONE O' HIS GIRLFRIENDS.
THAT JUST DON'T MAKE A LICK UH SENSE!
WHAT HE NEED WIT' A WIFE AND A GIRLFRIEND?
LOTTA THANGS GROWN FOLKS DO DON'T MAKE MUCH SENSE, BUT--?

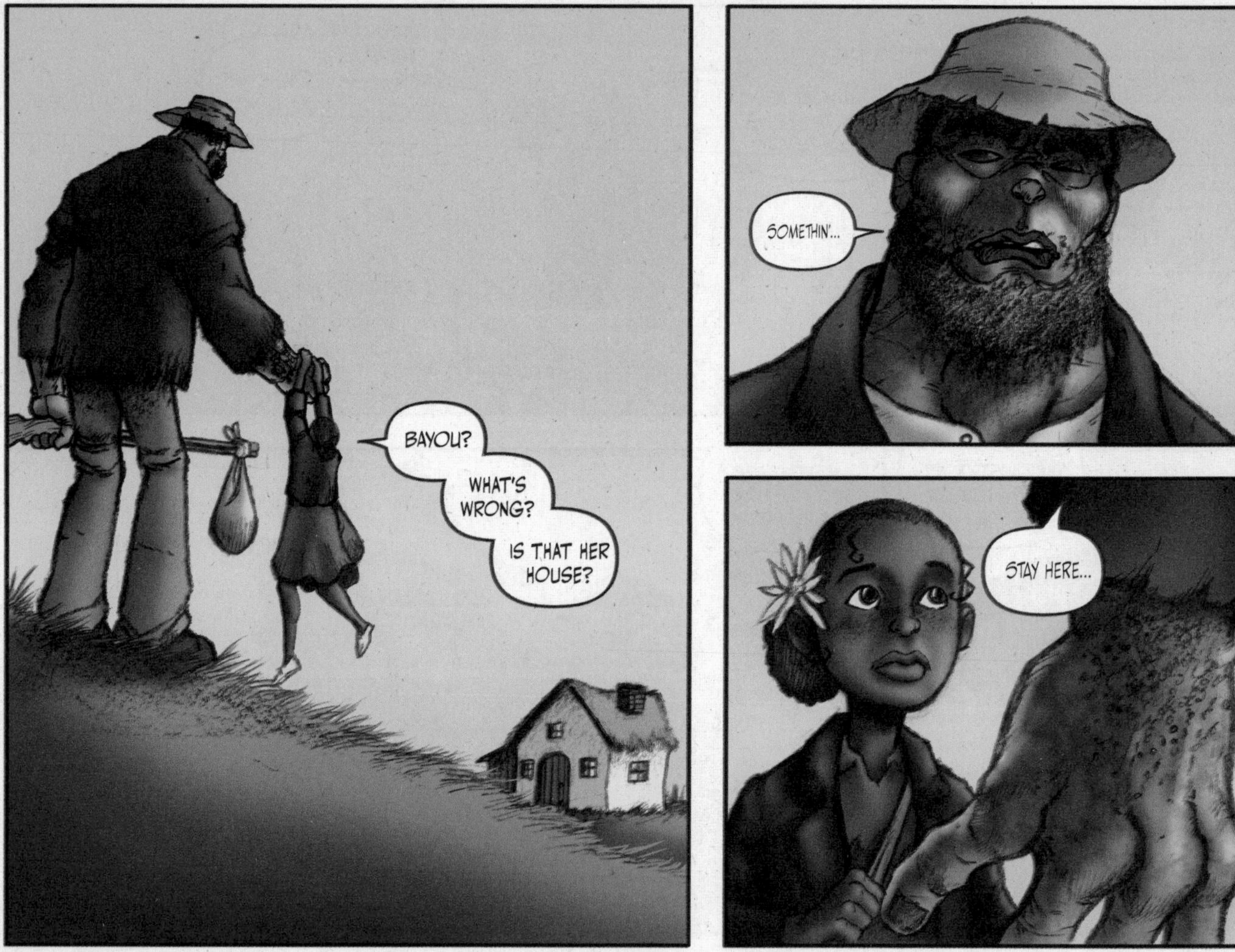
BAYOU?
WHAT'S WRONG?
IS THAT HER HOUSE?
SOMETHIN'...
STAY HERE...

BETTY?! MISS BETTY?! YOU HOME?

CREEAAK

Oh...

Lordy...

BAYOU! CAN I COME NOW?

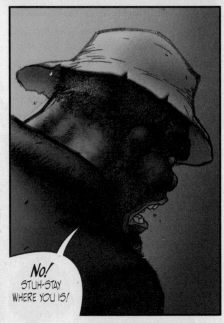

No! STUH-STAY WHERE YOU IS!

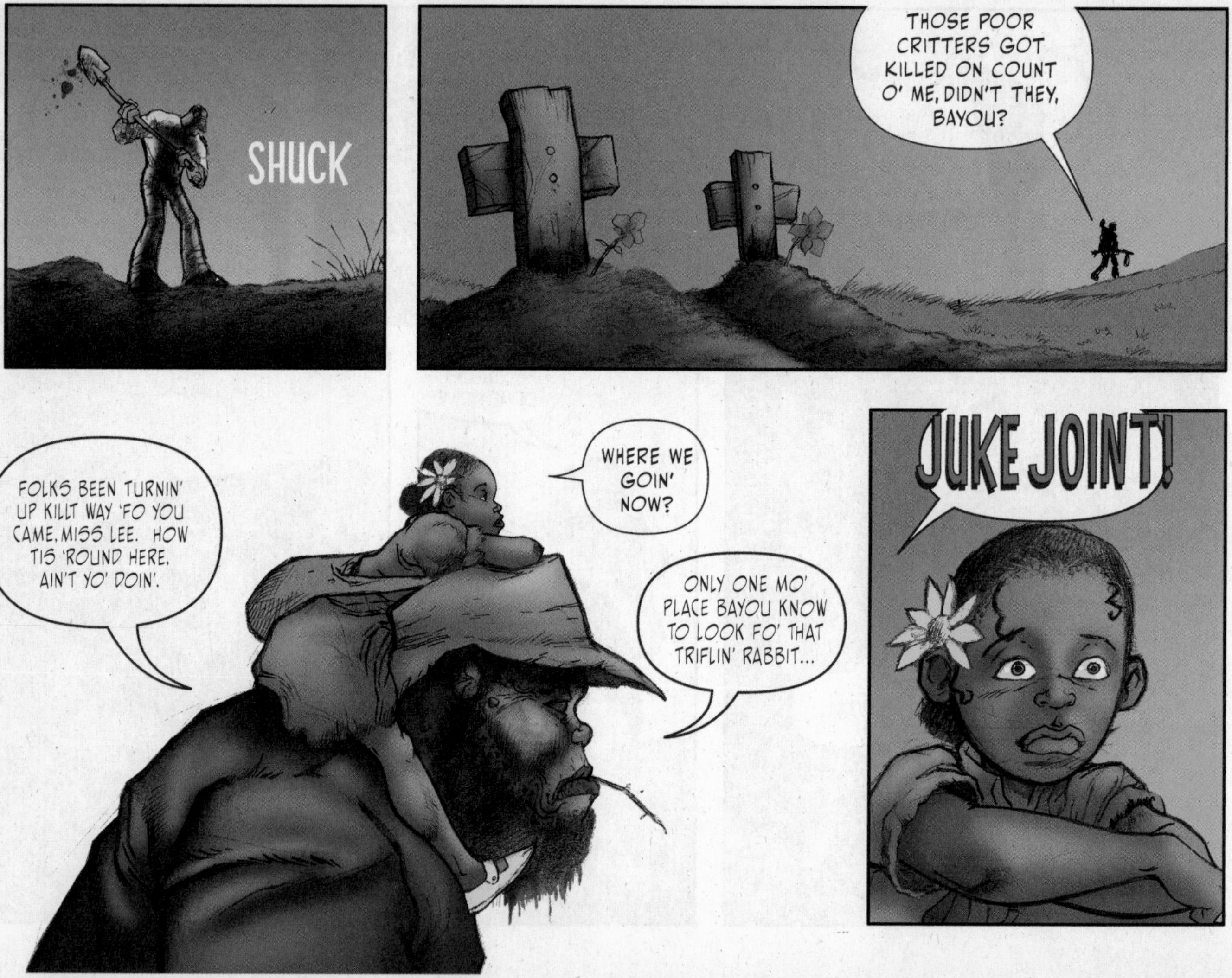
SHUCK
THOSE POOR CRITTERS GOT KILLED ON COUNT O' ME, DIDN'T THEY, BAYOU?
FOLKS BEEN TURNIN' UP KILLT WAY 'FO YOU CAME, MISS LEE. HOW TIS 'ROUND HERE, AIN'T YO' DOIN'.
WHERE WE GOIN' NOW?
ONLY ONE MO' PLACE BAYOU KNOW TO LOOK FO' THAT TRIFLIN' RABBIT...
JUKE JOINT!

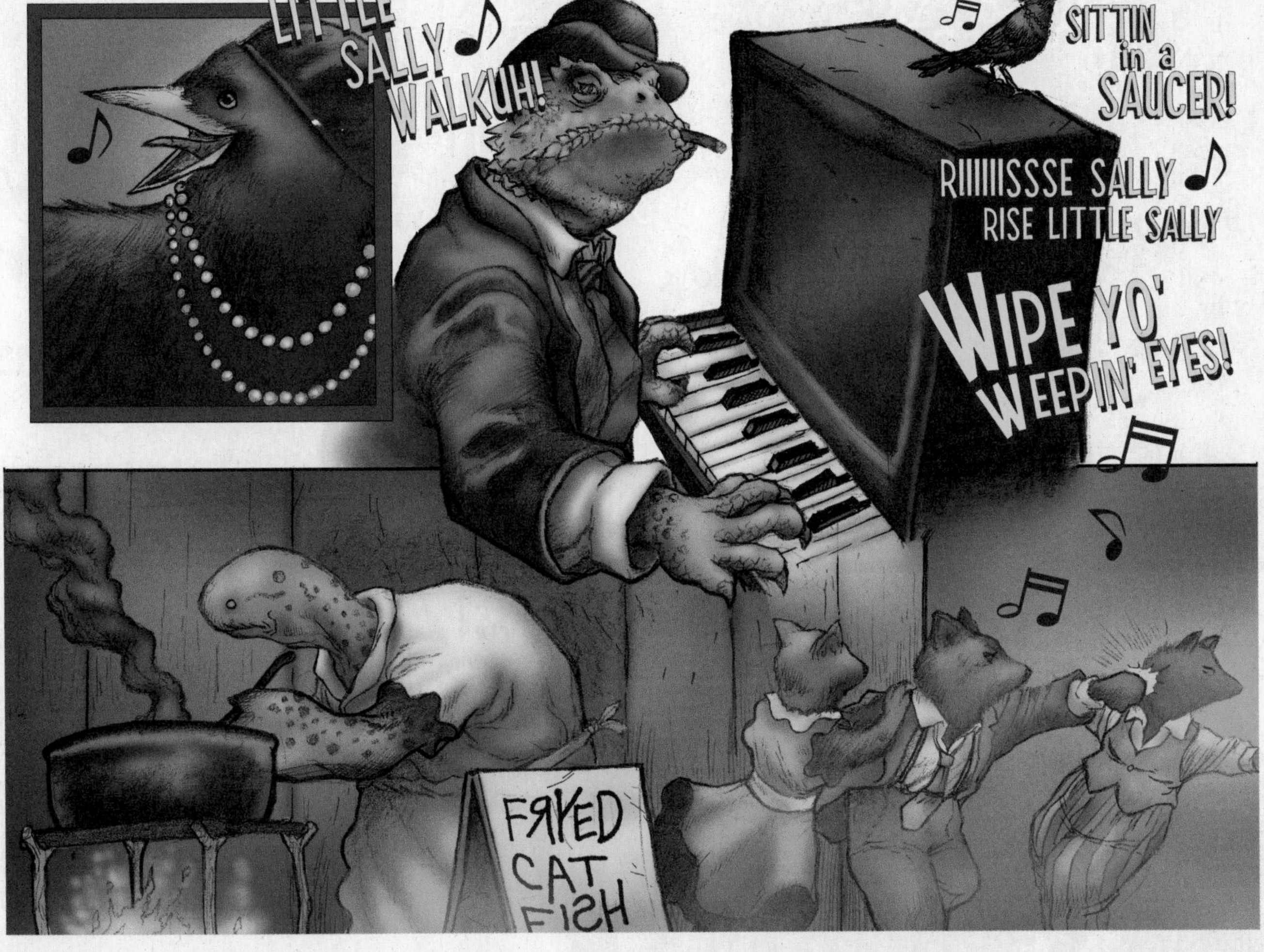
LITTLE SALLY WALKUH!
SITTIN in a SAUCER!
RIIIIIISSSE SALLY
RISE LITTLE SALLY
WIPE YO' WEEPIN' EYES!
FRYED CAT FISH

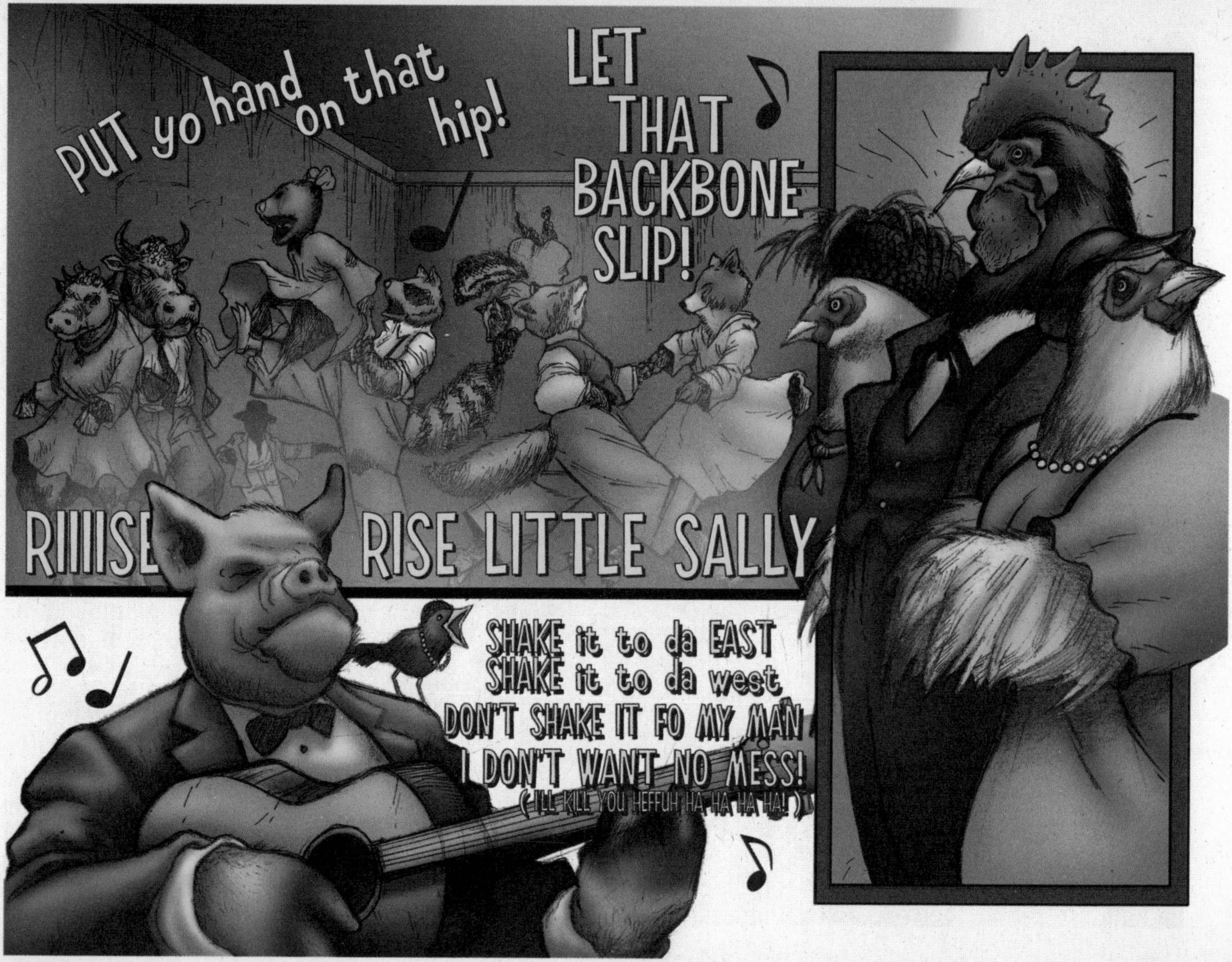
PUT yo hand on that hip!
LET THAT BACKBONE SLIP!
RIIISE
RISE LITTLE SALLY
SHAKE it to da EAST
SHAKE it to da west
DON'T SHAKE IT FO MY MAN
I DON'T WANT NO MESS!
(I'LL KILL YOU HEFFUH HA HA HA HA!)

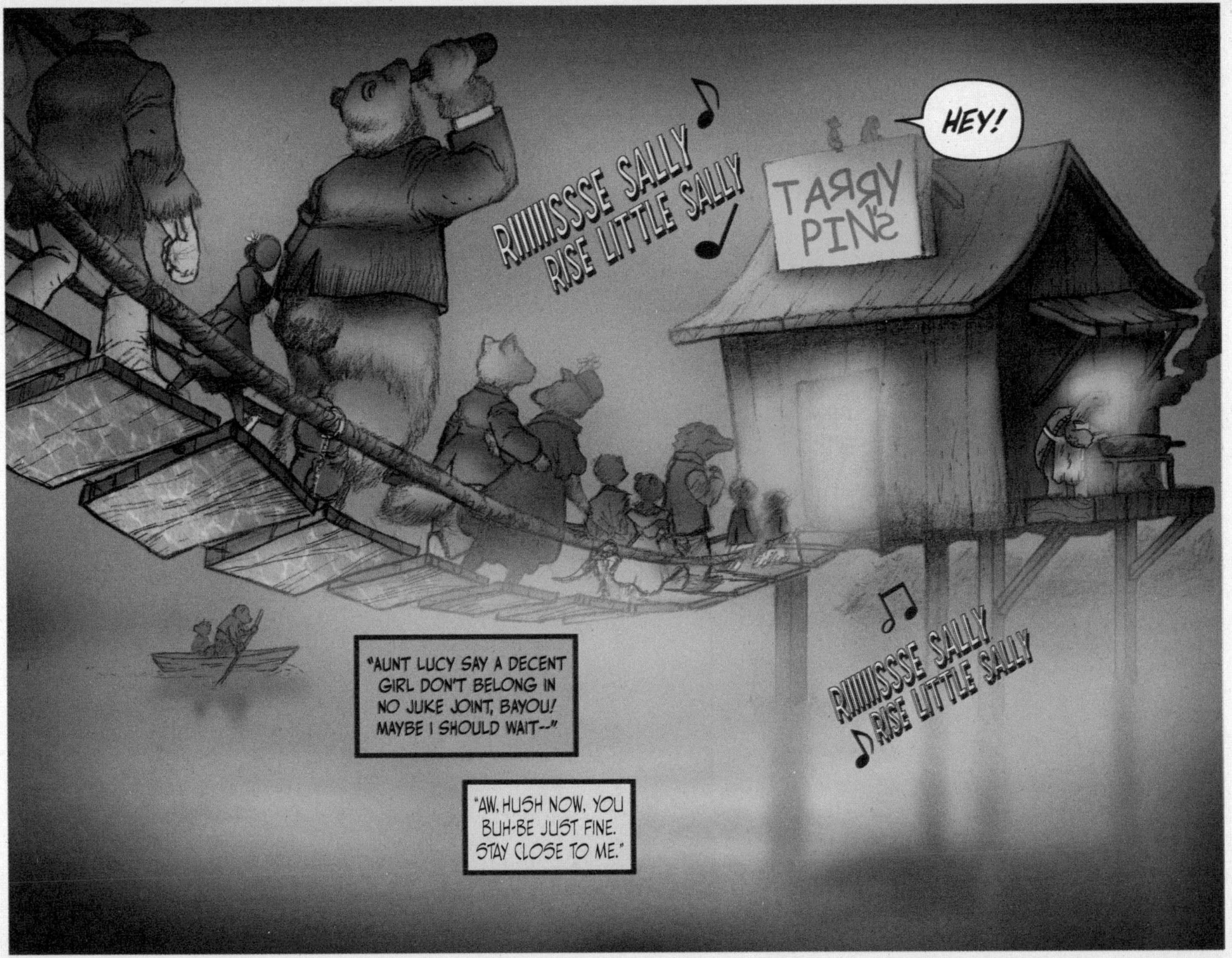
RIIIIISSSE SALLY RISE LITTLE SALLY
TARRY PIN'S
HEY!
RIIIIISSSE SALLY RISE LITTLE SALLY
"AUNT LUCY SAY A DECENT GIRL DON'T BELONG IN NO JUKE JOINT, BAYOU! MAYBE I SHOULD WAIT--"
"AW, HUSH NOW, YOU BUH-BE JUST FINE. STAY CLOSE TO ME."

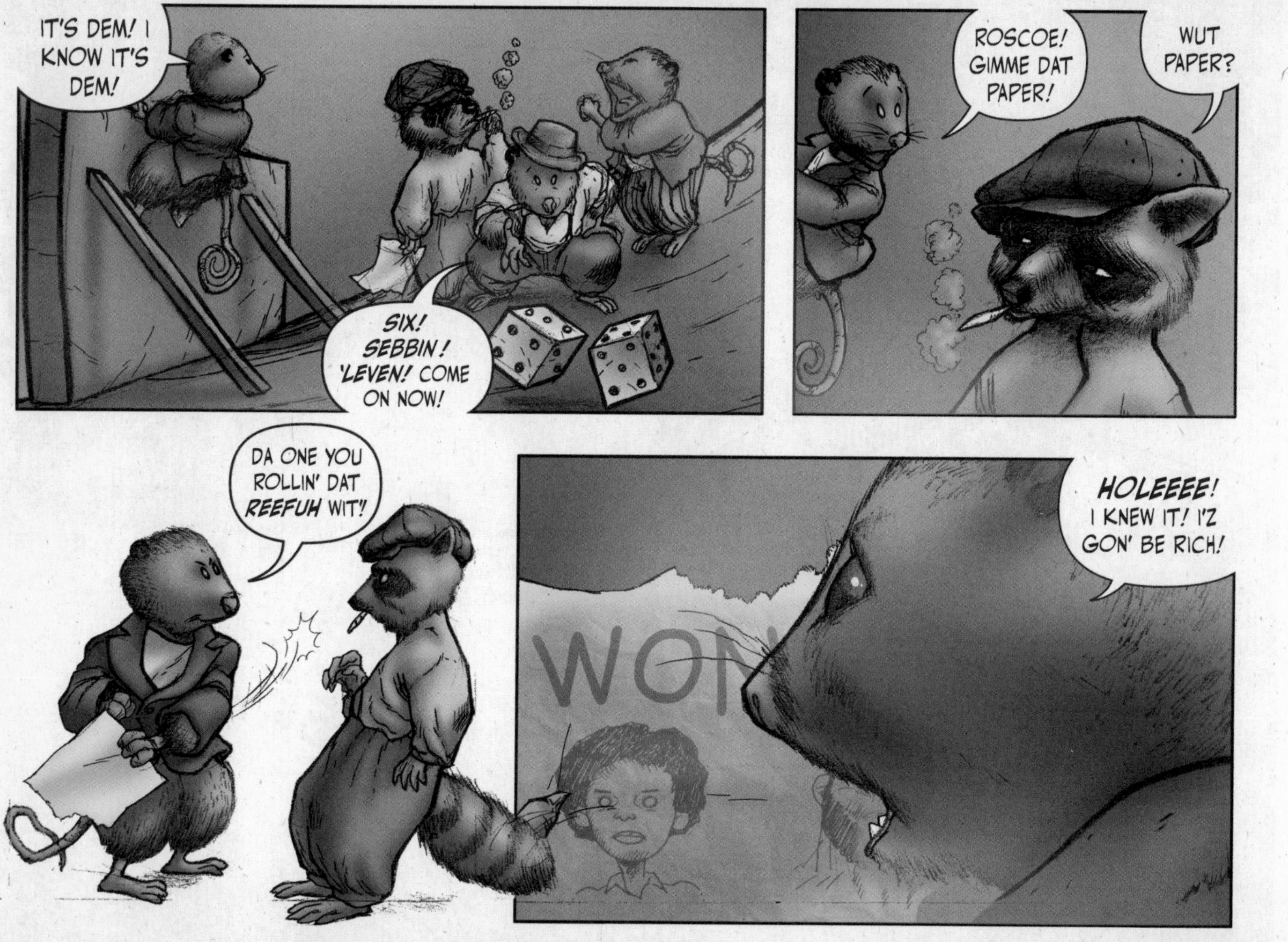

IT'S DEM! I KNOW IT'S DEM!
SIX! SEBBIN! 'LEVEN! COME ON NOW!
ROSCOE! GIMME DAT PAPER!
WUT PAPER?
DA ONE YOU ROLLIN' DAT REEFUH WIT'!
HOLEEEE! I KNEW IT! I'Z GON' BE RICH!
WON

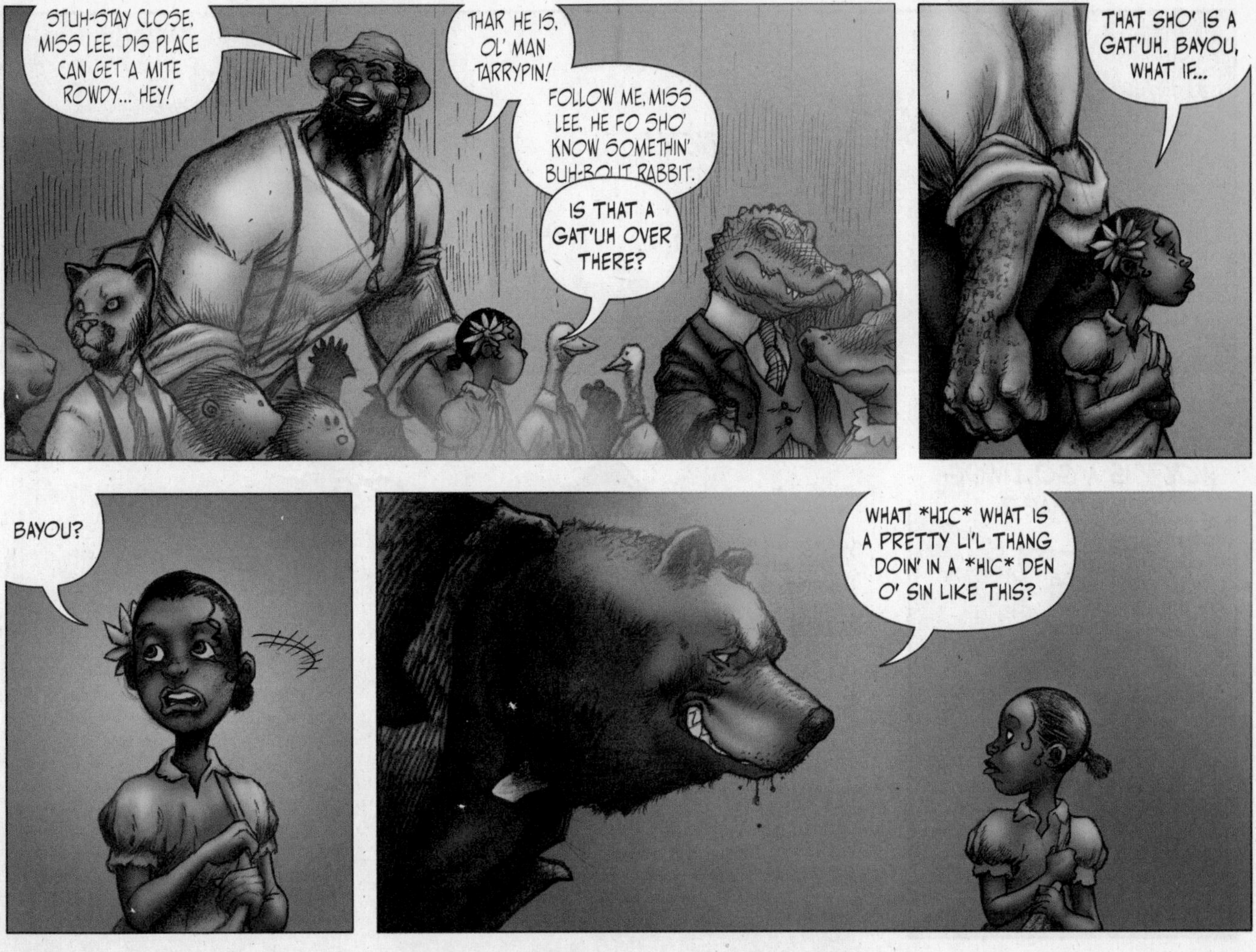
STUH-STAY CLOSE, MISS LEE. DIS PLACE CAN GET A MITE ROWDY... HEY!
THAR HE IS, OL' MAN TARRYPIN!
FOLLOW ME, MISS LEE. HE FO SHO' KNOW SOMETHIN' BUH-BOUT RABBIT.
IS THAT A GAT'UH OVER THERE?
THAT SHO' IS A GAT'UH. BAYOU, WHAT IF...
BAYOU?
WHAT *HIC* WHAT IS A PRETTY LI'L THANG DOIN' IN A *HIC* DEN O' SIN LIKE THIS?

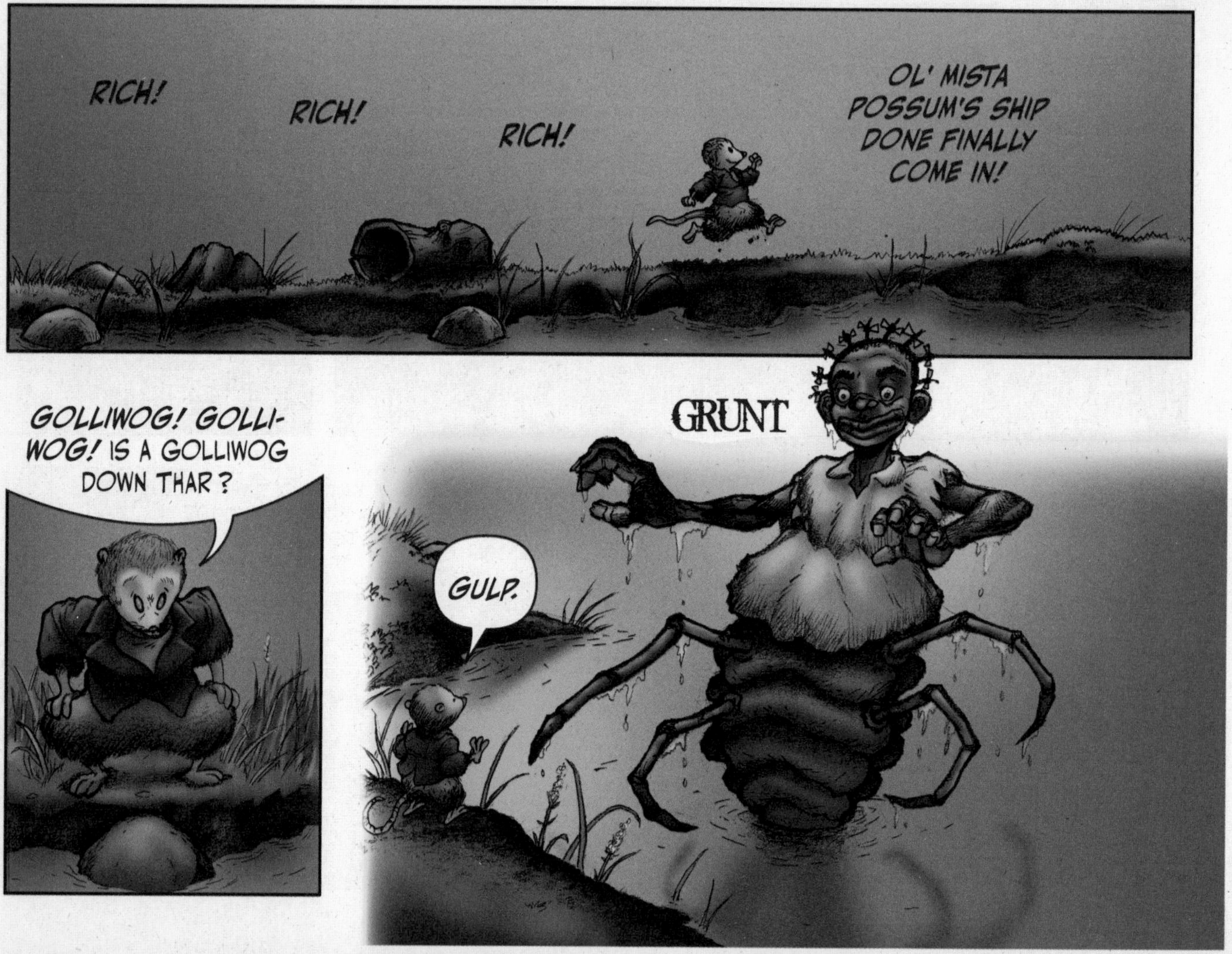
RICH!
RICH!
RICH!
OL' MISTA POSSUM'S SHIP DONE FINALLY COME IN!
GOLLIWOG! GOLLI-WOG! IS A GOLLIWOG DOWN THAR?
GRUNT
GULP.

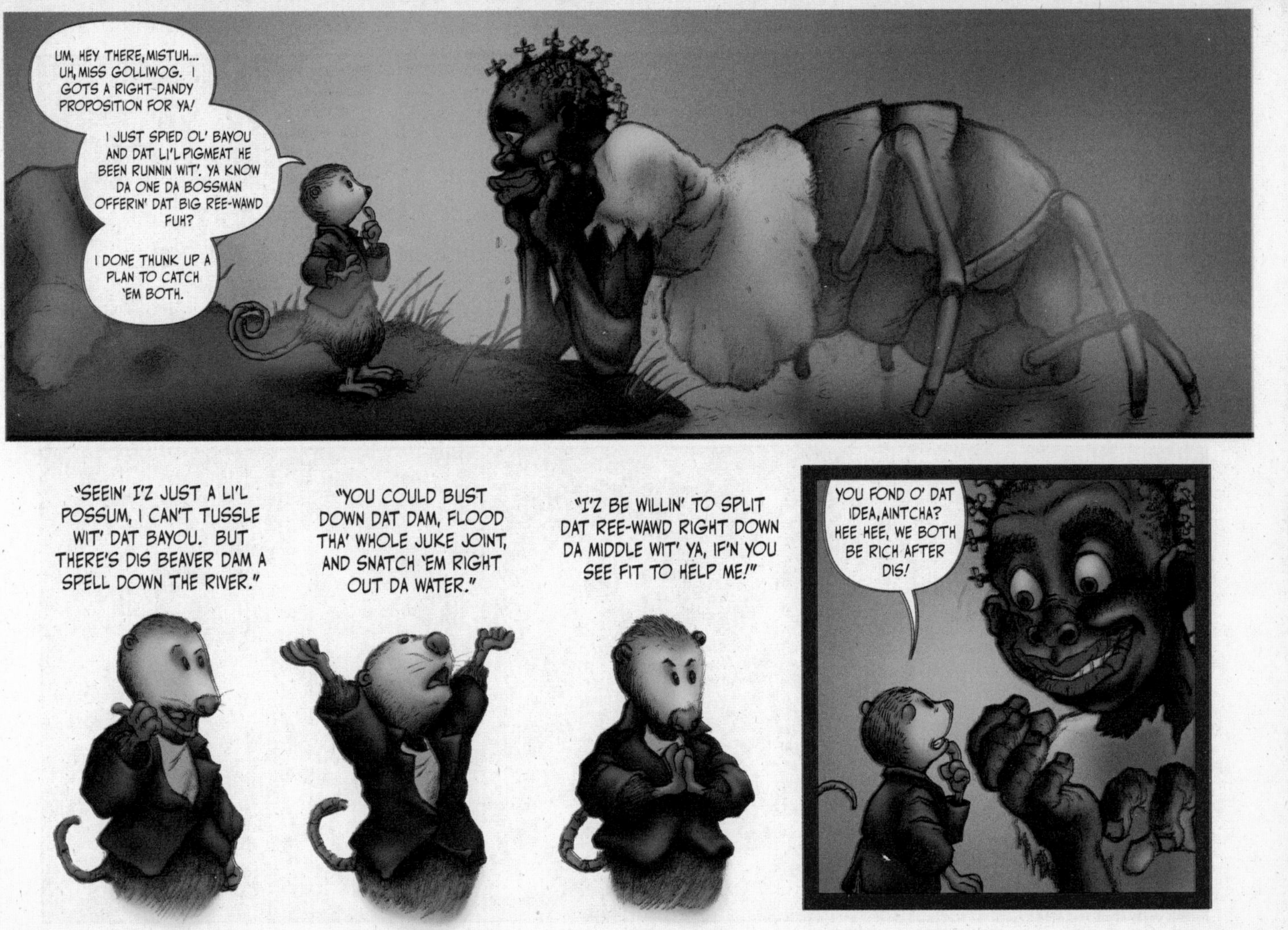
UM, HEY THERE, MISTUH... UH, MISS GOLLIWOG. I GOTS A RIGHT DANDY PROPOSITION FOR YA!
I JUST SPIED OL' BAYOU AND DAT LI'L PIGMEAT HE BEEN RUNNIN WIT'. YA KNOW DA ONE DA BOSSMAN OFFERIN' DAT BIG REE-WAWD FUH?
I DONE THUNK UP A PLAN TO CATCH 'EM BOTH.
"SEEIN' I'Z JUST A LI'L POSSUM, I CAN'T TUSSLE WIT' DAT BAYOU. BUT THERE'S DIS BEAVER DAM A SPELL DOWN THE RIVER."
"YOU COULD BUST DOWN DAT DAM, FLOOD THA' WHOLE JUKE JOINT, AND SNATCH 'EM RIGHT OUT DA WATER."
"I'Z BE WILLIN' TO SPLIT DAT REE-WAWD RIGHT DOWN DA MIDDLE WIT' YA, IF'N YOU SEE FIT TO HELP ME!"
YOU FOND O' DAT IDEA, AINTCHA? HEE HEE, WE BOTH BE RICH AFTER DIS!

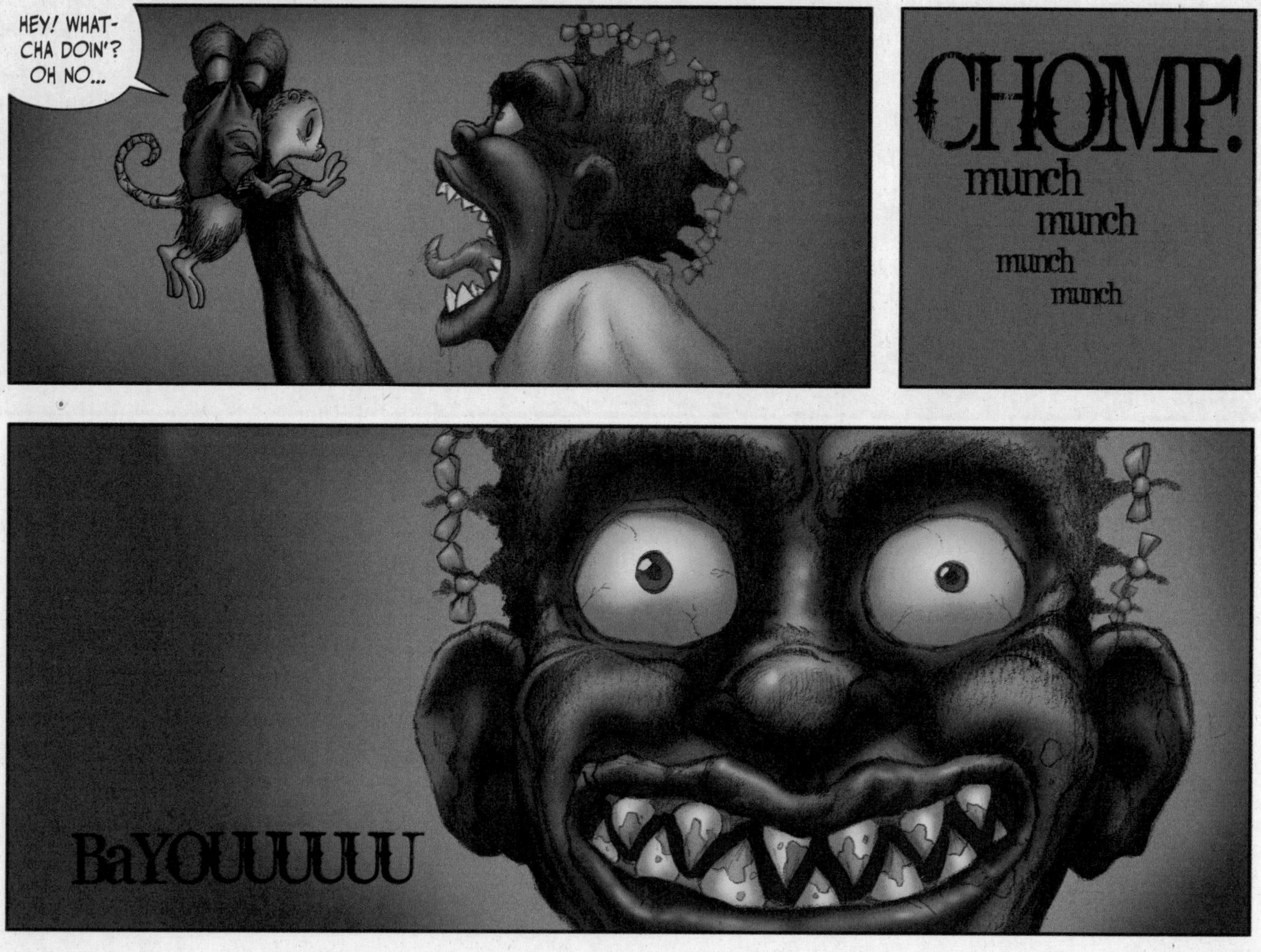
HEY! WHAT-CHA DOIN'? OH NO...
CHOMP!
munch
munch
munch
munch
BaYOUUUUUU

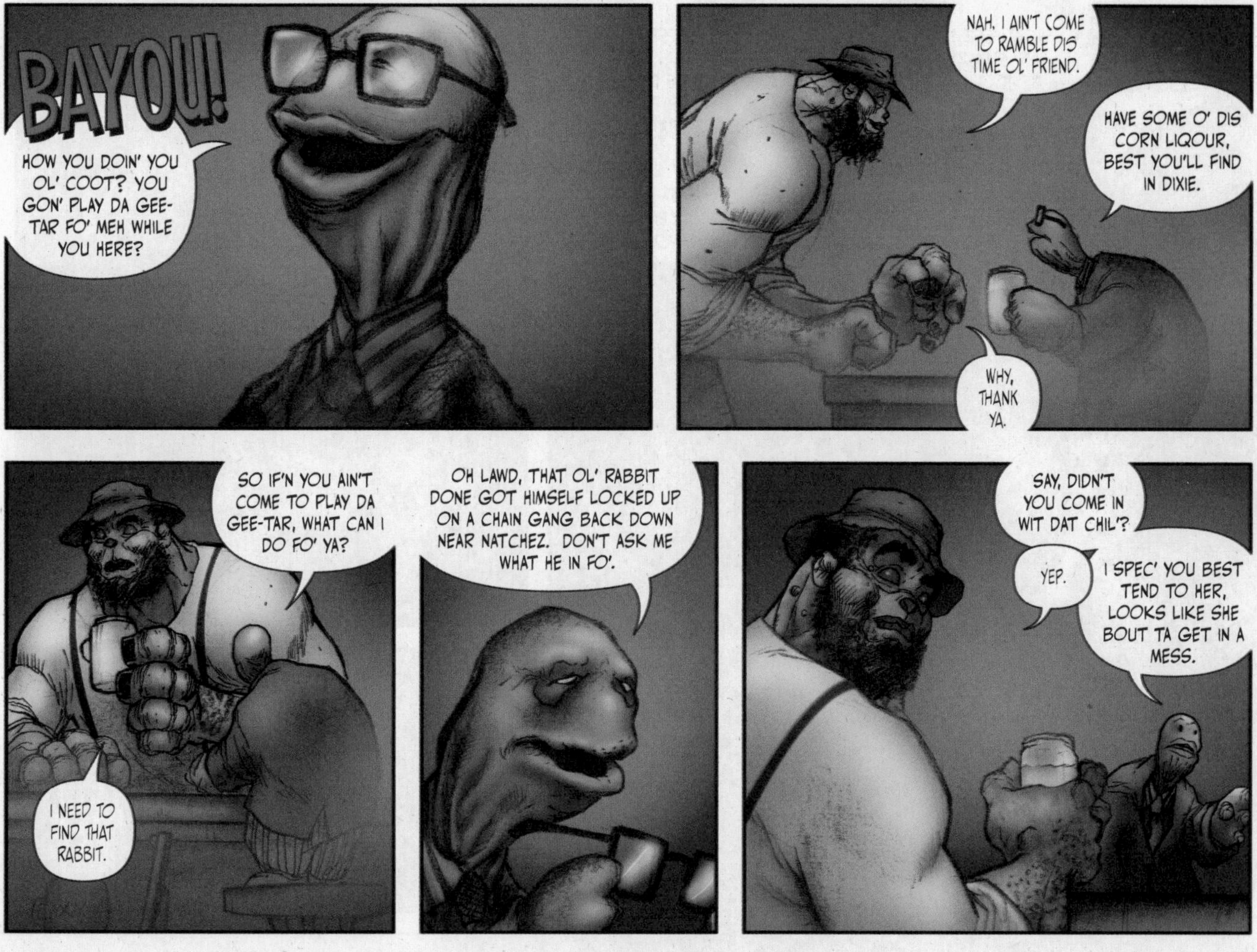
BAYOU!
HOW YOU DOIN' YOU OL' COOT? YOU GON' PLAY DA GEE-TAR FO' MEH WHILE YOU HERE?
NAH, I AIN'T COME TO RAMBLE DIS TIME OL' FRIEND.
HAVE SOME O' DIS CORN LIQOUR, BEST YOU'LL FIND IN DIXIE.
WHY, THANK YA.
SO IF'N YOU AIN'T COME TO PLAY DA GEE-TAR, WHAT CAN I DO FO' YA?
I NEED TO FIND THAT RABBIT.
OH LAWD, THAT OL' RABBIT DONE GOT HIMSELF LOCKED UP ON A CHAIN GANG BACK DOWN NEAR NATCHEZ. DON'T ASK ME WHAT HE IN FO'.
SAY, DIDN'T YOU COME IN WIT DAT CHIL'?
YEP.
I SPEC' YOU BEST TEND TO HER, LOOKS LIKE SHE BOUT TA GET IN A MESS.

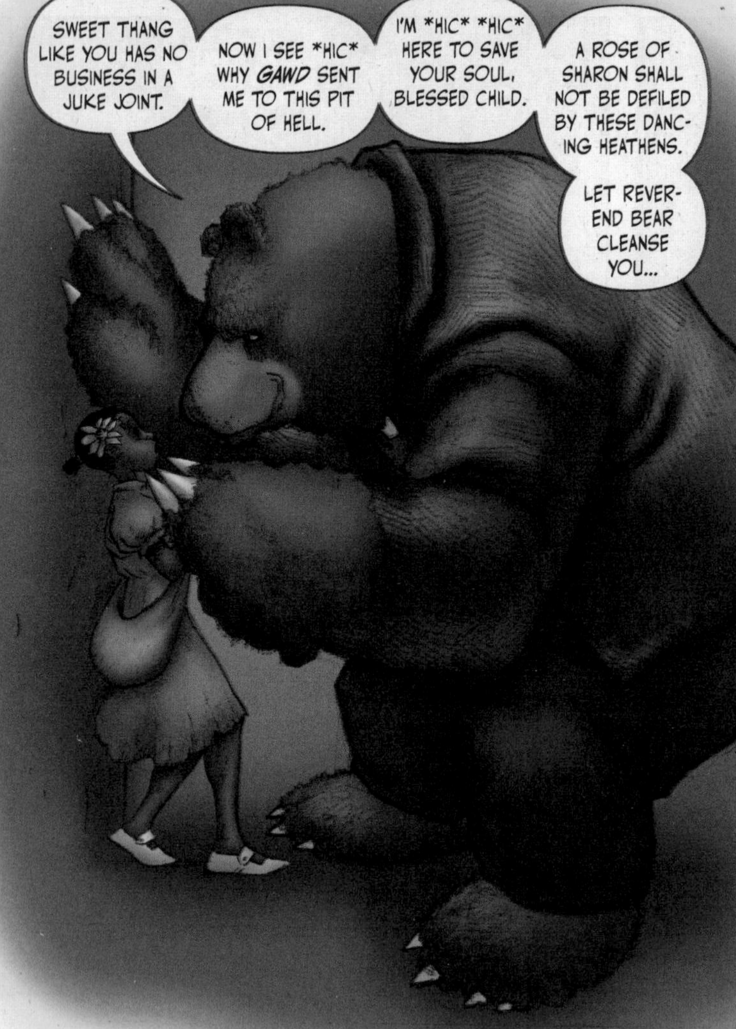
SWEET THANG LIKE YOU HAS NO BUSINESS IN A JUKE JOINT.
NOW I SEE *HIC* WHY *GAWD* SENT ME TO THIS PIT OF HELL.
I'M *HIC* *HIC* HERE TO SAVE YOUR SOUL, BLESSED CHILD.
A ROSE OF SHARON SHALL NOT BE DEFILED BY THESE DANCING HEATHENS.
LET REVEREND BEAR CLEANSE YOU...

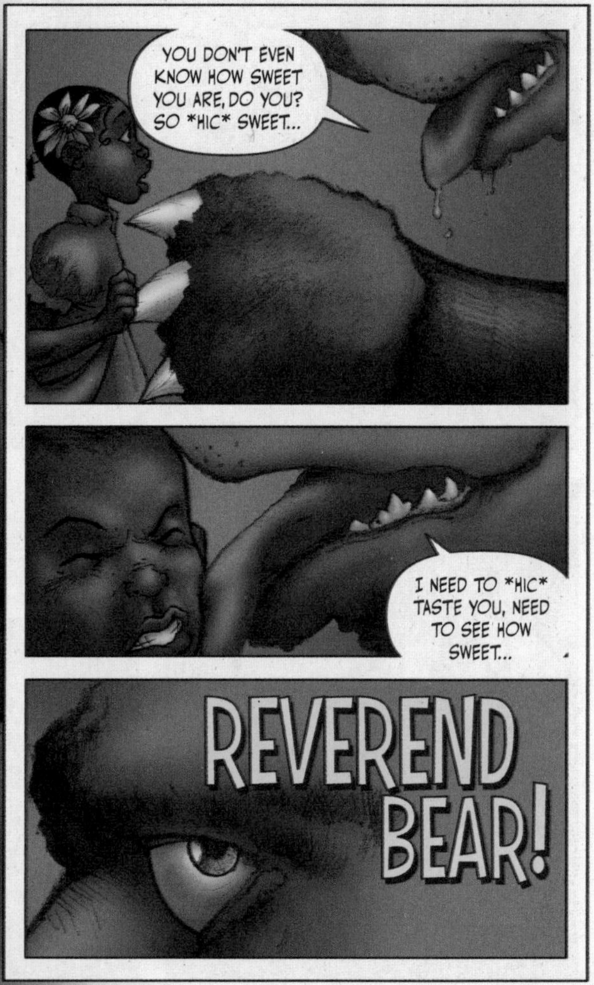
YOU DON'T EVEN KNOW HOW SWEET YOU ARE, DO YOU? SO *HIC* SWEET...
I NEED TO *HIC* TASTE YOU, NEED TO SEE HOW SWEET...
REVEREND BEAR!

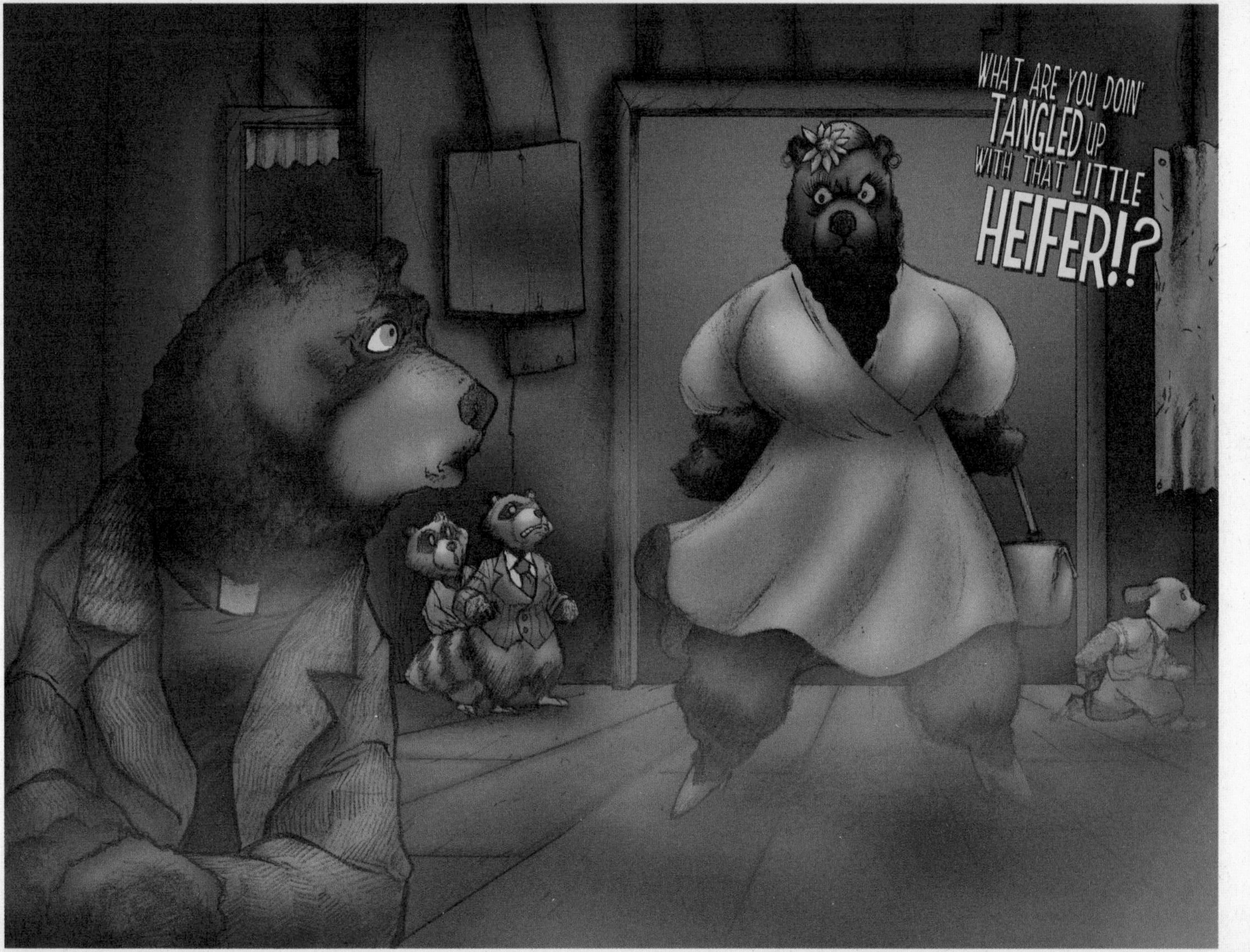
WHAT ARE YOU DOIN' TANGLED UP WITH THAT LITTLE HEIFER!?

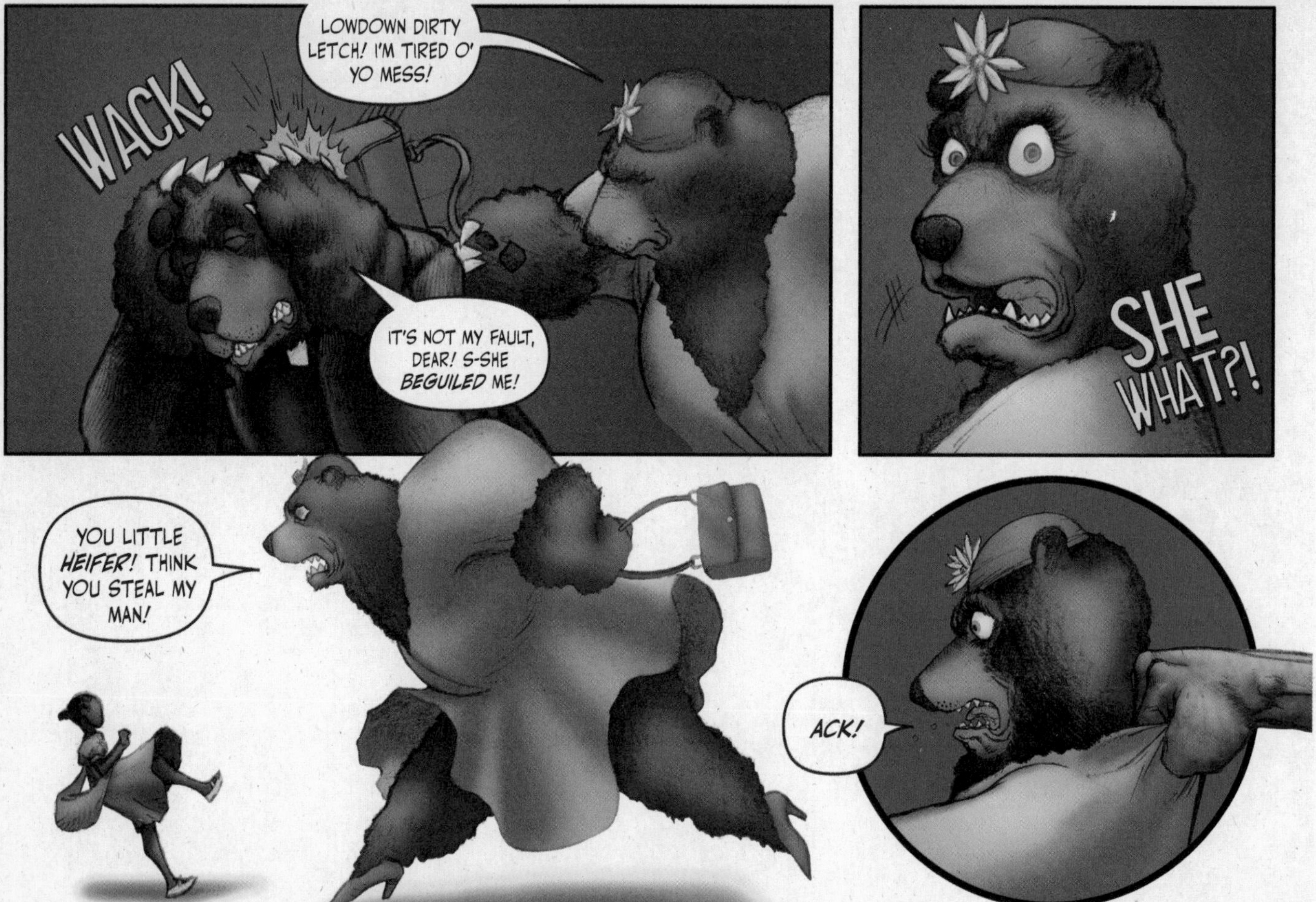
LOWDOWN DIRTY LETCH! I'M TIRED O' YO MESS!
WACK!
IT'S NOT MY FAULT, DEAR! S-SHE *BEGUILED* ME!
SHE WHAT?!
YOU LITTLE *HEIFER!* THINK YOU STEAL MY MAN!
ACK!

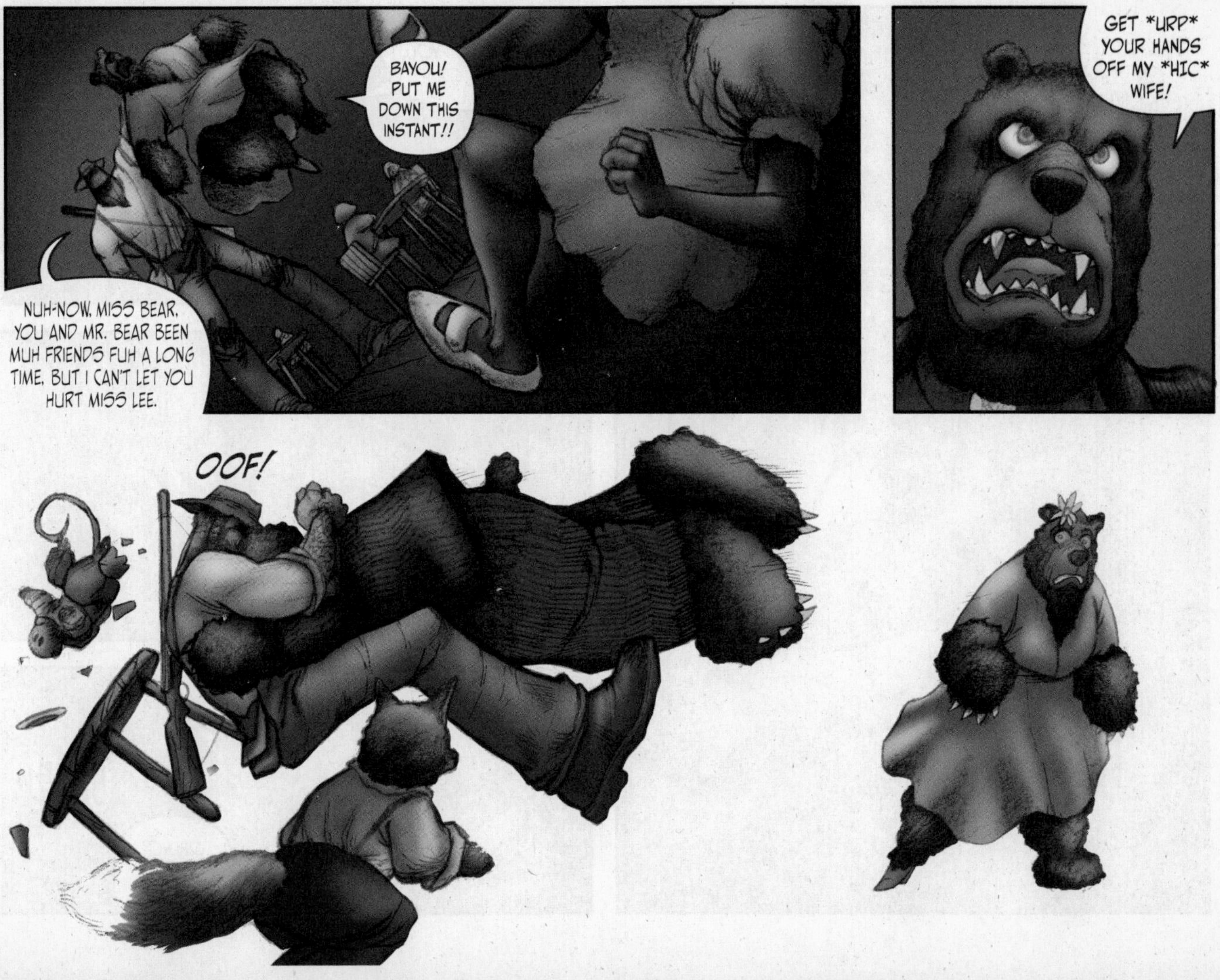
BAYOU! PUT ME DOWN THIS INSTANT!!
NUH-NOW, MISS BEAR, YOU AND MR. BEAR BEEN MUH FRIENDS FUH A LONG TIME, BUT I CAN'T LET YOU HURT MISS LEE.
GET *URP* YOUR HANDS OFF MY *HIC* WIFE!
OOF!

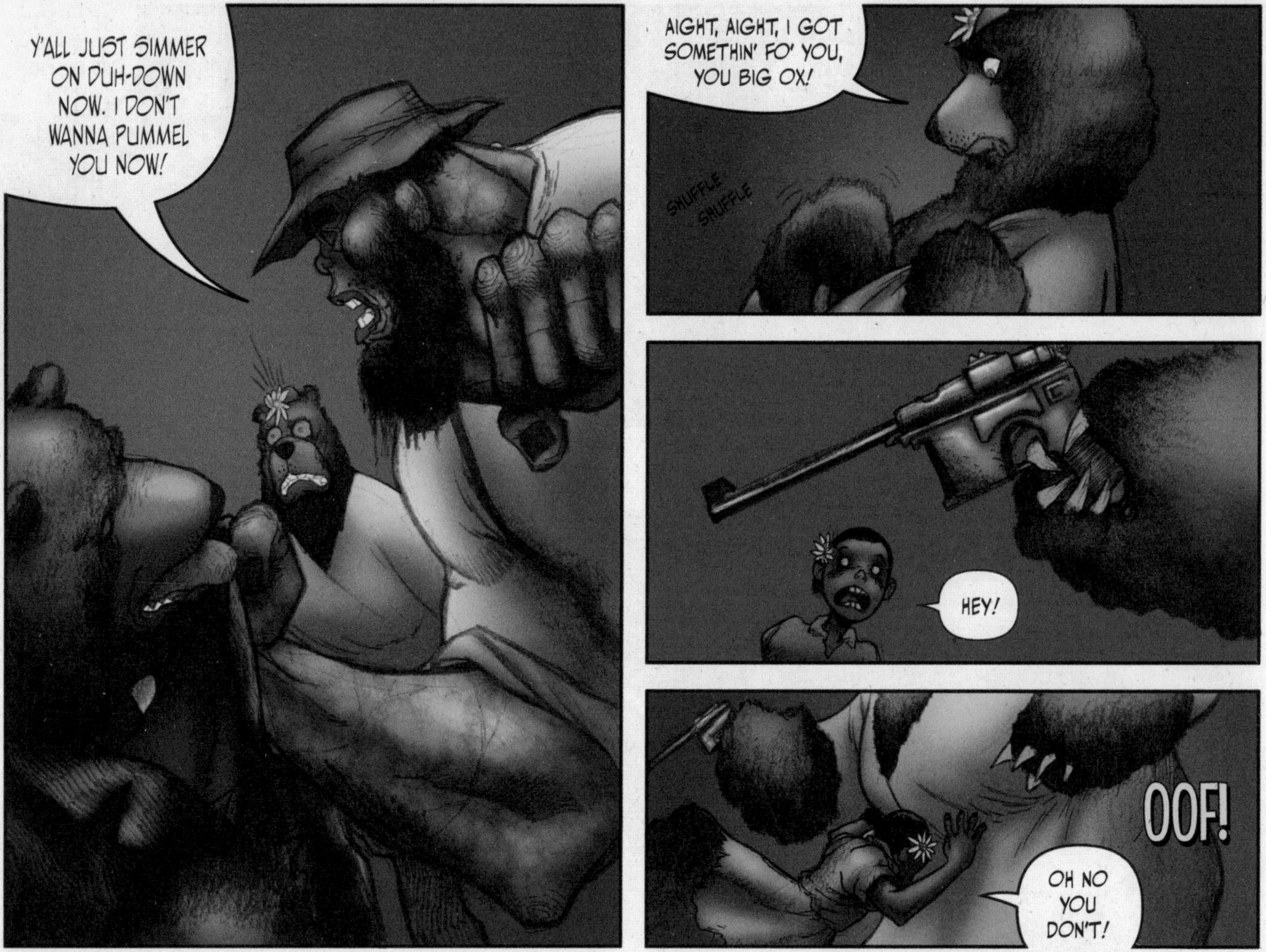
Y'ALL JUST SIMMER ON DUH-DOWN NOW. I DON'T WANNA PUMMEL YOU NOW!
AIGHT, AIGHT, I GOT SOMETHIN' FO' YOU, YOU BIG OX!
SHUFFLE SHUFFLE
HEY!
OOF!
OH NO YOU DON'T!

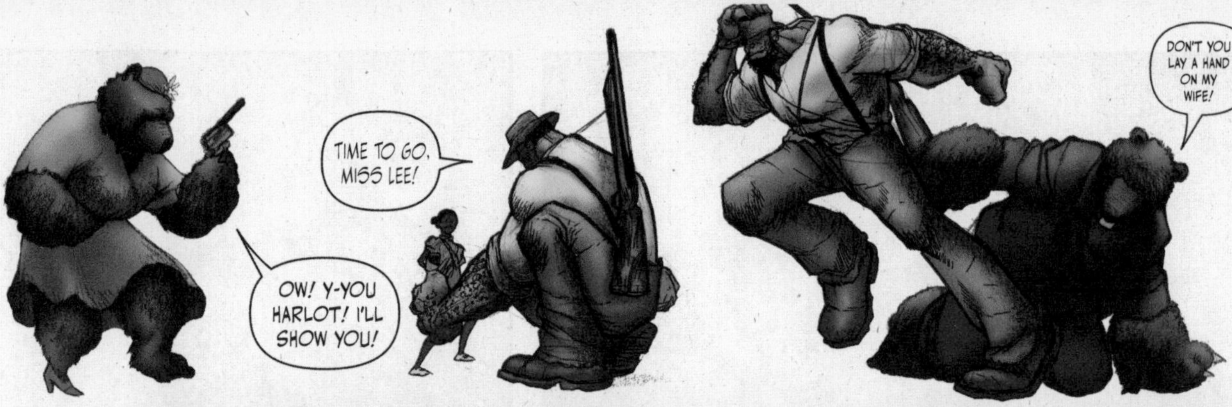
TIME TO GO, MISS LEE!
OW! Y-YOU HARLOT! I'LL SHOW YOU!
DON'T YOU LAY A HAND ON MY WIFE!

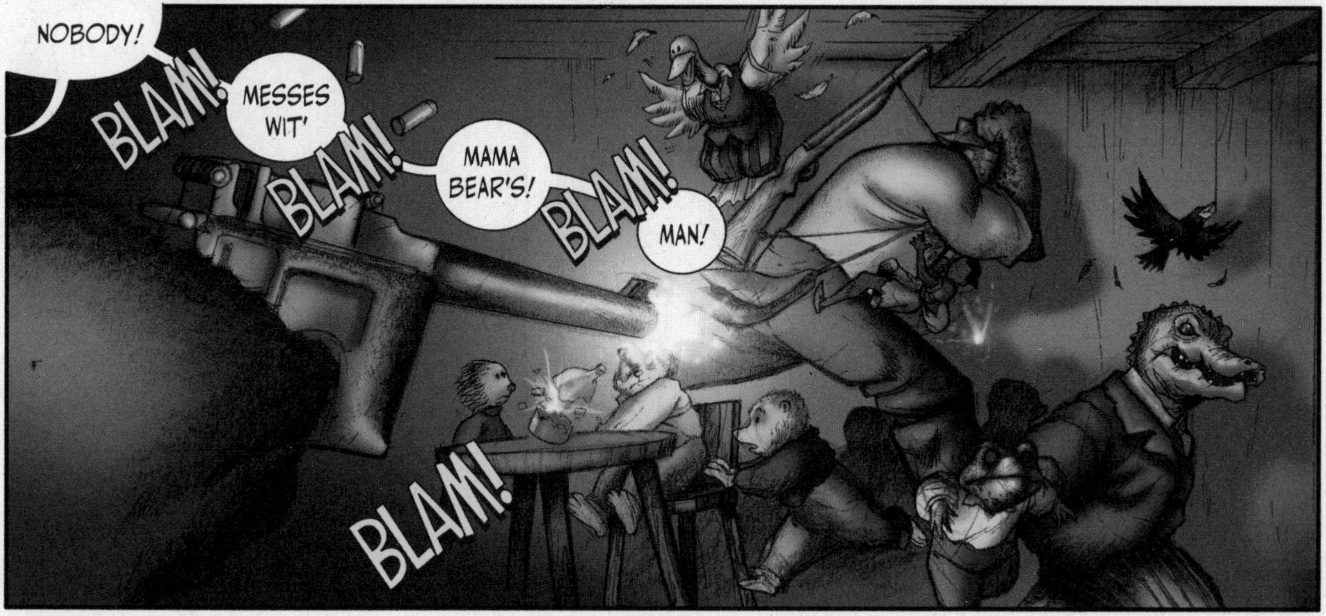
NOBODY!
BLAM!
MESSES WIT'
BLAM!
MAMA BEAR'S!
BLAM!
MAN!
BLAM!

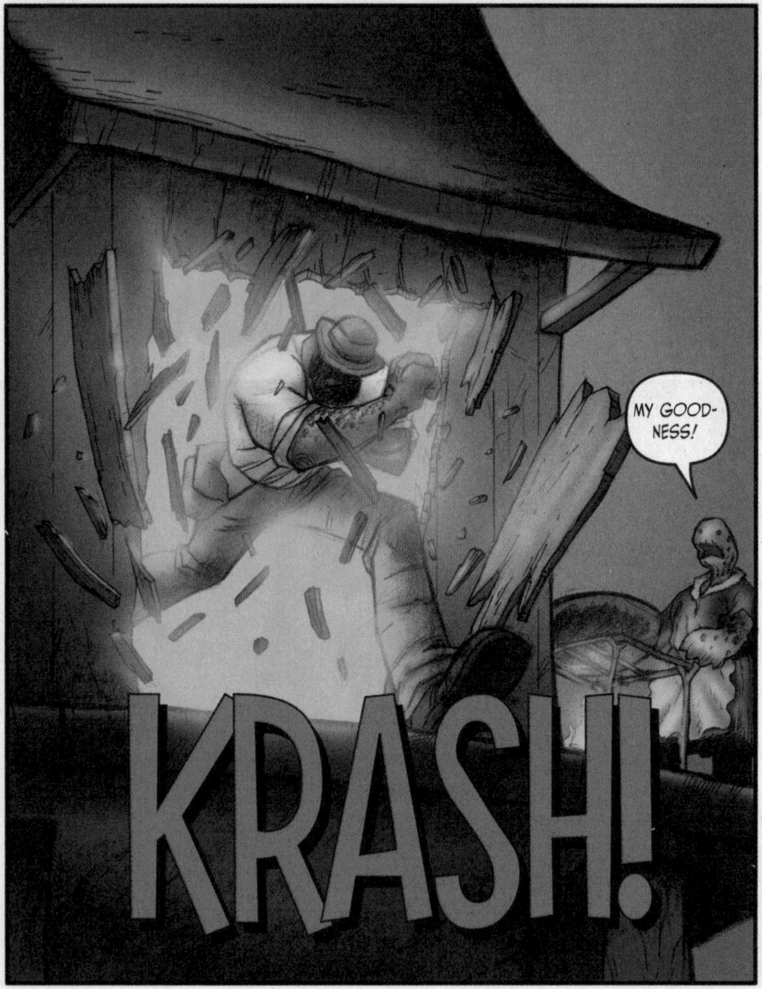
MY GOOD-
NESS!
KRASH!

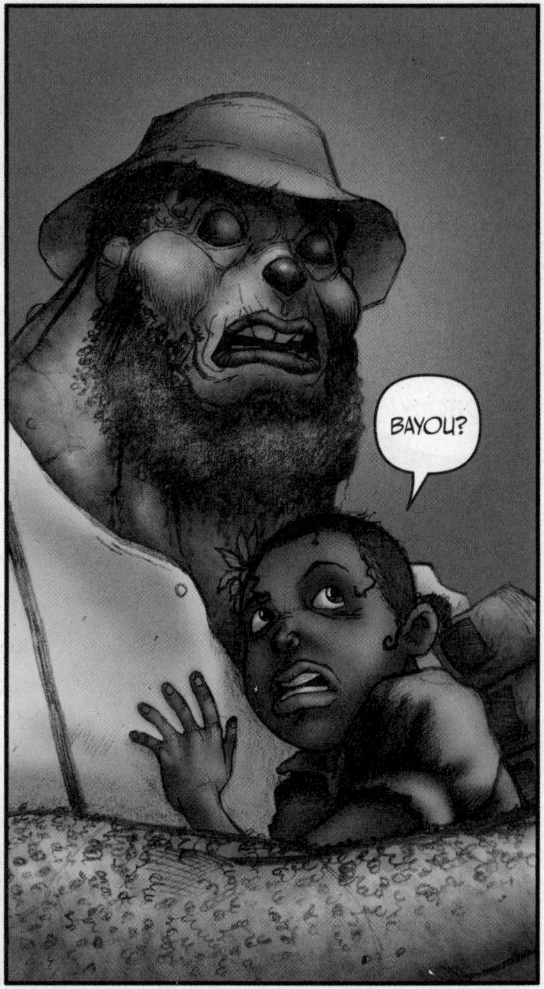
BAYOU?

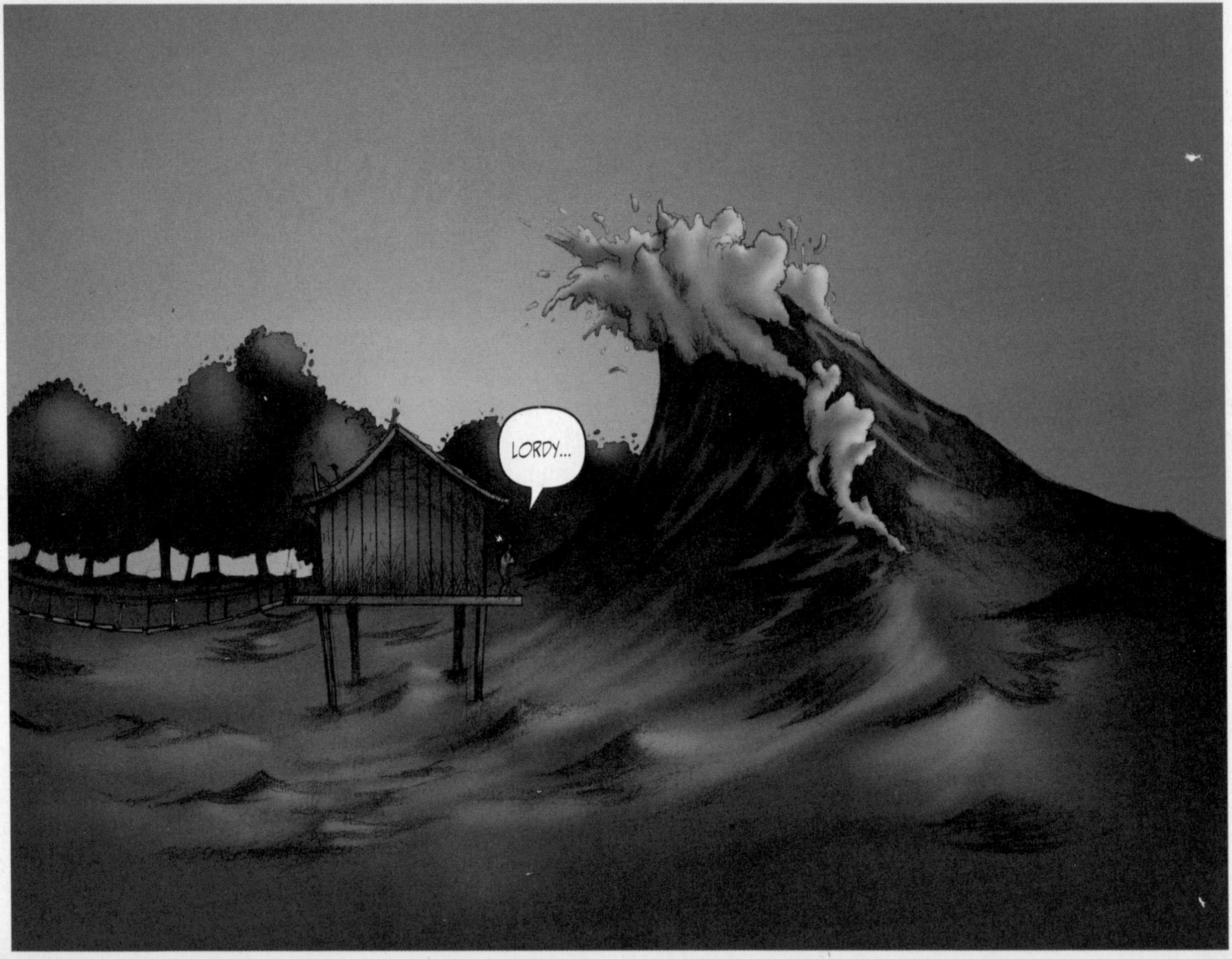
LORDY...

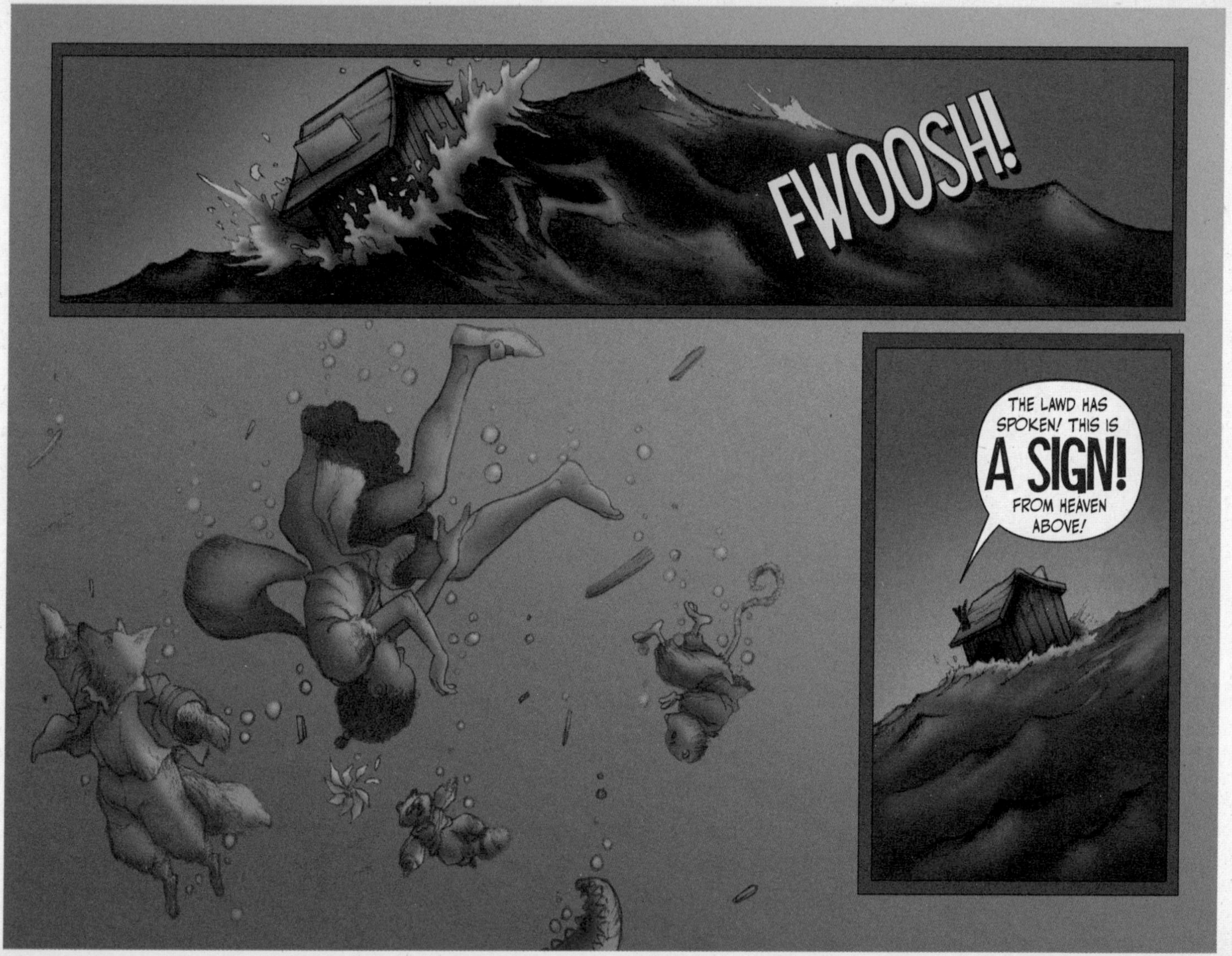
FWOOSH!
THE LAWD HAS SPOKEN! THIS IS A SIGN! FROM HEAVEN ABOVE!

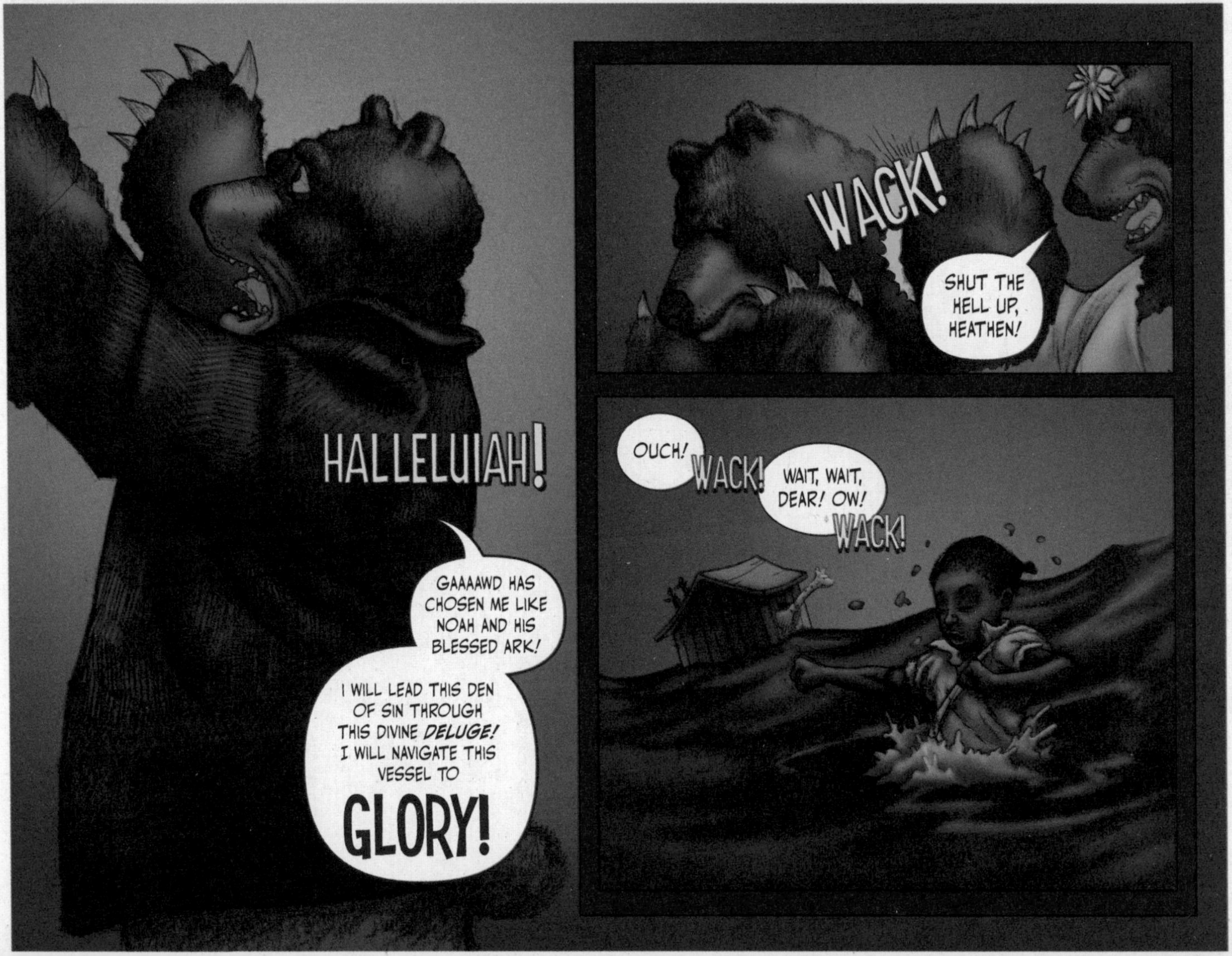
HALLELUIAH!
GAAAAWD HAS CHOSEN ME LIKE NOAH AND HIS BLESSED ARK!
I WILL LEAD THIS DEN OF SIN THROUGH THIS DIVINE *DELUGE!* I WILL NAVIGATE THIS VESSEL TO GLORY!
WACK!
SHUT THE HELL UP, HEATHEN!
OUCH!
WACK!
WAIT, WAIT, DEAR! OW!
WACK!

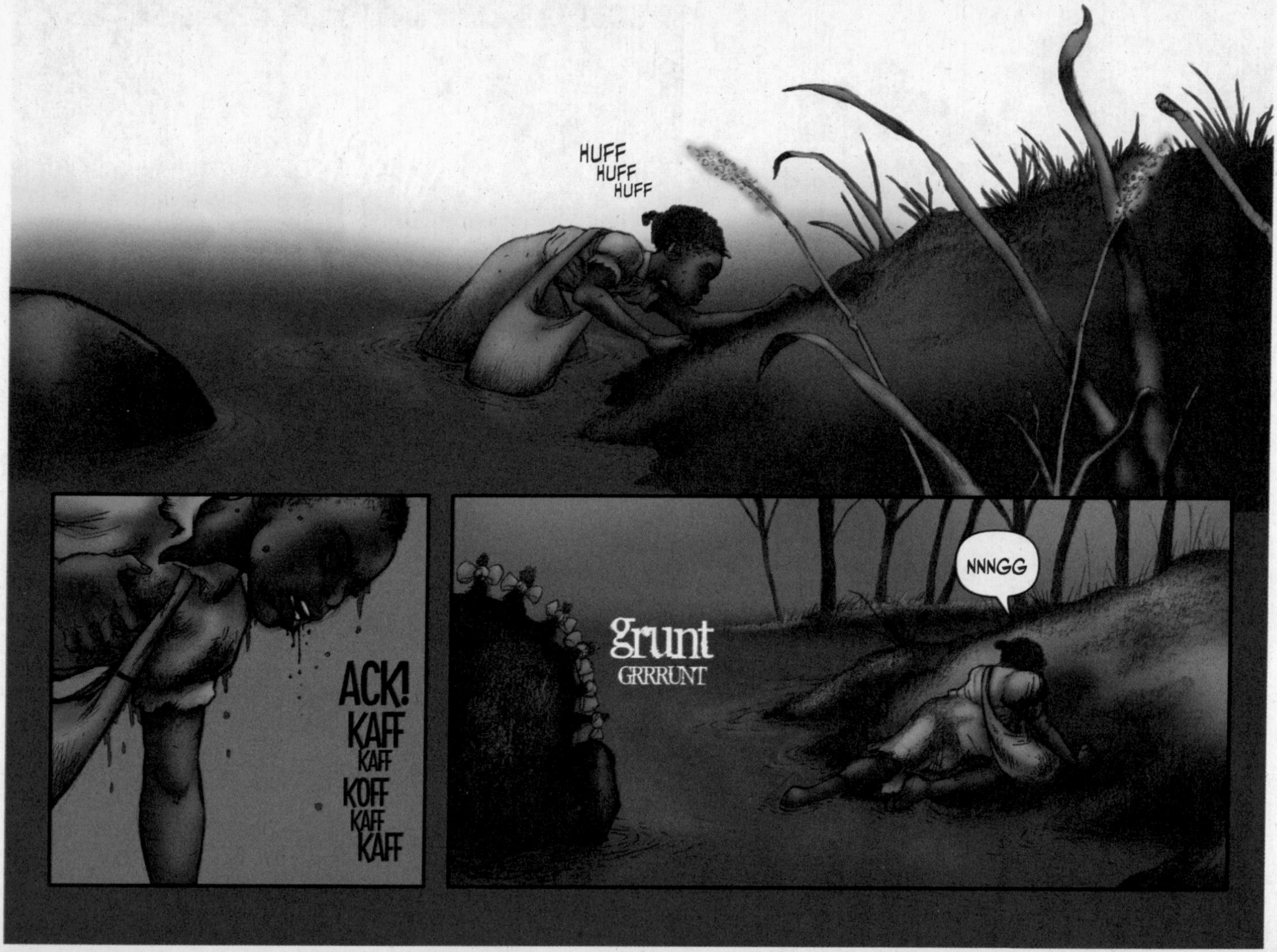
HUFF
HUFF
HUFF
ACK!
KAFF
KAFF
KOFF
KAFF
KAFF
grunt
GRRRUNT
NNNGG

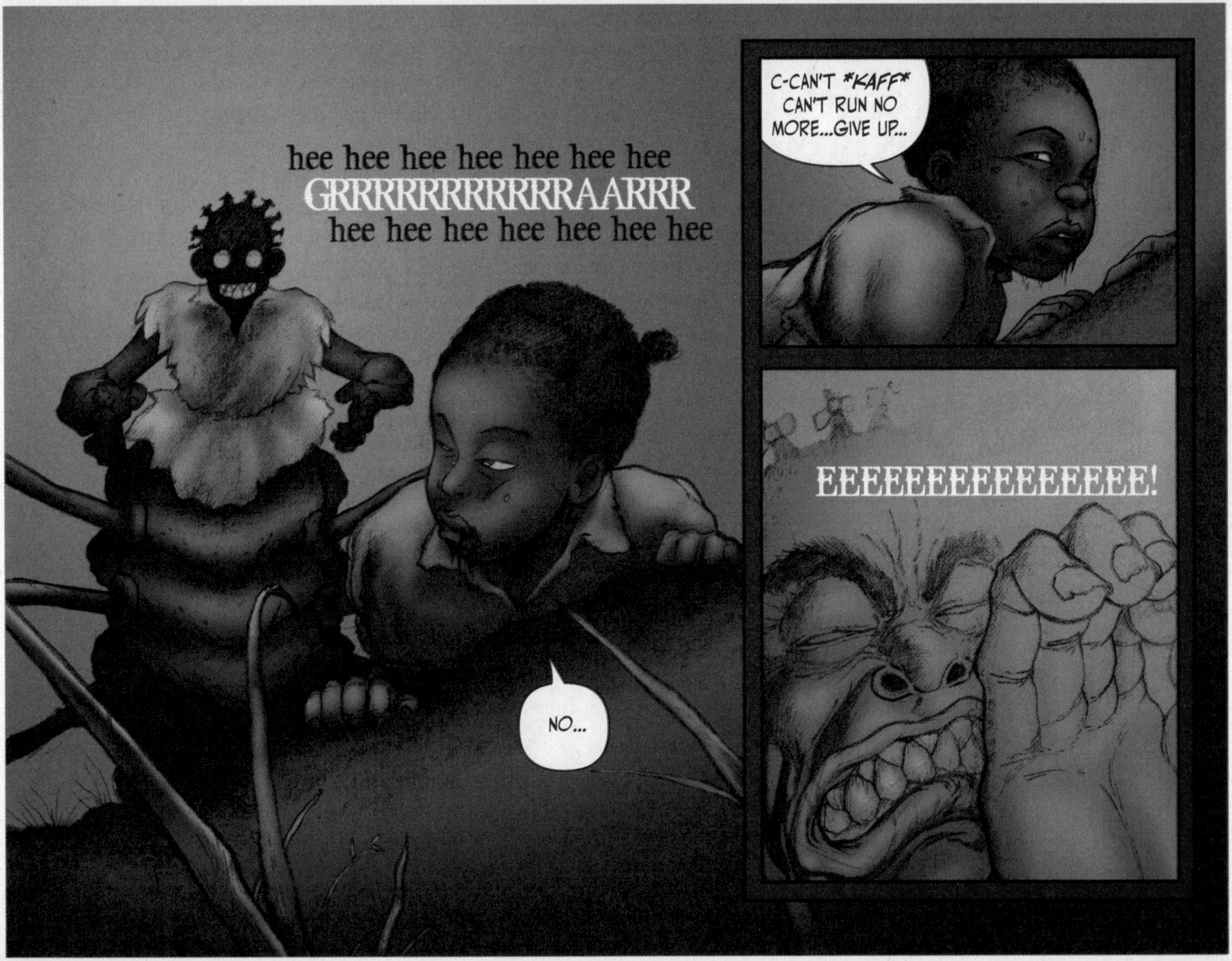
hee hee hee hee hee hee hee
GRRRRRRRRRRRAARRR
hee hee hee hee hee hee hee
NO...
C-CAN'T *KAFF* CAN'T RUN NO MORE...GIVE UP...
EEEEEEEEEEEEEEE!

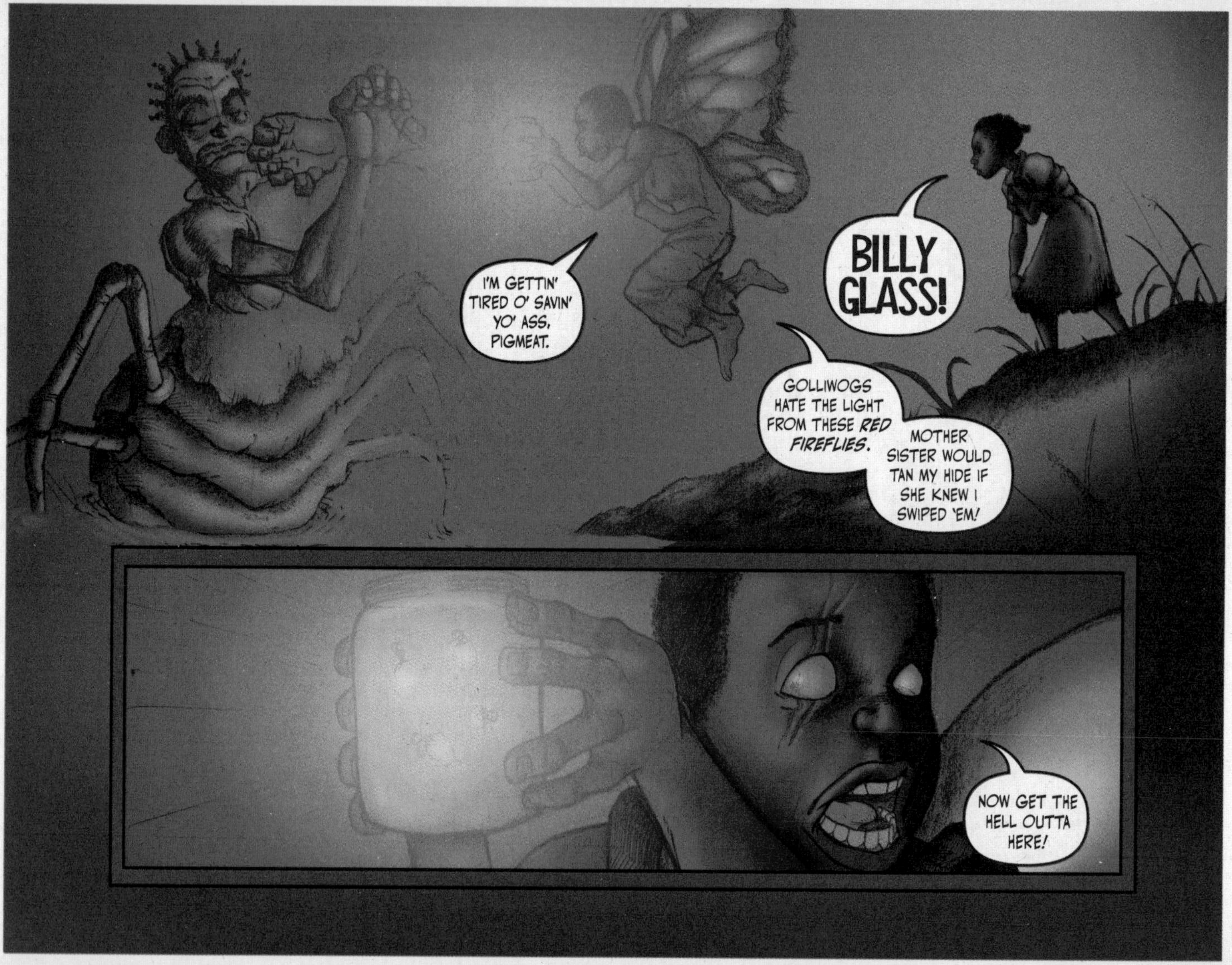
I'M GETTIN' TIRED O' SAVIN' YO' ASS, PIGMEAT.
BILLY GLASS!
GOLLIWOGS HATE THE LIGHT FROM THESE *RED FIREFLIES.*
MOTHER SISTER WOULD TAN MY HIDE IF SHE KNEW I SWIPED 'EM!
NOW GET THE HELL OUTTA HERE!

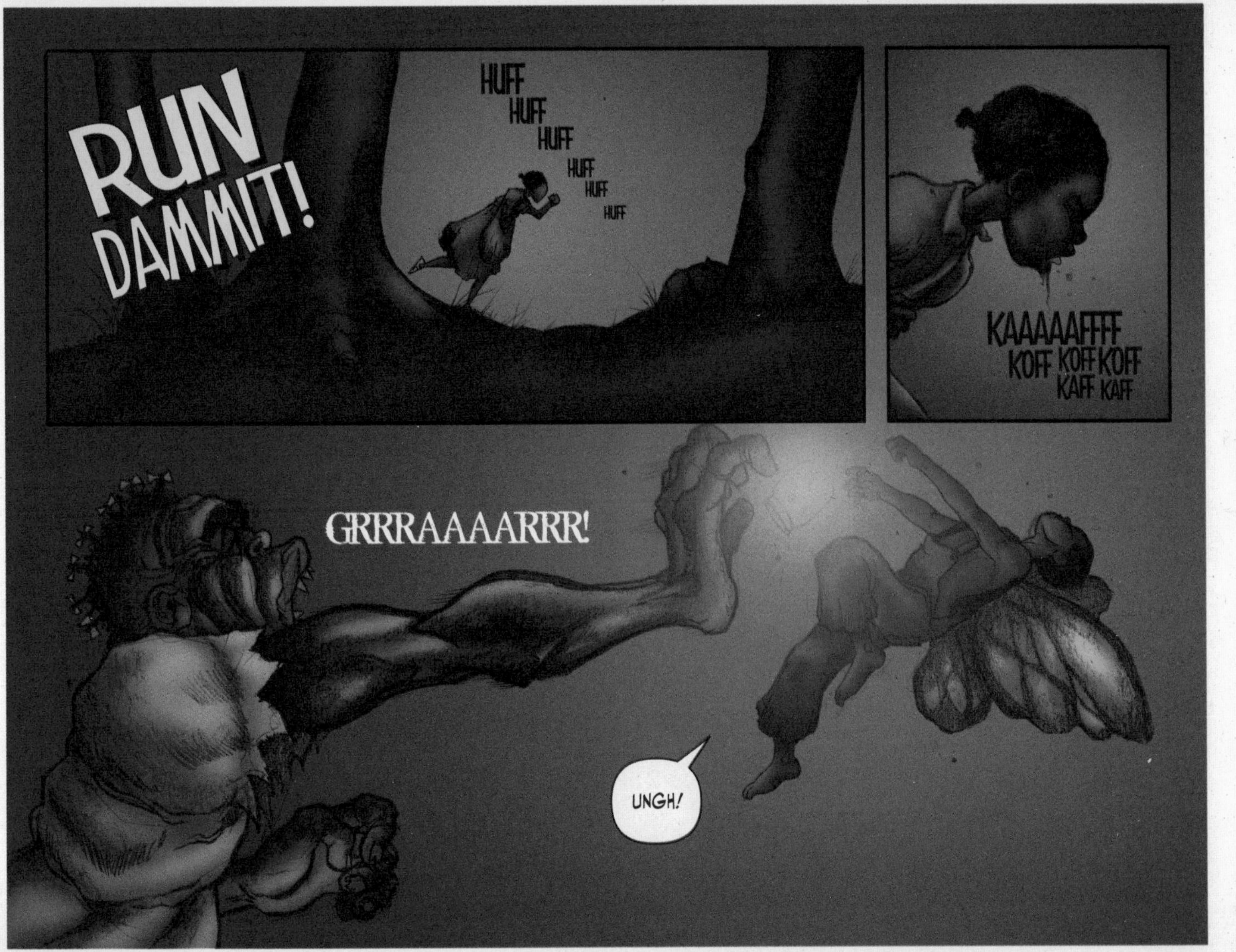
RUN DAMMIT!
HUFF
HUFF
HUFF
HUFF
HUFF
HUFF
KAAAAAFFFF
KOFF KOFF KOFF
KAFF KAFF
GRRRAAAARRR!
UNGH!

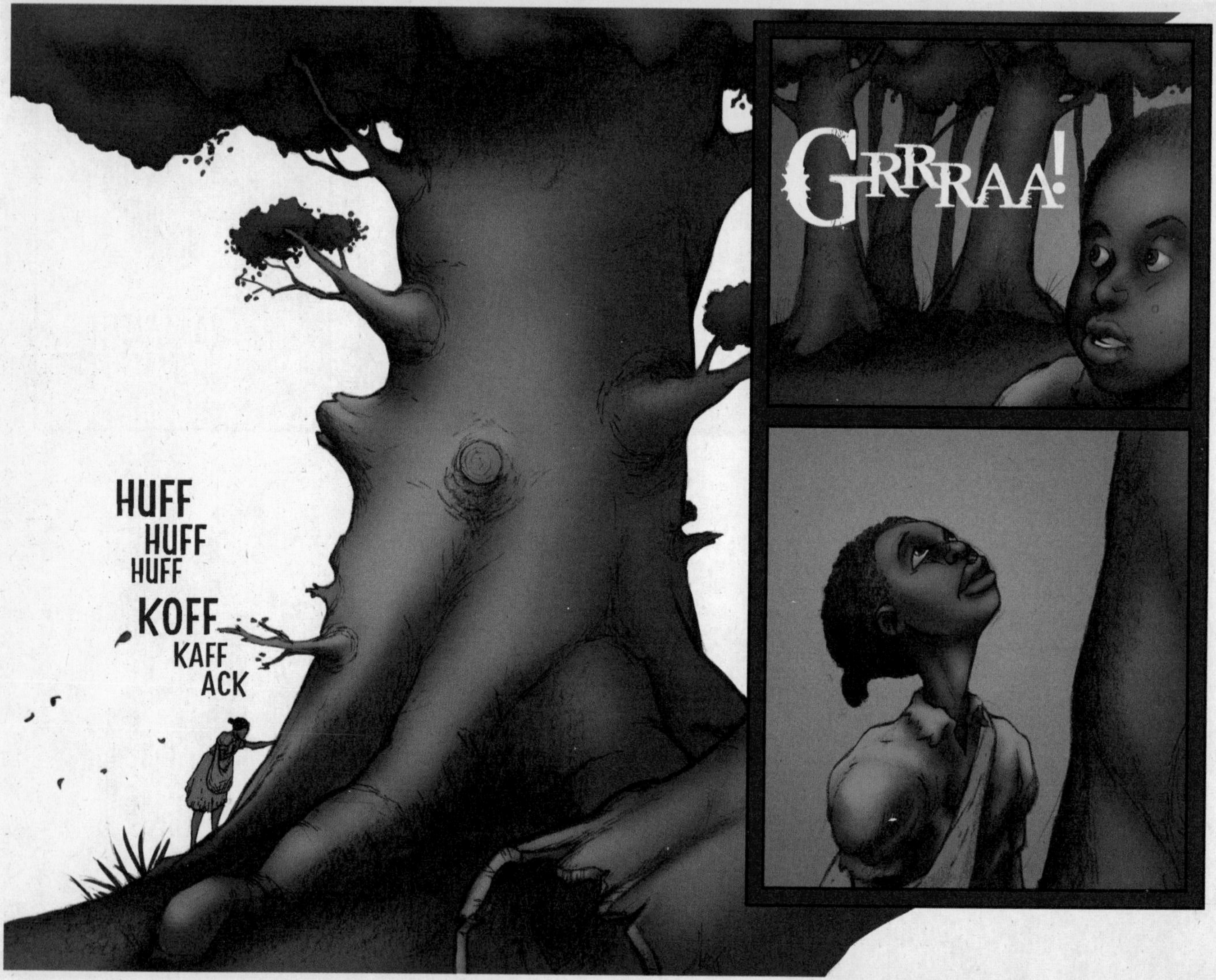
HUFF
HUFF
HUFF
KOFF
KAFF
ACK
GRRRAA!

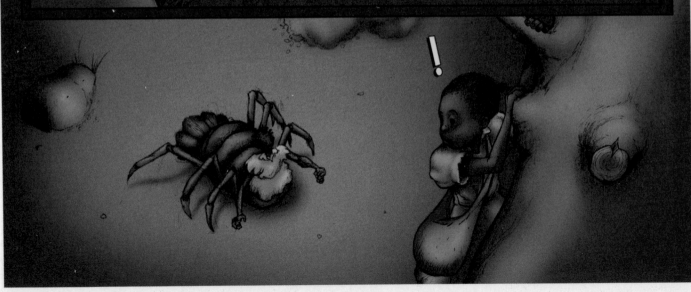

GRUNT GRUNT GRUNT GRUNT SNORT GRUNT GRUNT GRUNT

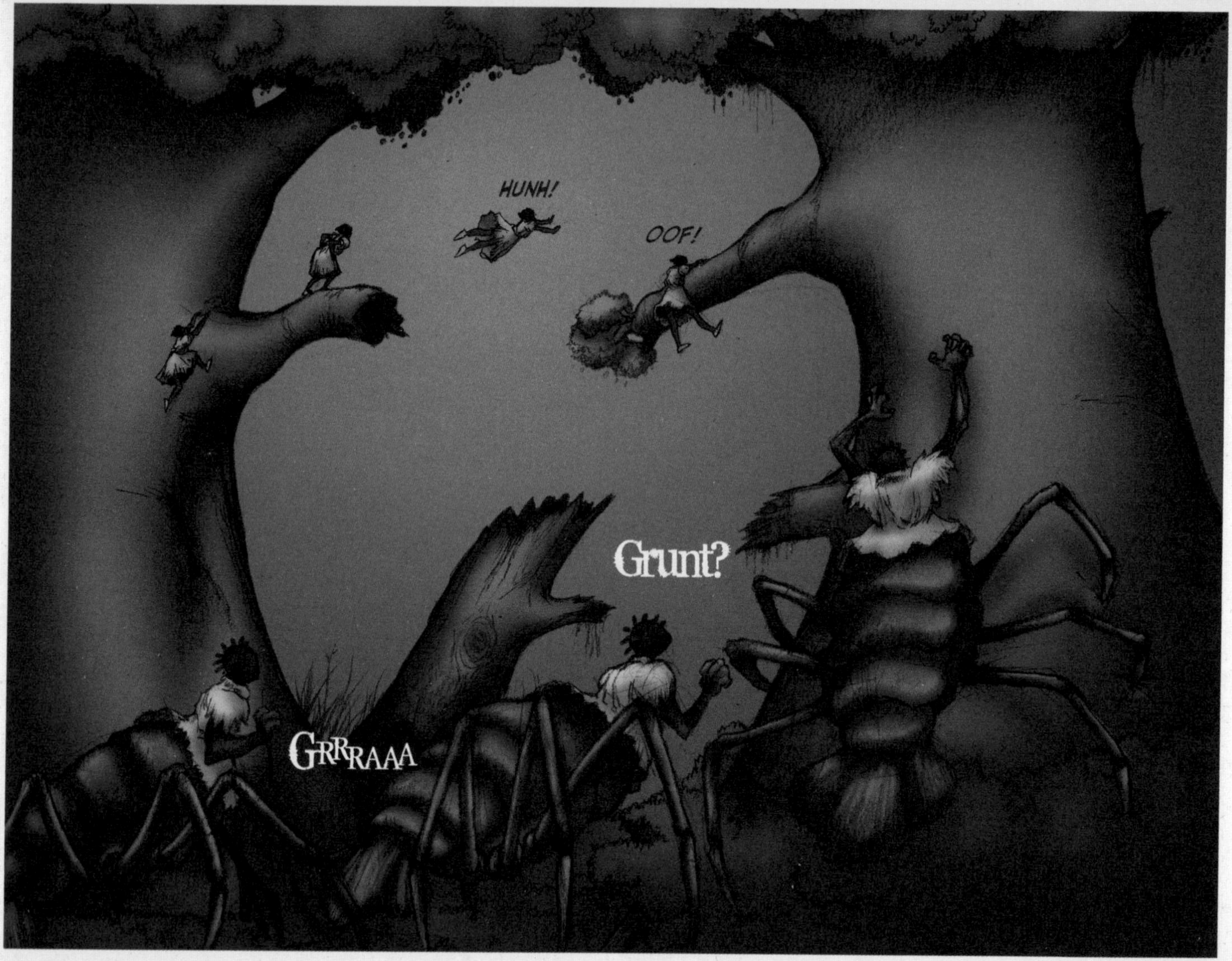
HUNH!
OOF!
Grunt?
GRRRAAA

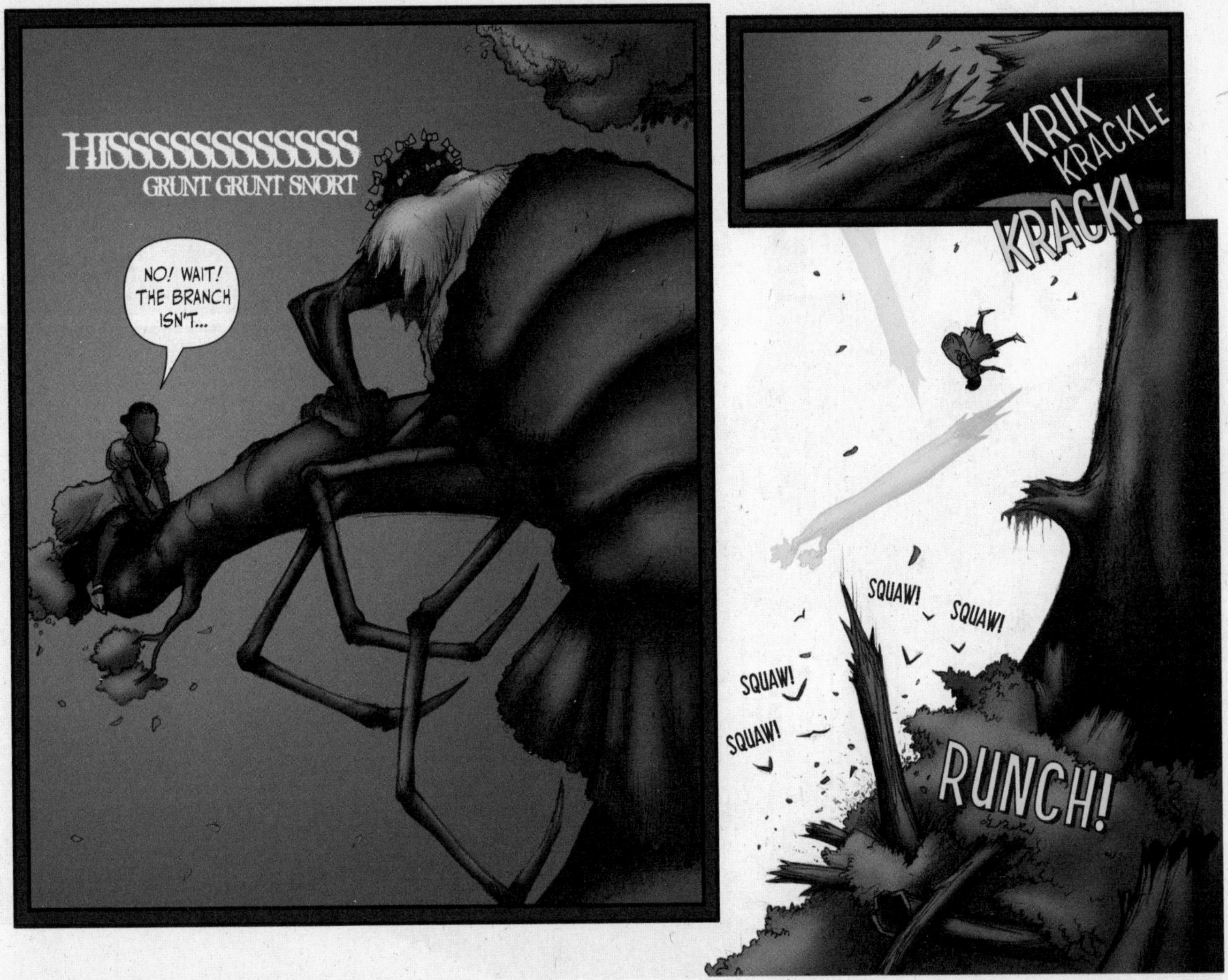
HISSSSSSSSSSSS
GRUNT GRUNT SNORT
NO! WAIT! THE BRANCH ISN'T...
KRIK
KRACKLE
KRACK!
SQUAW!
SQUAW!
SQUAW!
SQUAW!
RUNCH!

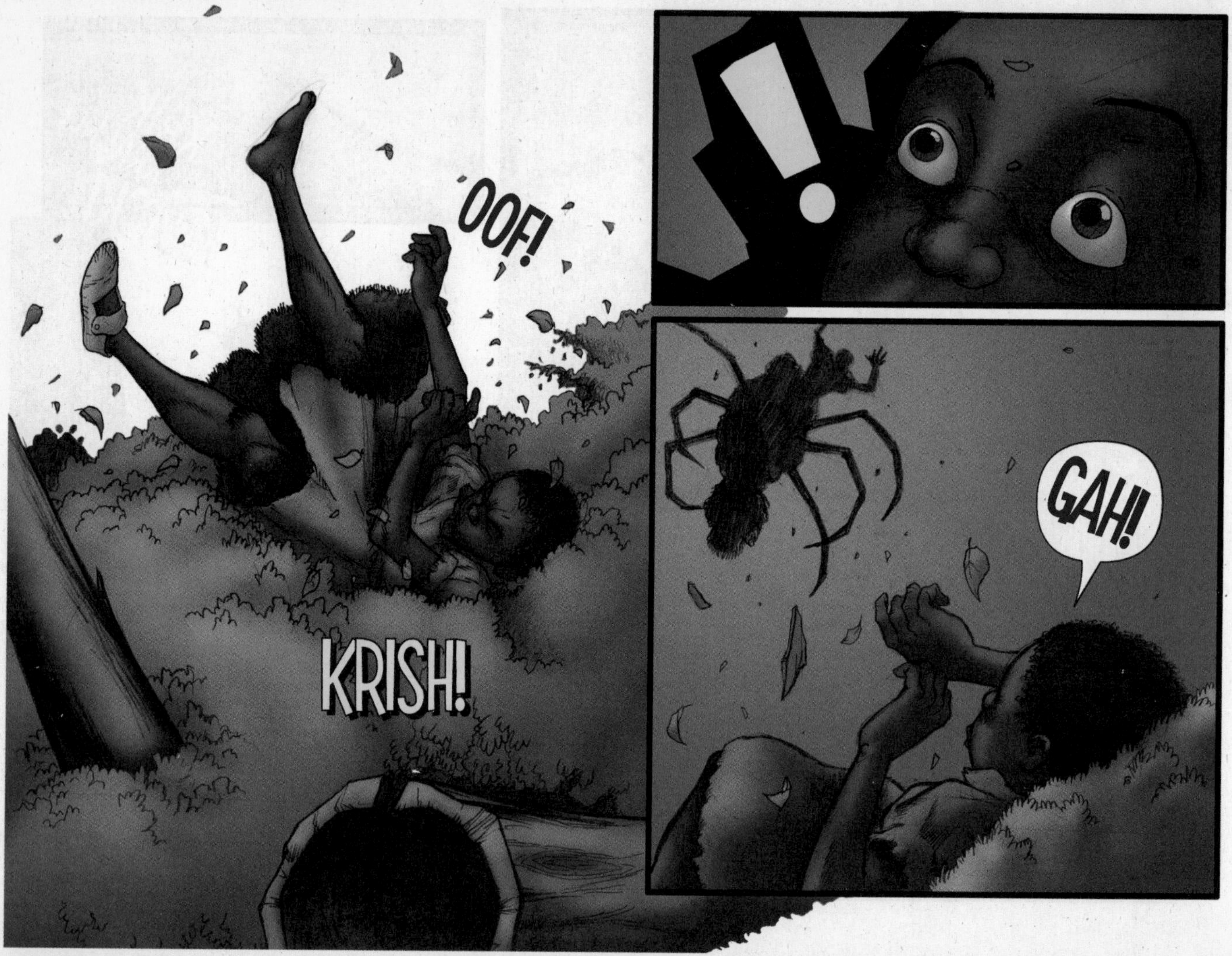
OOF!
KRISH!
!
GAH!

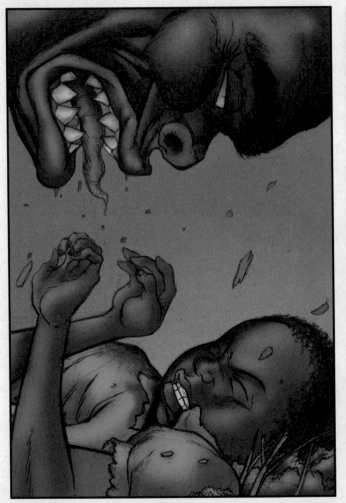

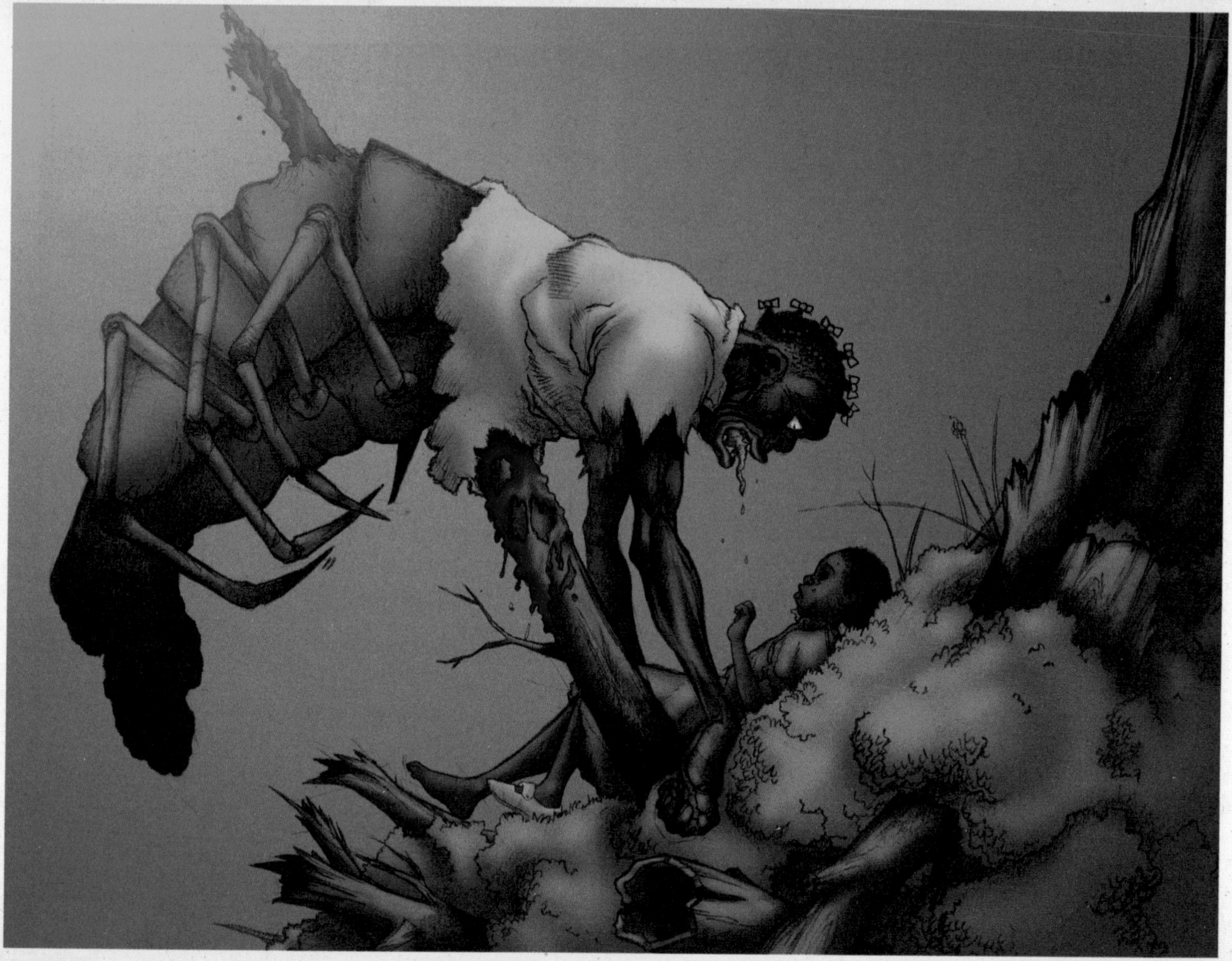

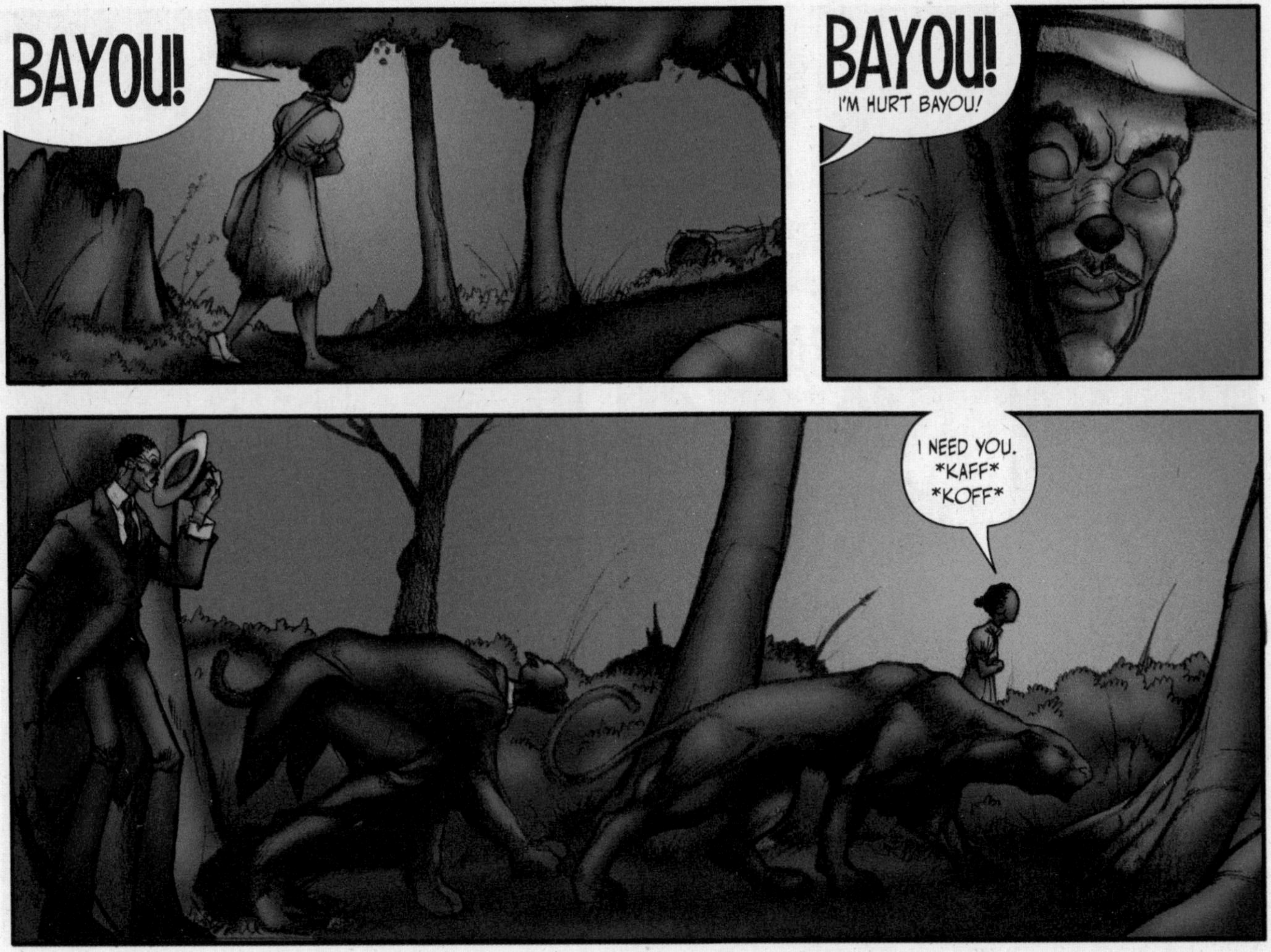
BAYOU!
BAYOU!
I'M HURT BAYOU!
I NEED YOU. *KAFF* *KOFF*

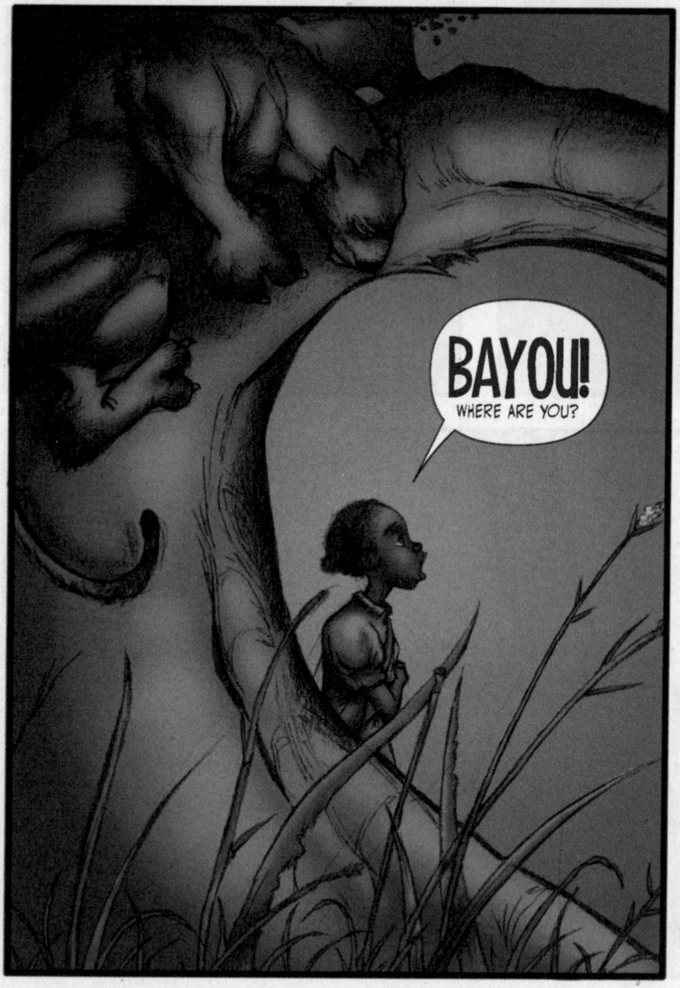
BAYOU!
WHERE ARE YOU?

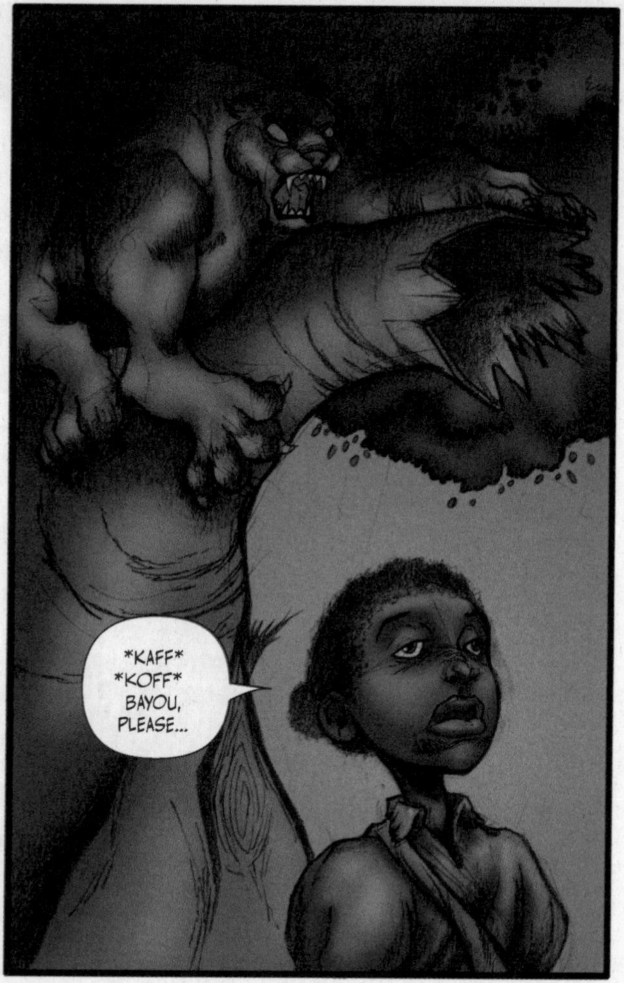
KAFF *KOFF* BAYOU, PLEASE...

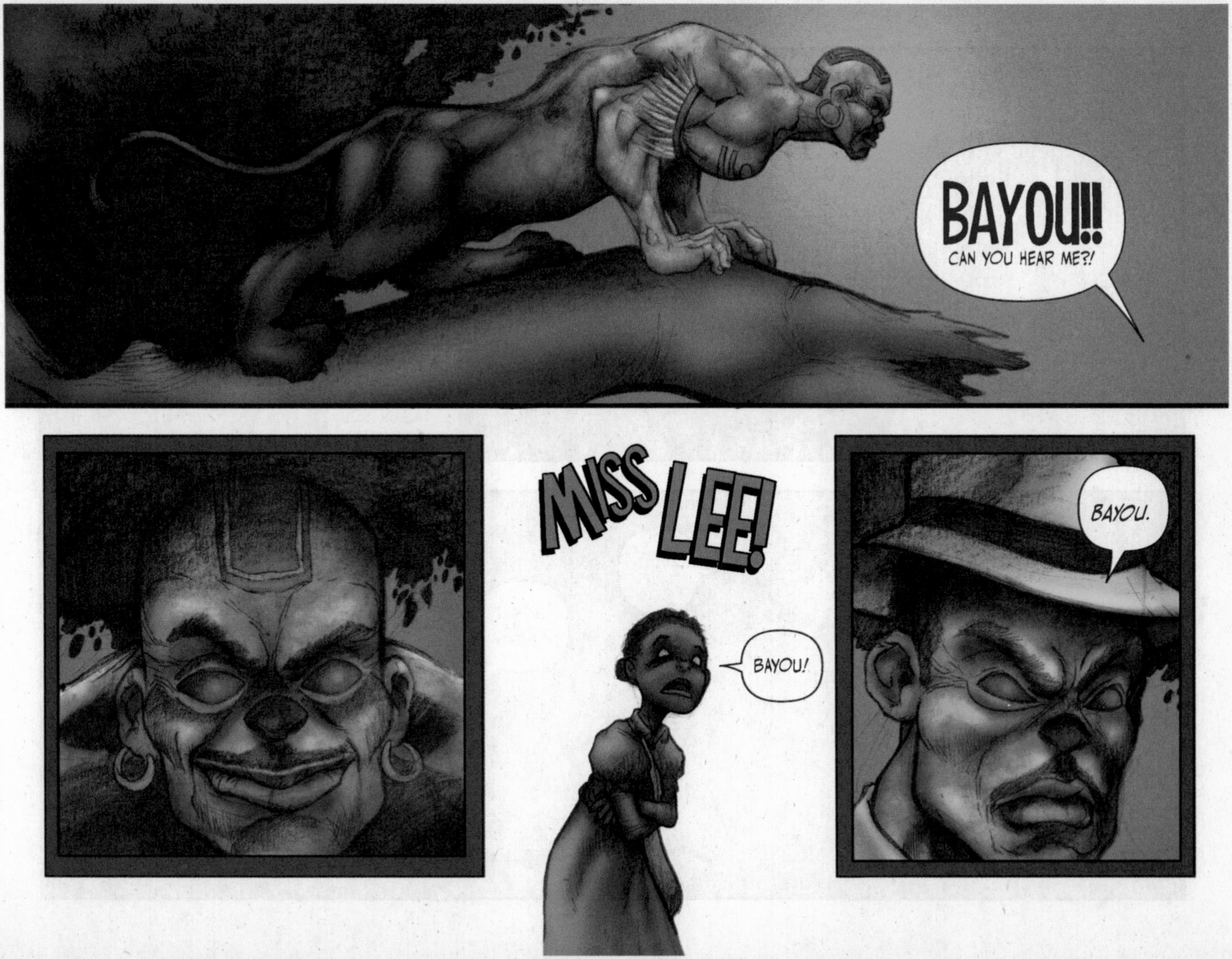
BAYOU!!
CAN YOU HEAR ME?!
MISS LEE!
BAYOU!
BAYOU.

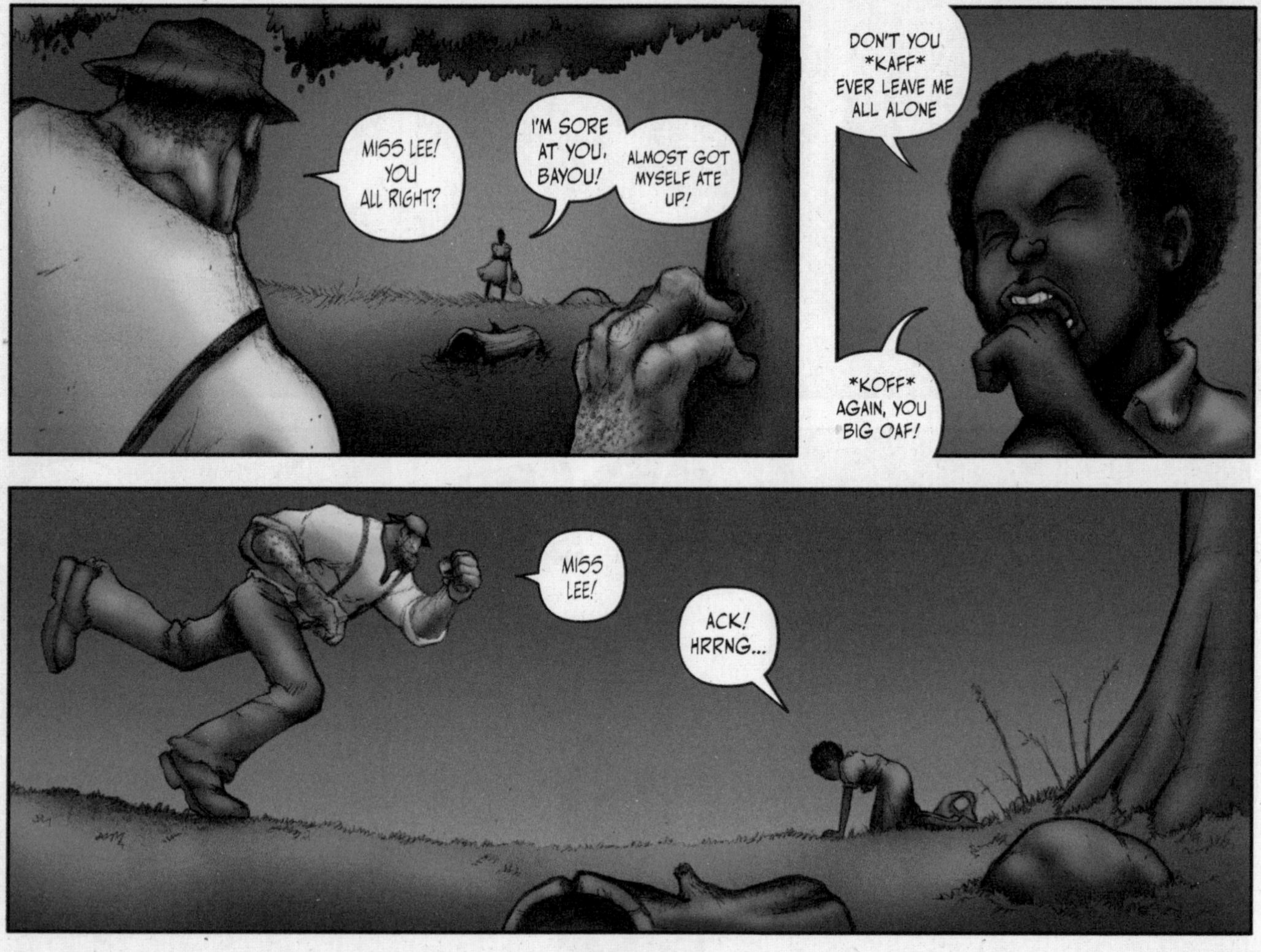
MISS LEE! YOU ALL RIGHT?
I'M SORE AT YOU, BAYOU!
ALMOST GOT MYSELF ATE UP!
DON'T YOU *KAFF* EVER LEAVE ME ALL ALONE
KOFF AGAIN, YOU BIG OAF!
MISS LEE!
ACK! HRRNG...

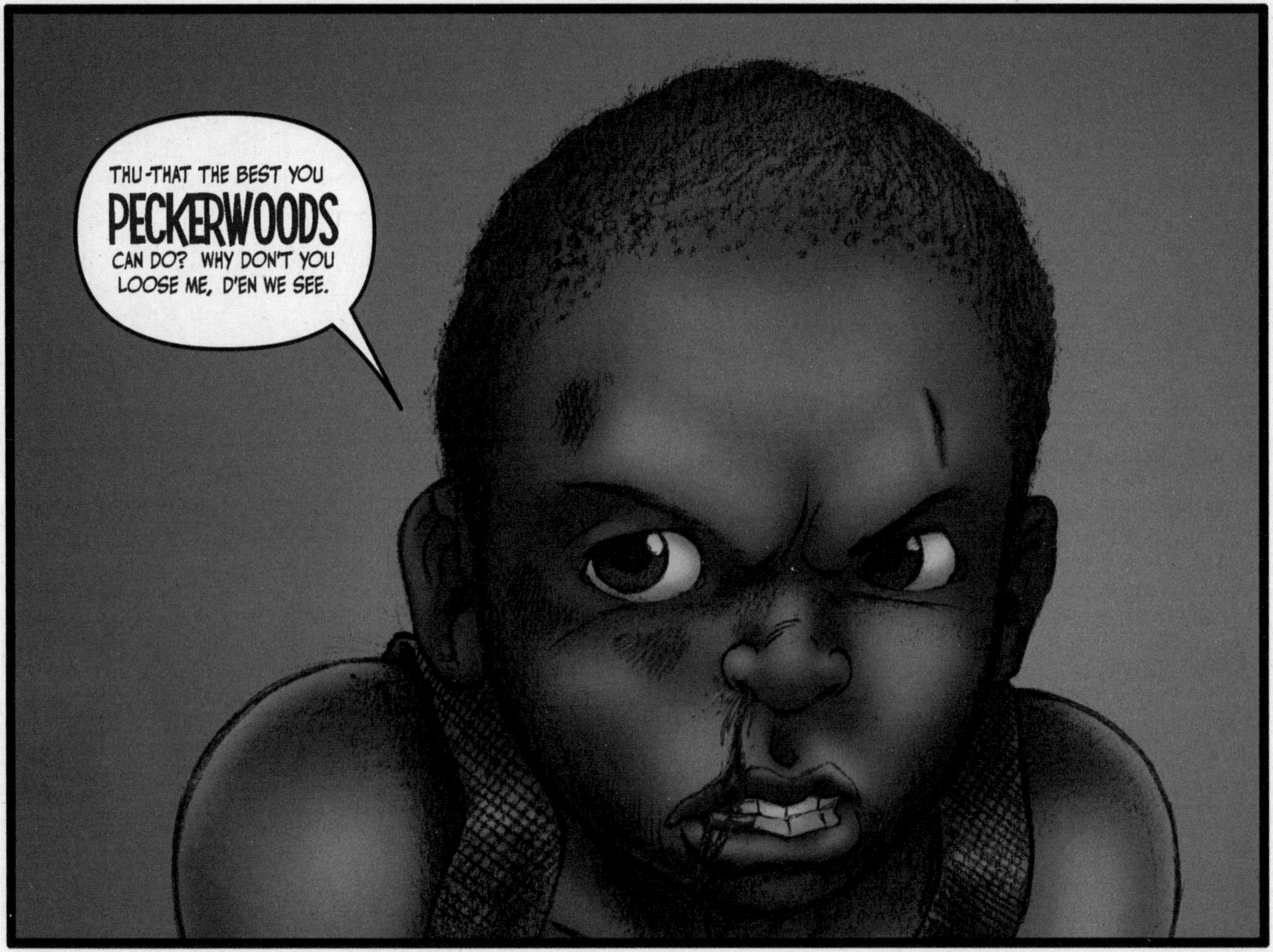
THU-THAT THE BEST YOU PECKERWOODS CAN DO? WHY DON'T YOU LOOSE ME, D'EN WE SEE.

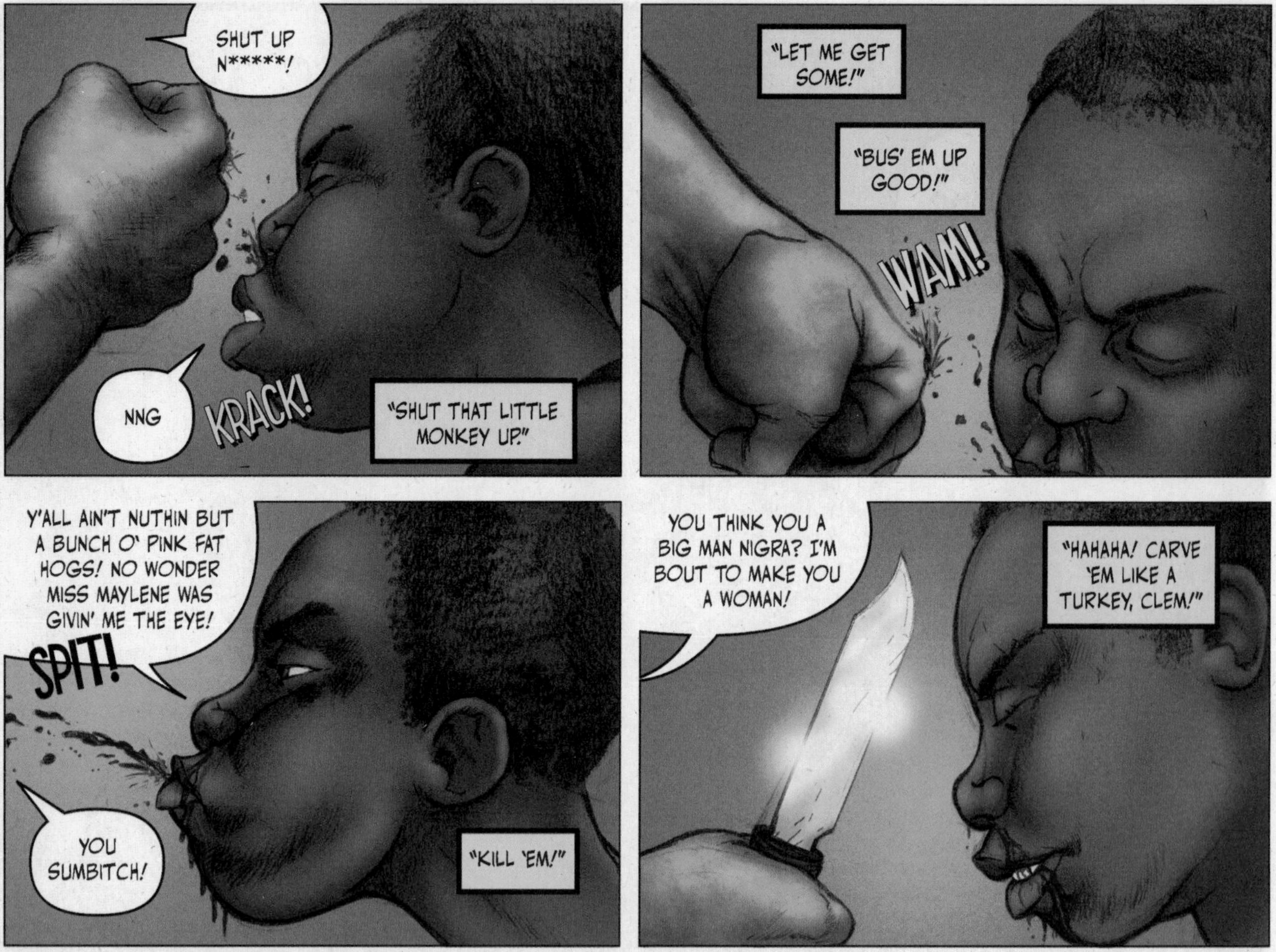
SHUT UP N*****!
NNG
KRACK!
"SHUT THAT LITTLE MONKEY UP."
"LET ME GET SOME!"
"BUS' EM UP GOOD!"
WAM!
Y'ALL AIN'T NUTHIN BUT A BUNCH O' PINK FAT HOGS! NO WONDER MISS MAYLENE WAS GIVIN' ME THE EYE!
SPIT!
YOU SUMBITCH!
"KILL 'EM!"
YOU THINK YOU A BIG MAN NIGRA? I'M BOUT TO MAKE YOU A WOMAN!
"HAHAHA! CARVE 'EM LIKE A TURKEY, CLEM!"

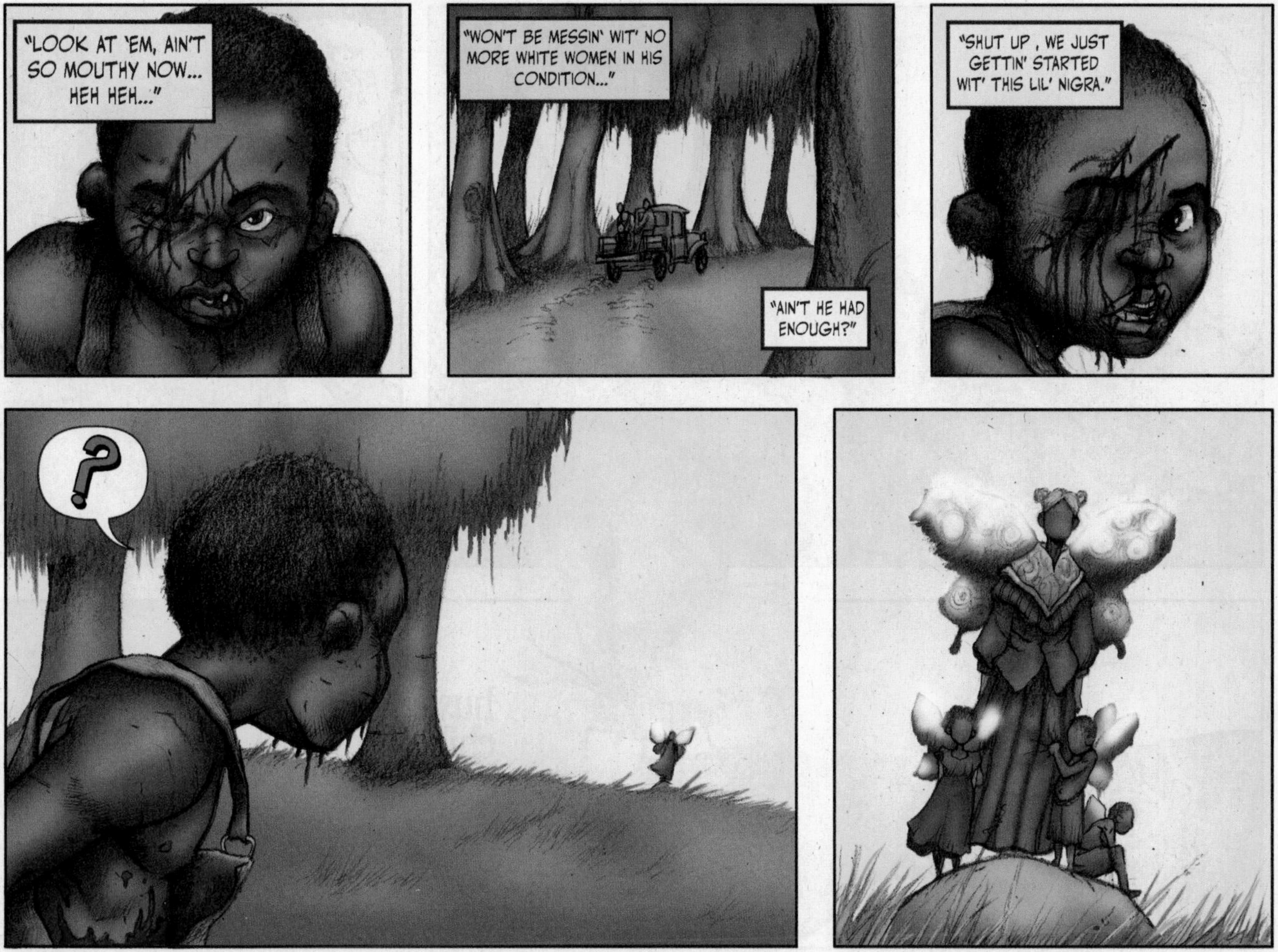
"LOOK AT 'EM, AIN'T SO MOUTHY NOW... HEH HEH..."
"WON'T BE MESSIN' WIT' NO MORE WHITE WOMEN IN HIS CONDITION..."
"AIN'T HE HAD ENOUGH?"
"SHUT UP , WE JUST GETTIN' STARTED WIT' THIS LIL' NIGRA."
?

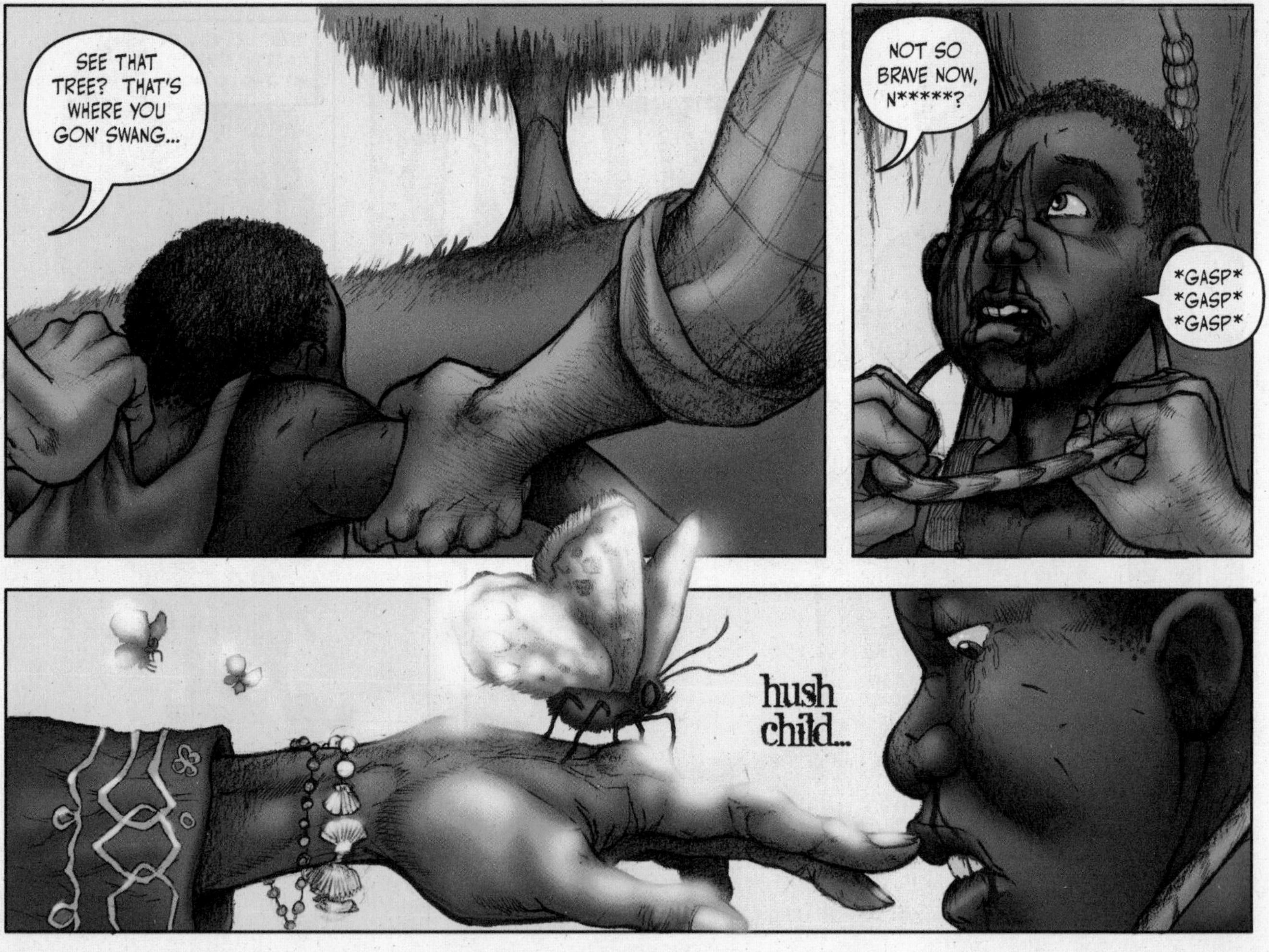
SEE THAT TREE? THAT'S WHERE YOU GON' SWANG...
NOT SO BRAVE NOW, N*****?
GASP *GASP* *GASP*
hush child...

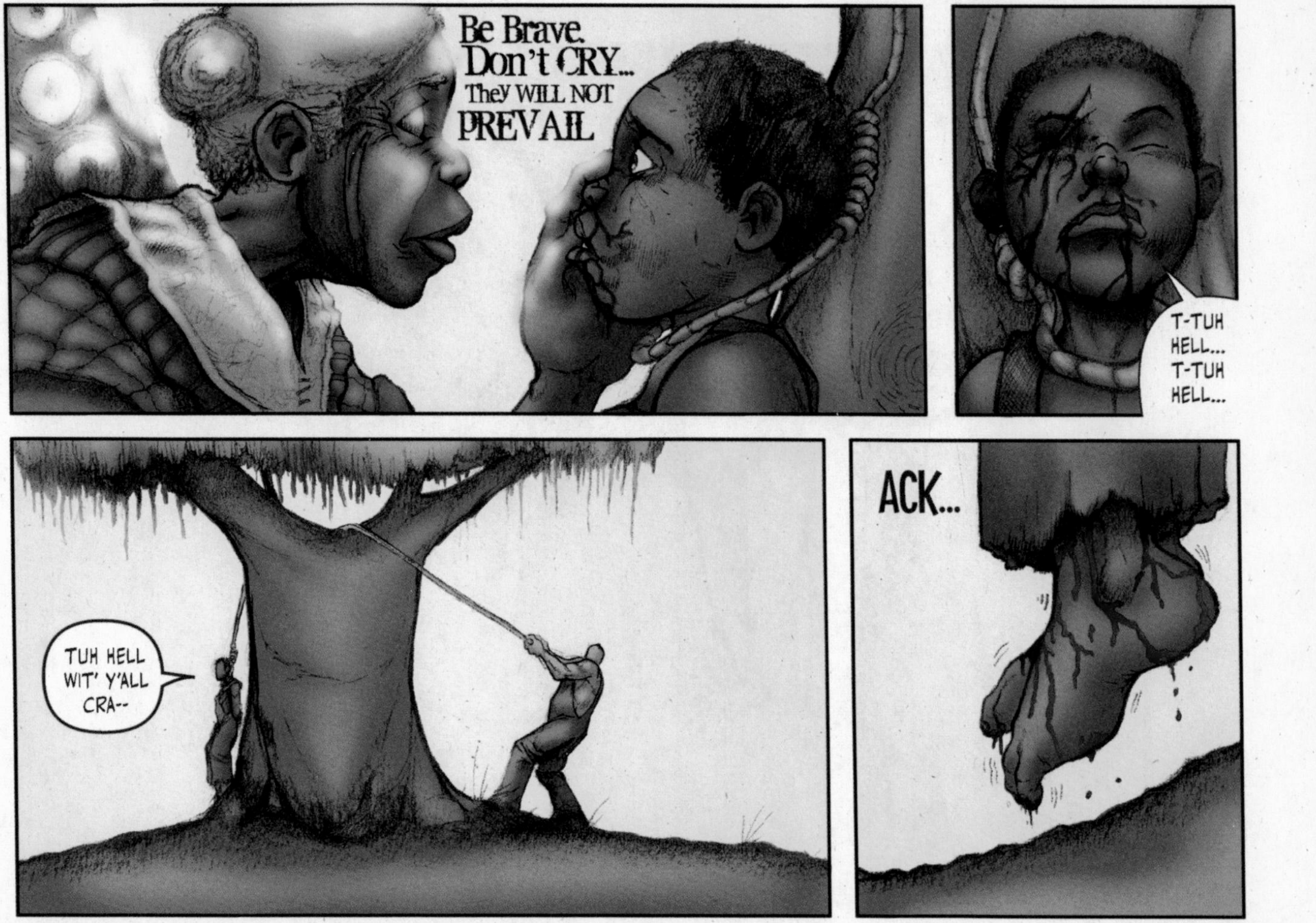
Be Brave. Don't CRY... They WILL NOT PREVAIL
T-TUH HELL... T-TUH HELL...
TUH HELL WIT' Y'ALL CRA--
ACK...

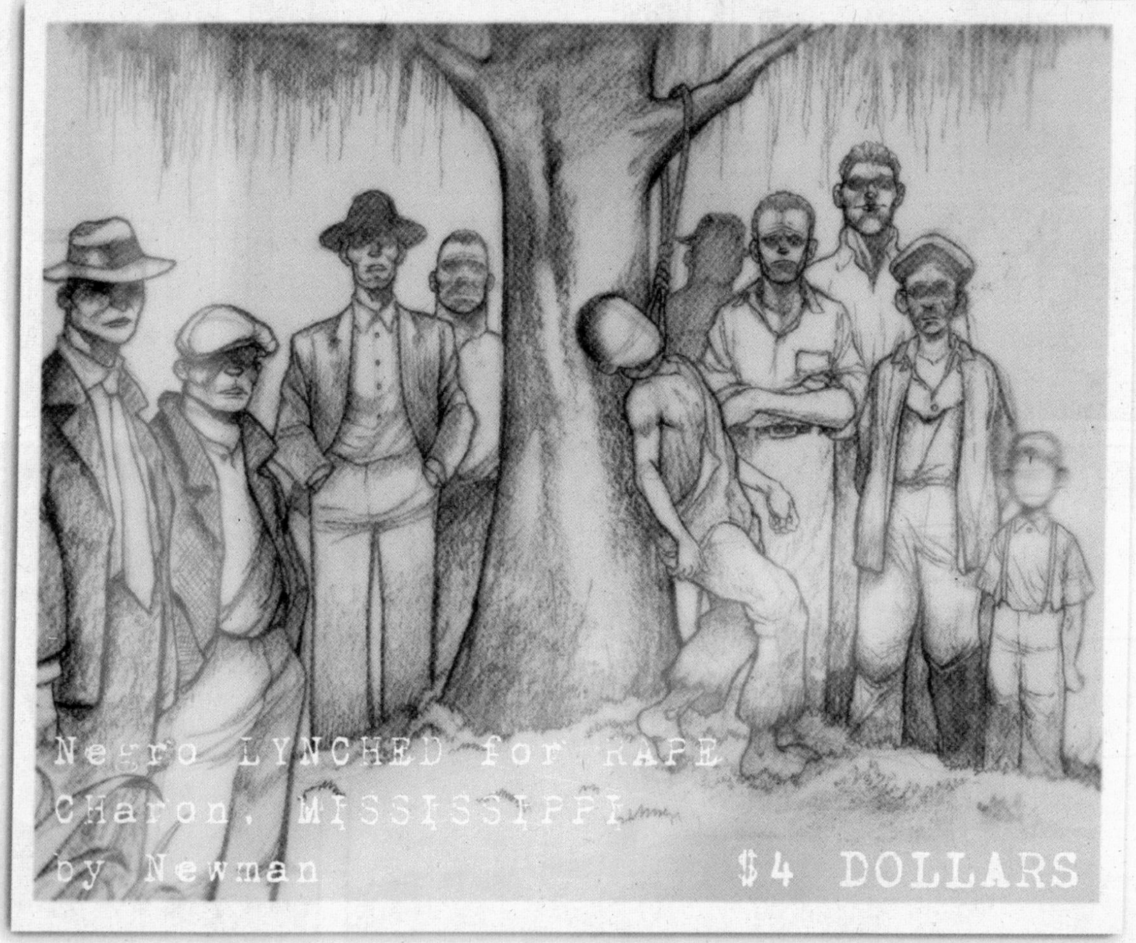
Negro LYNCHED for RAPE
CHaron, MISSISSIPPI
by Newman
$4 DOLLARS

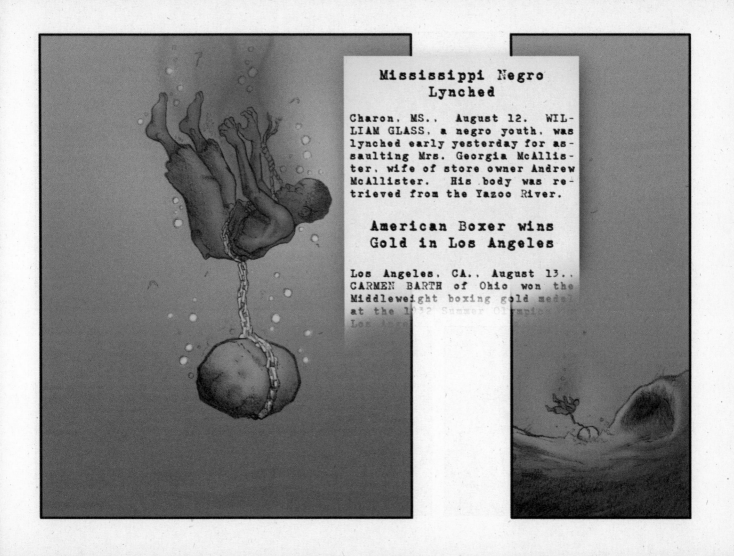

Mississippi Negro Lynched

Charon, MS., August 12. WIL-
LIAM GLASS, a negro youth, was
lynched early yesterday for as-
saulting Mrs. Georgia McAllister, wife of store owner Andrew
McAllister. His body was re-
trieved from the Yazoo River.

American Boxer wins Gold in Los Angeles

Los Angeles, CA., August 13..
CARMEN BARTH of Ohio won the
Middleweight boxing gold medal
at the 1932 Summer Olympics in
Los Angeles.

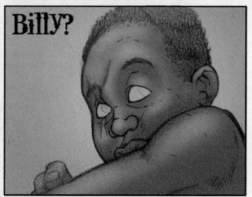

Billy?

come on over with me, BILLY, everything will be ok...

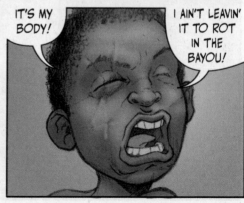

IT'S MY BODY!

I AIN'T LEAVIN' IT TO ROT IN THE BAYOU!

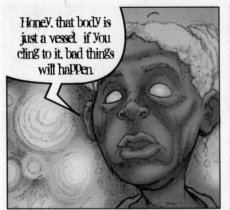

Honey, that body is just a vessel. If you cling to it, bad things will happen.

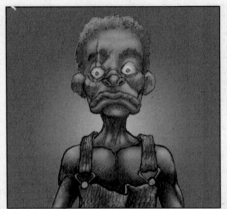

T'AINT FAIR. MY MAMA... SHE GON' BE TORE UP IF I AIN'T LAID TO REST PROPER...

WAIT!

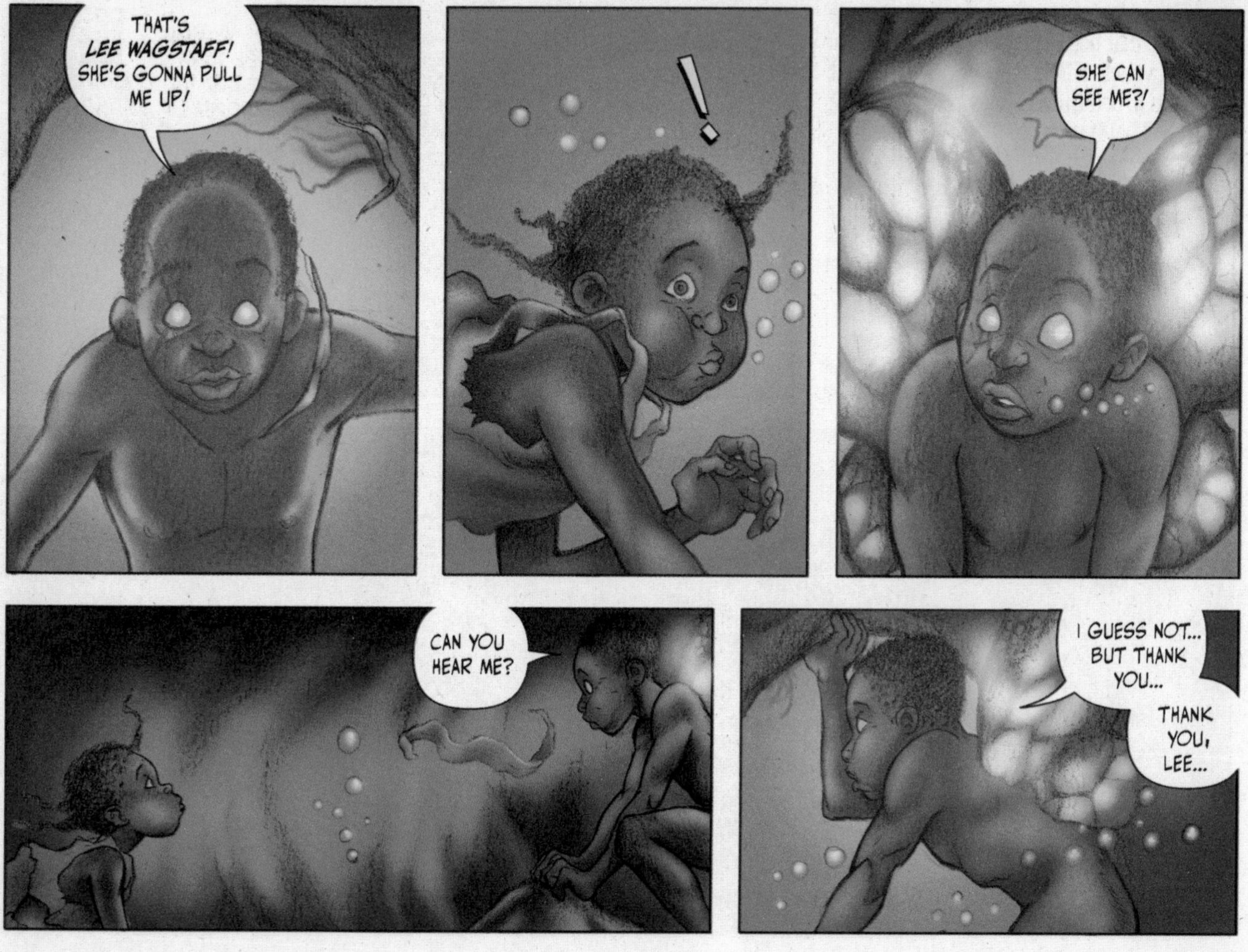
THAT'S *LEE WAGSTAFF!* SHE'S GONNA PULL ME UP!
!
SHE CAN SEE ME?!
CAN YOU HEAR ME?
I GUESS NOT... BUT THANK YOU...
THANK YOU, LEE...

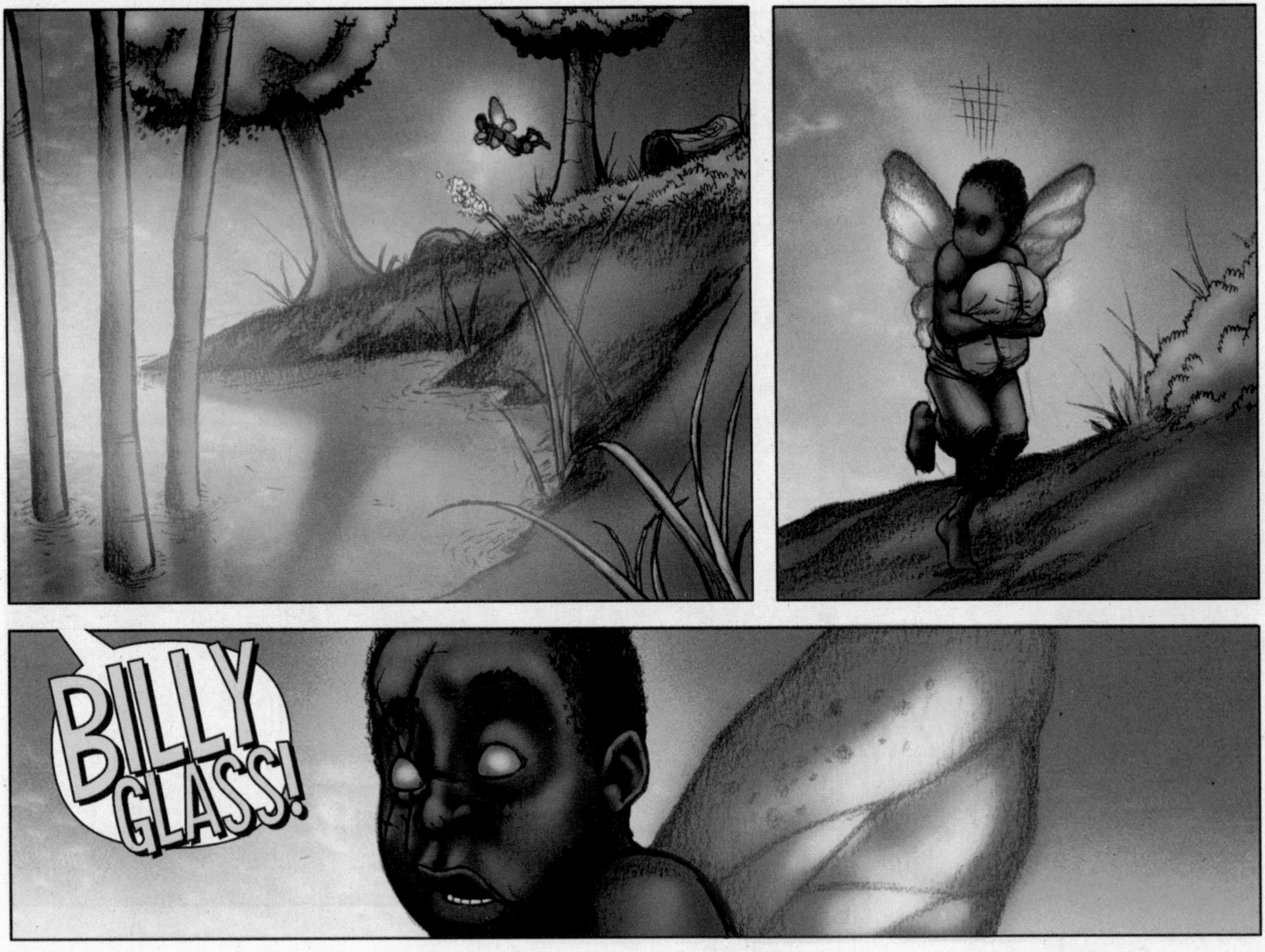
BILLY GLASS!

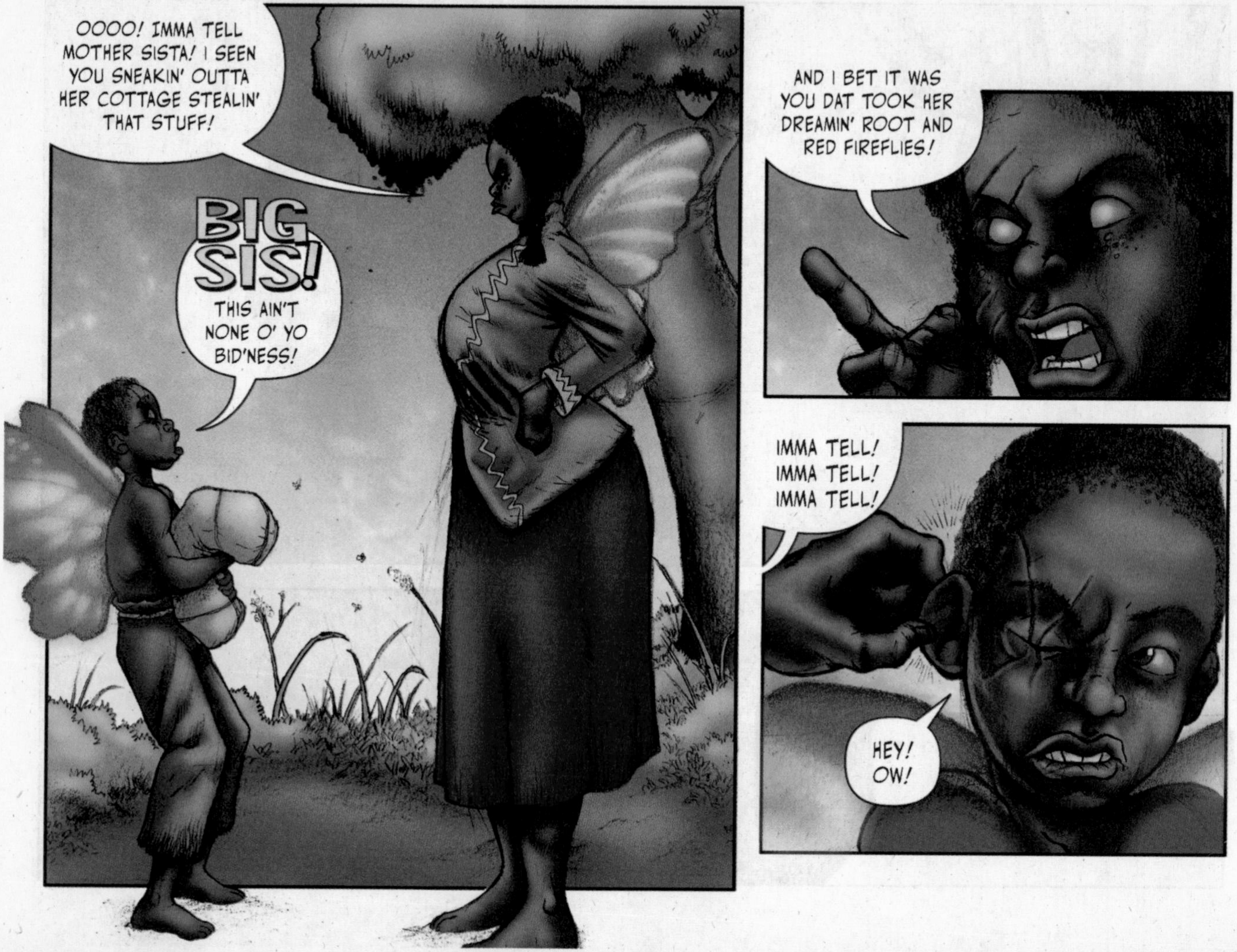
OOOO! IMMA TELL MOTHER SISTA! I SEEN YOU SNEAKIN' OUTTA HER COTTAGE STEALIN' THAT STUFF!
BIG SIS! THIS AIN'T NONE O' YO BID'NESS!
AND I BET IT WAS YOU DAT TOOK HER DREAMIN' ROOT AND RED FIREFLIES!
IMMA TELL! IMMA TELL! IMMA TELL!
HEY! OW!

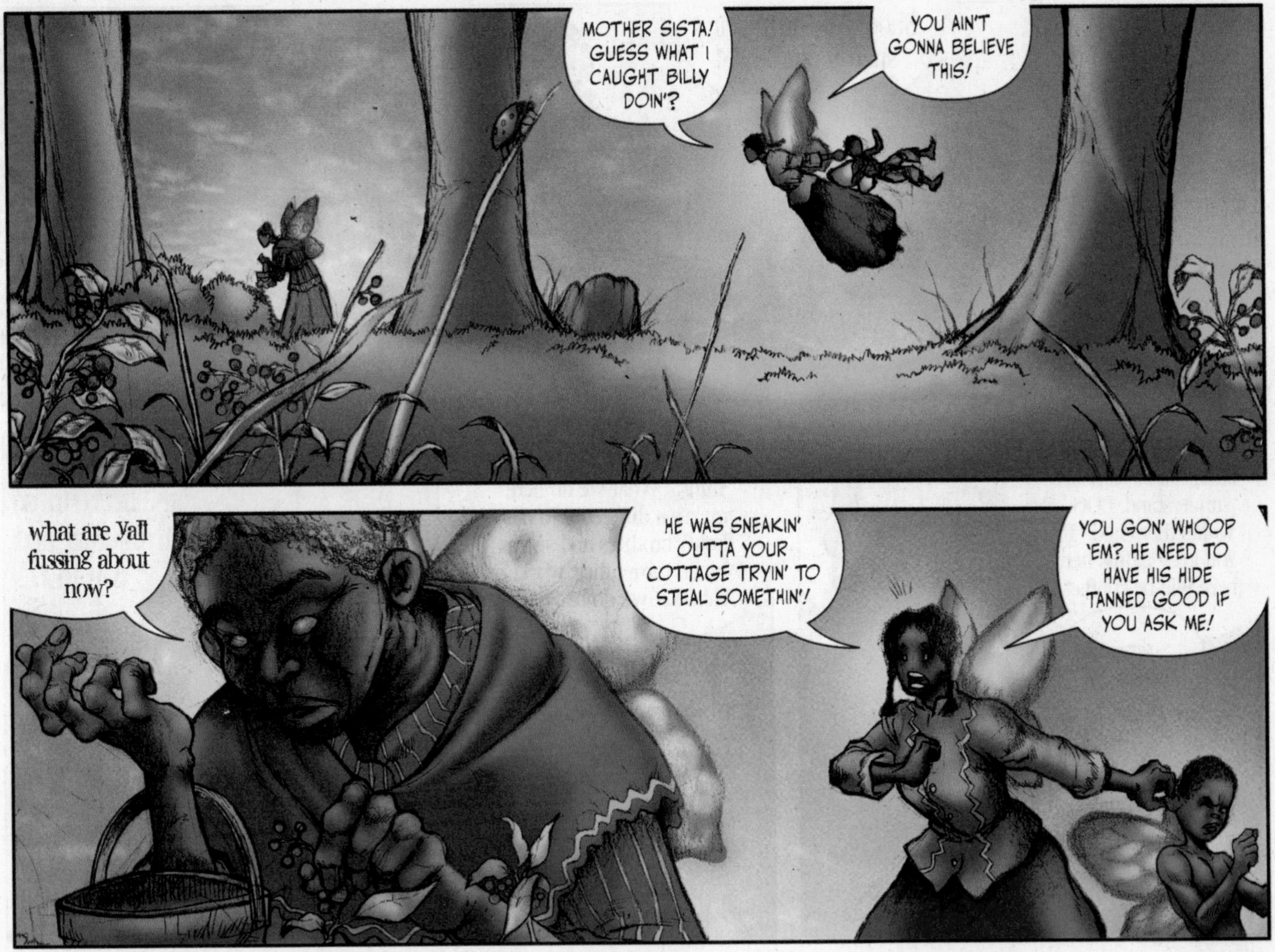
MOTHER SISTA! GUESS WHAT I CAUGHT BILLY DOIN'?
YOU AIN'T GONNA BELIEVE THIS!
what are Yall fussing about now?
HE WAS SNEAKIN' OUTTA YOUR COTTAGE TRYIN' TO STEAL SOMETHIN'!
YOU GON' WHOOP 'EM? HE NEED TO HAVE HIS HIDE TANNED GOOD IF YOU ASK ME!

MOTHER SISTA, I WAS JUST TRYIN' TA GET LEE SOME DRY CLOTHES AND MEDICINE...

Shoo! And stop being such a busybody!

I WOULDN'TA BEEN LAID TO REST PROPER IF'N SHE DIDN'T FISH ME OUT THE BAYOU.

I know why you did it, child. But you gotta understand, BOG wants that child. If you keep aiding her, there will be conflict...

YOU AFRAID O' BOG?

Conflict with BOG is no easy thing. What we do here makes a difference to our fleshly brothers and sisters. We can throw their world in CHAOS if we do battle here.

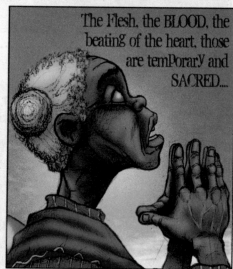

The Flesh, the BLOOD, the beating of the heart, those are temporary and SACRED....

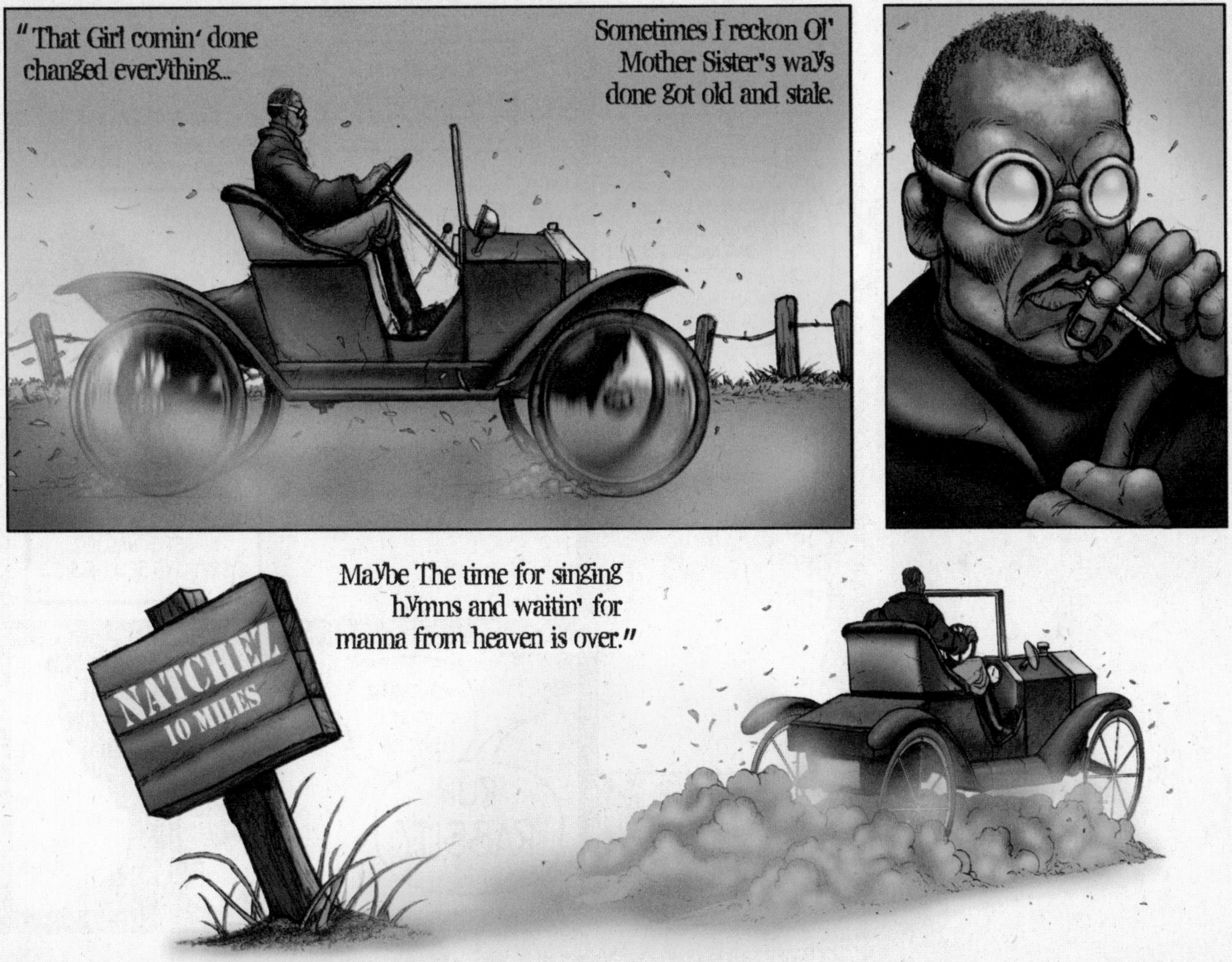
"That Girl comin' done changed everything...
Sometimes I reckon Ol' Mother Sister's ways done got old and stale.
Maybe The time for singing hymns and waitin' for manna from heaven is over."
NATCHEZ
10 MILES

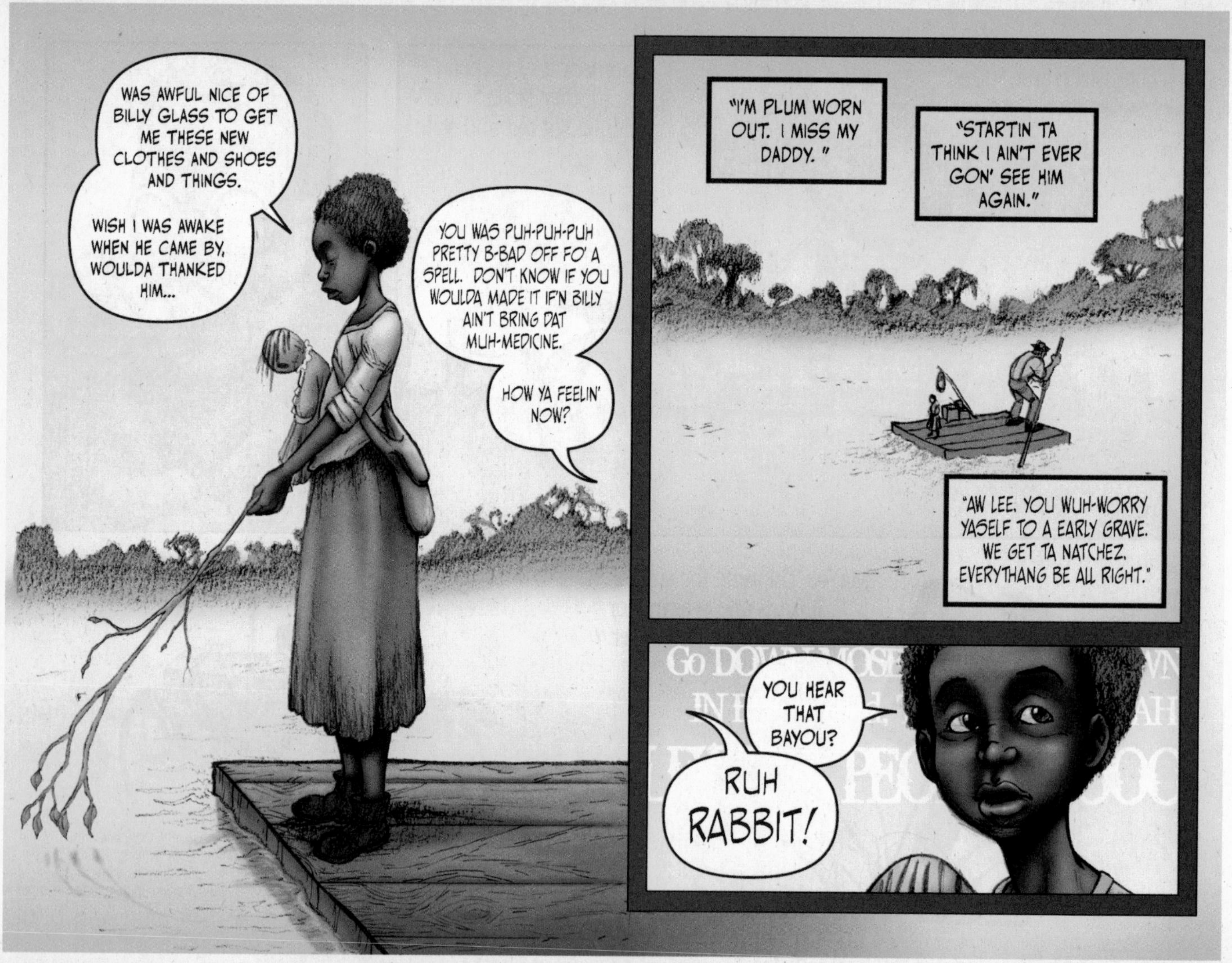
WAS AWFUL NICE OF BILLY GLASS TO GET ME THESE NEW CLOTHES AND SHOES AND THINGS.
WISH I WAS AWAKE WHEN HE CAME BY, WOULDA THANKED HIM...
YOU WAS PUH-PUH-PUH PRETTY B-BAD OFF FO' A SPELL. DON'T KNOW IF YOU WOULDA MADE IT IF'N BILLY AIN'T BRING DAT MUH-MEDICINE.
HOW YA FEELIN' NOW?
"I'M PLUM WORN OUT. I MISS MY DADDY."
"STARTIN TA THINK I AIN'T EVER GON' SEE HIM AGAIN."
"AW LEE. YOU WUH-WORRY YASELF TO A EARLY GRAVE. WE GET TA NATCHEZ, EVERYTHANG BE ALL RIGHT."
YOU HEAR THAT BAYOU?
RUH RABBIT!

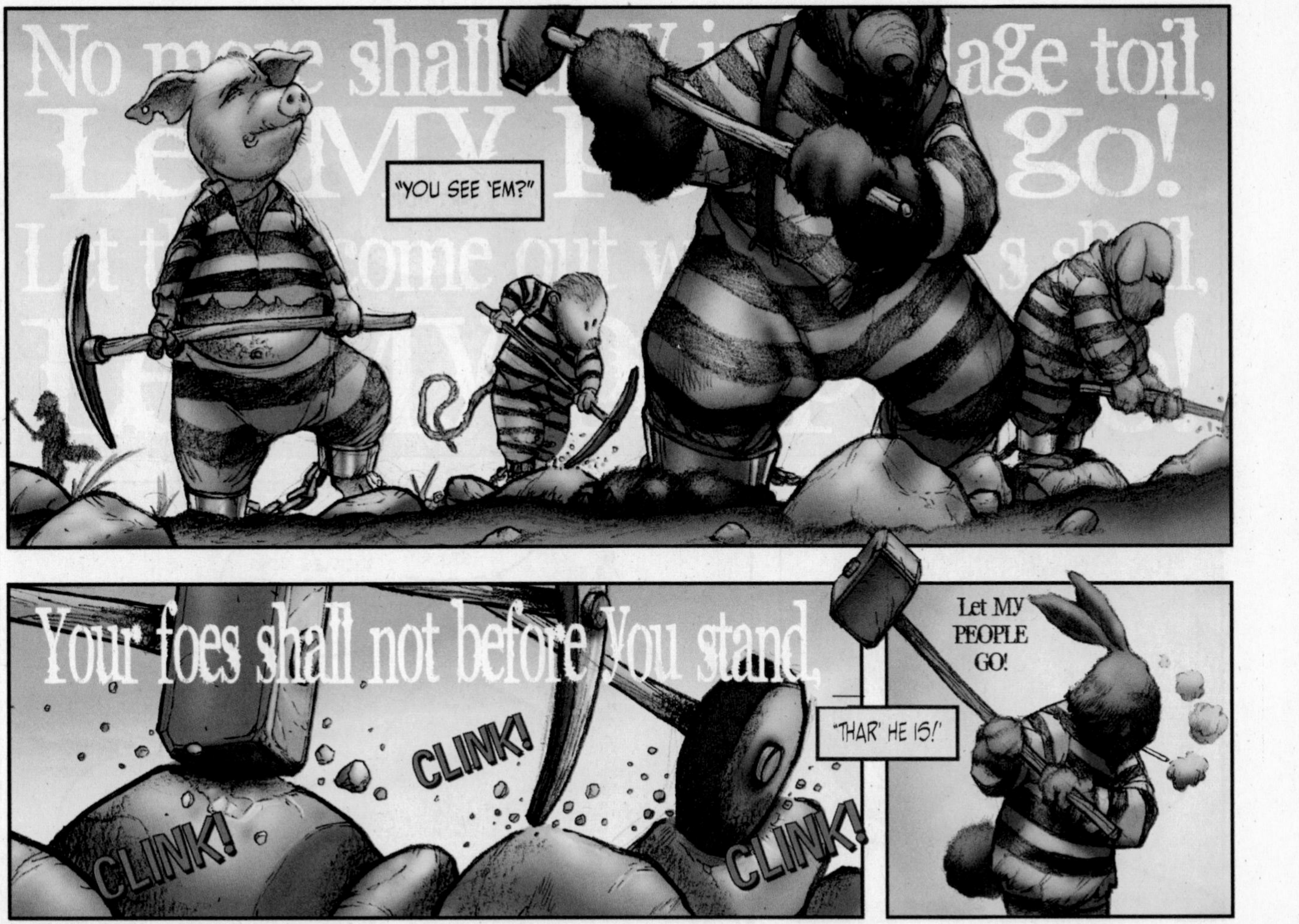
"YOU SEE 'EM?"
Your foes shall not before You stand,
CLINK!
CLINK!
CLINK!
"THAR' HE IS!'
Let MY PEOPLE GO!

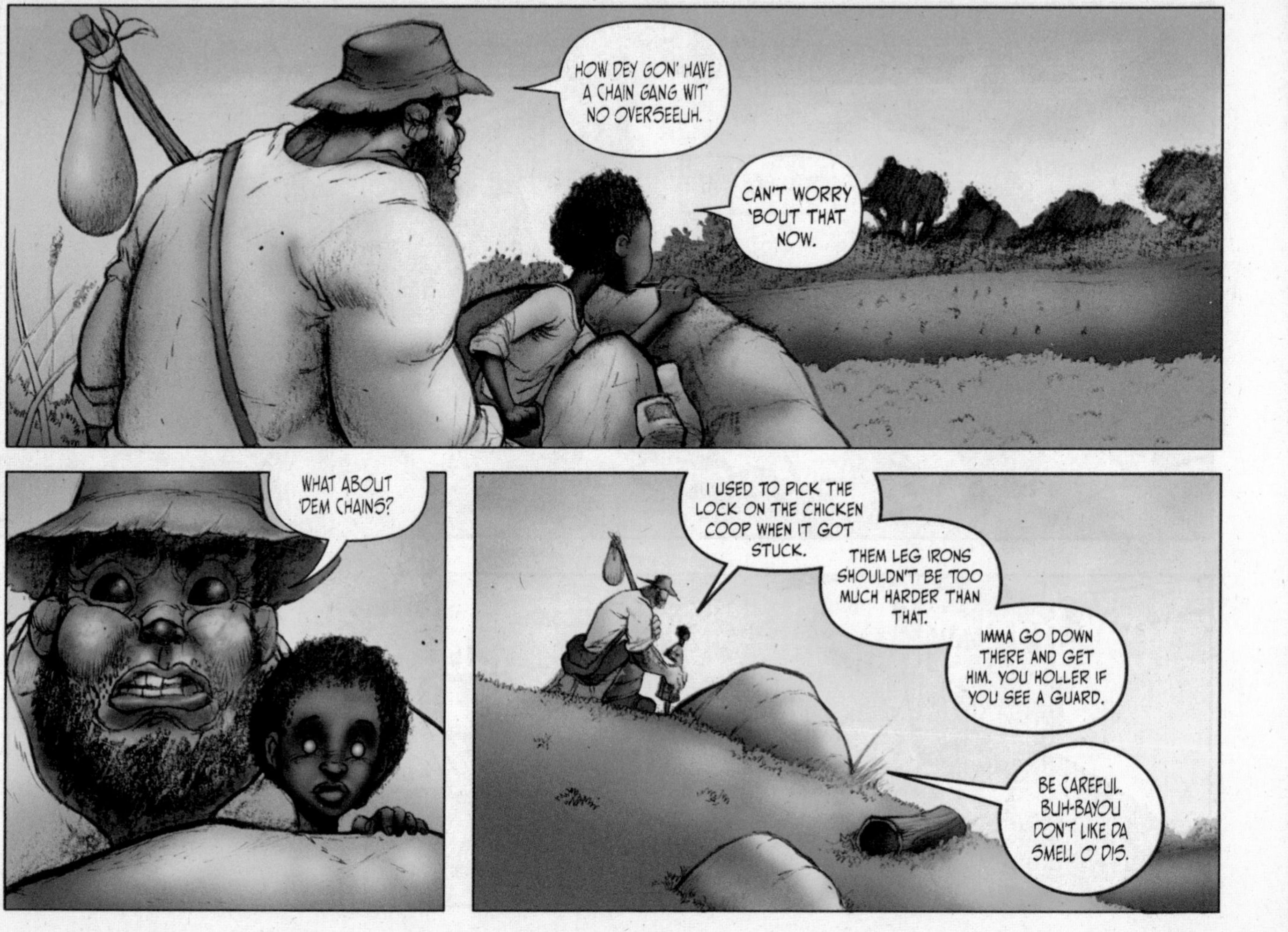
HOW DEY GON' HAVE A CHAIN GANG WIT' NO OVERSEEUH.
CAN'T WORRY 'BOUT THAT NOW.
WHAT ABOUT 'DEM CHAINS?
I USED TO PICK THE LOCK ON THE CHICKEN COOP WHEN IT GOT STUCK.
THEM LEG IRONS SHOULDN'T BE TOO MUCH HARDER THAN THAT.
IMMA GO DOWN THERE AND GET HIM. YOU HOLLER IF YOU SEE A GUARD.
BE CAREFUL. BUH-BAYOU DON'T LIKE DA SMELL O' DIS.

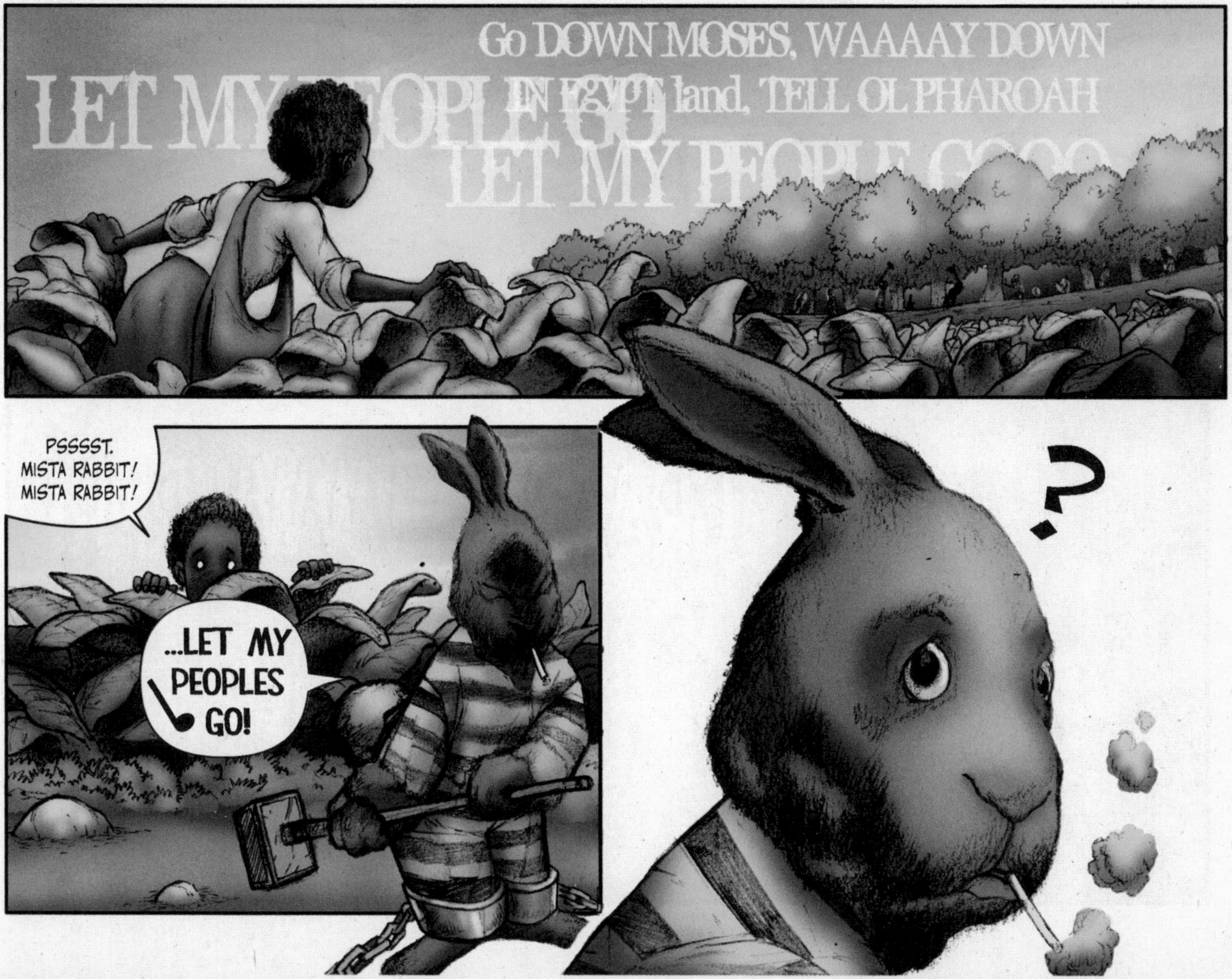
Go DOWN MOSES, WAAAAY DOWN
land, TELL OL PHAROAH
LET MY
LET MY
PSSSST. MISTA RABBIT! MISTA RABBIT!
...LET MY PEOPLES GO!
?

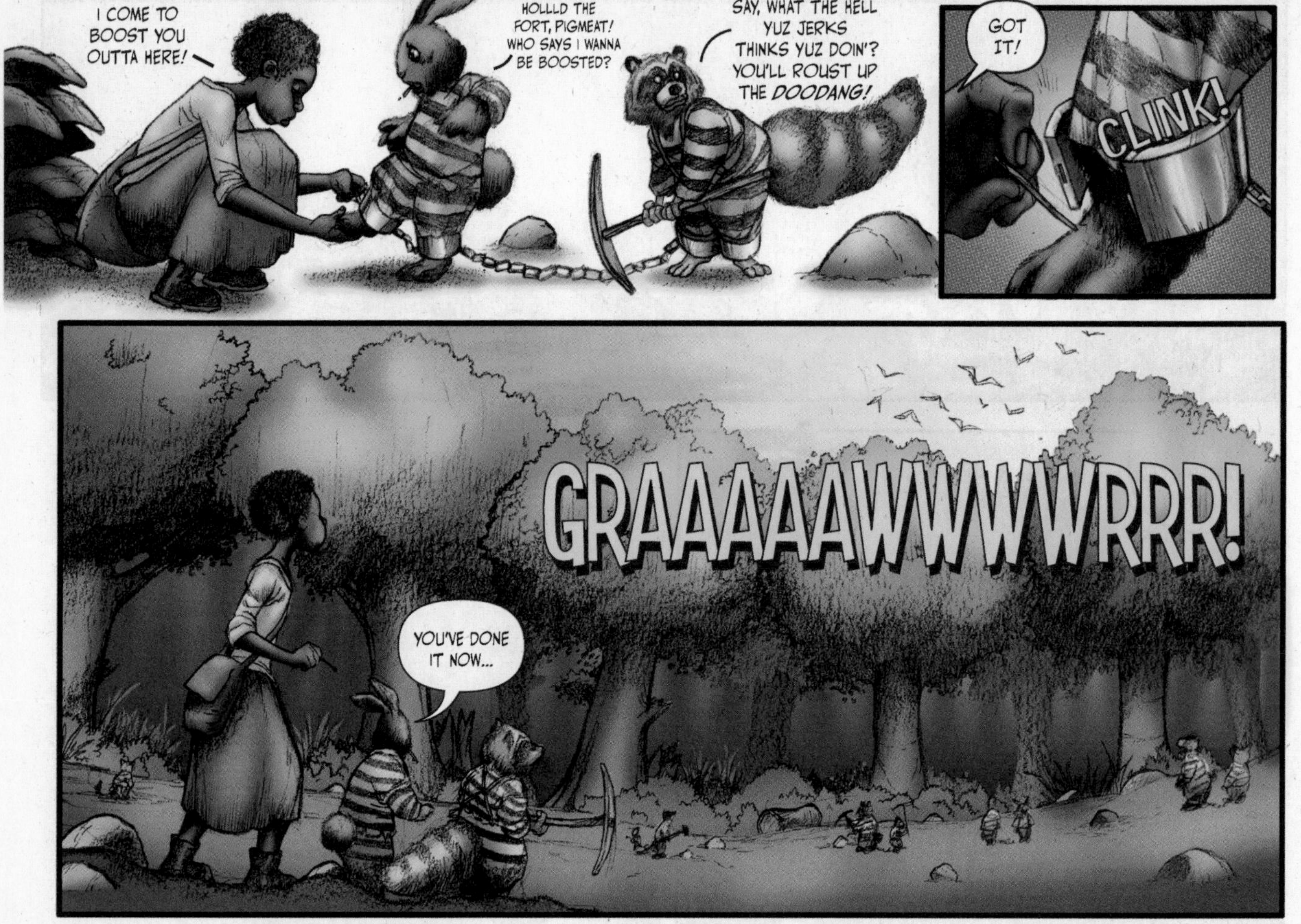
I COME TO BOOST YOU OUTTA HERE!
HOLLLD THE FORT, PIGMEAT! WHO SAYS I WANNA BE BOOSTED?
SAY, WHAT THE HELL YUZ JERKS THINKS YUZ DOIN'? YOU'LL ROUST UP THE *DOODANG!*
GOT IT!
CLINK!
GRAAAAAAWWWWWRRR!
YOU'VE DONE IT NOW...

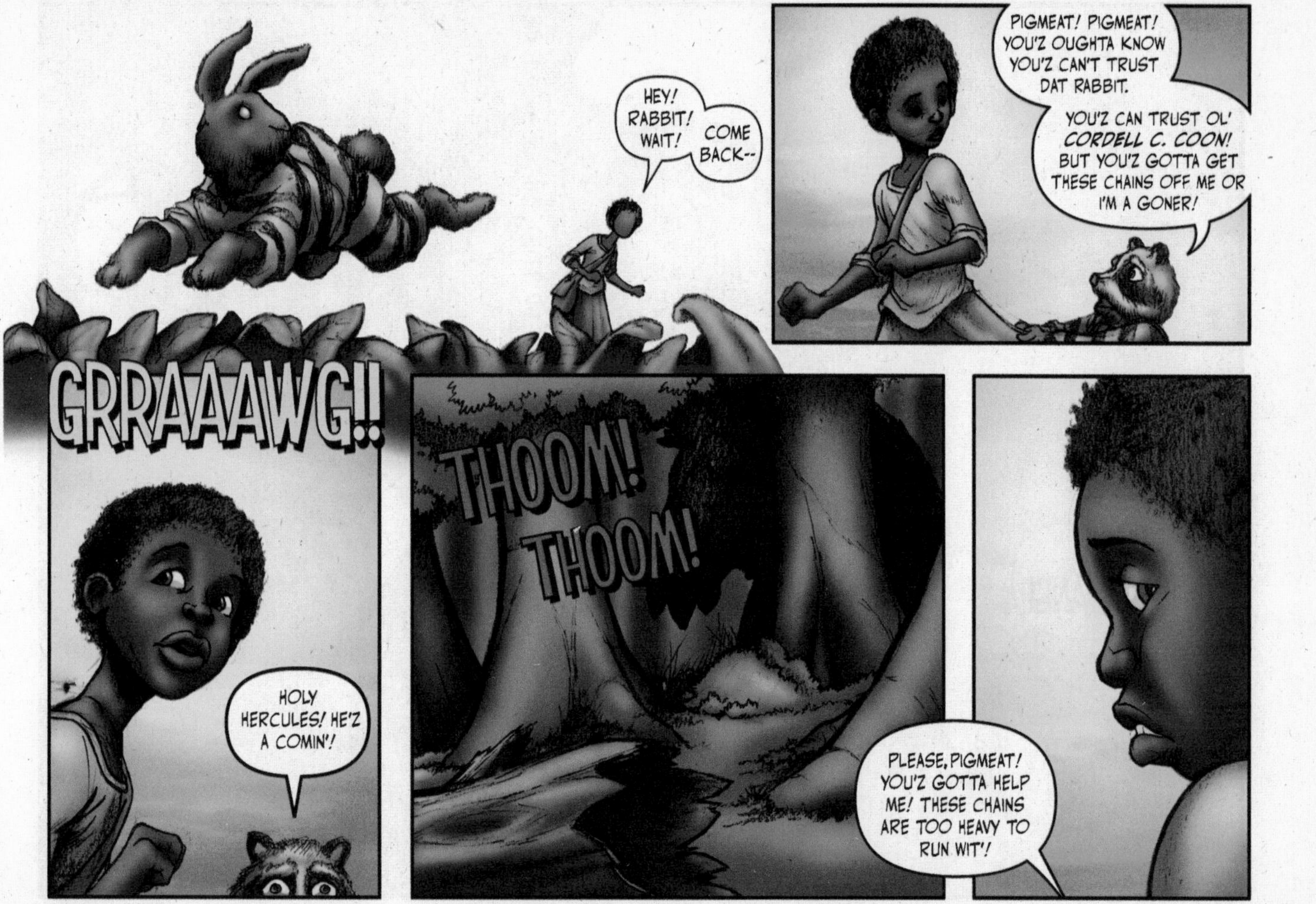
HEY! RABBIT! WAIT!
COME BACK--
PIGMEAT! PIGMEAT! YOU'Z OUGHTA KNOW YOU'Z CAN'T TRUST DAT RABBIT.
YOU'Z CAN TRUST OL' CORDELL C. COON! BUT YOU'Z GOTTA GET THESE CHAINS OFF ME OR I'M A GONER!
GRRAAAWG!!
HOLY HERCULES! HE'Z A COMIN'!
THOOM! THOOM!
PLEASE, PIGMEAT! YOU'Z GOTTA HELP ME! THESE CHAINS ARE TOO HEAVY TO RUN WIT'!

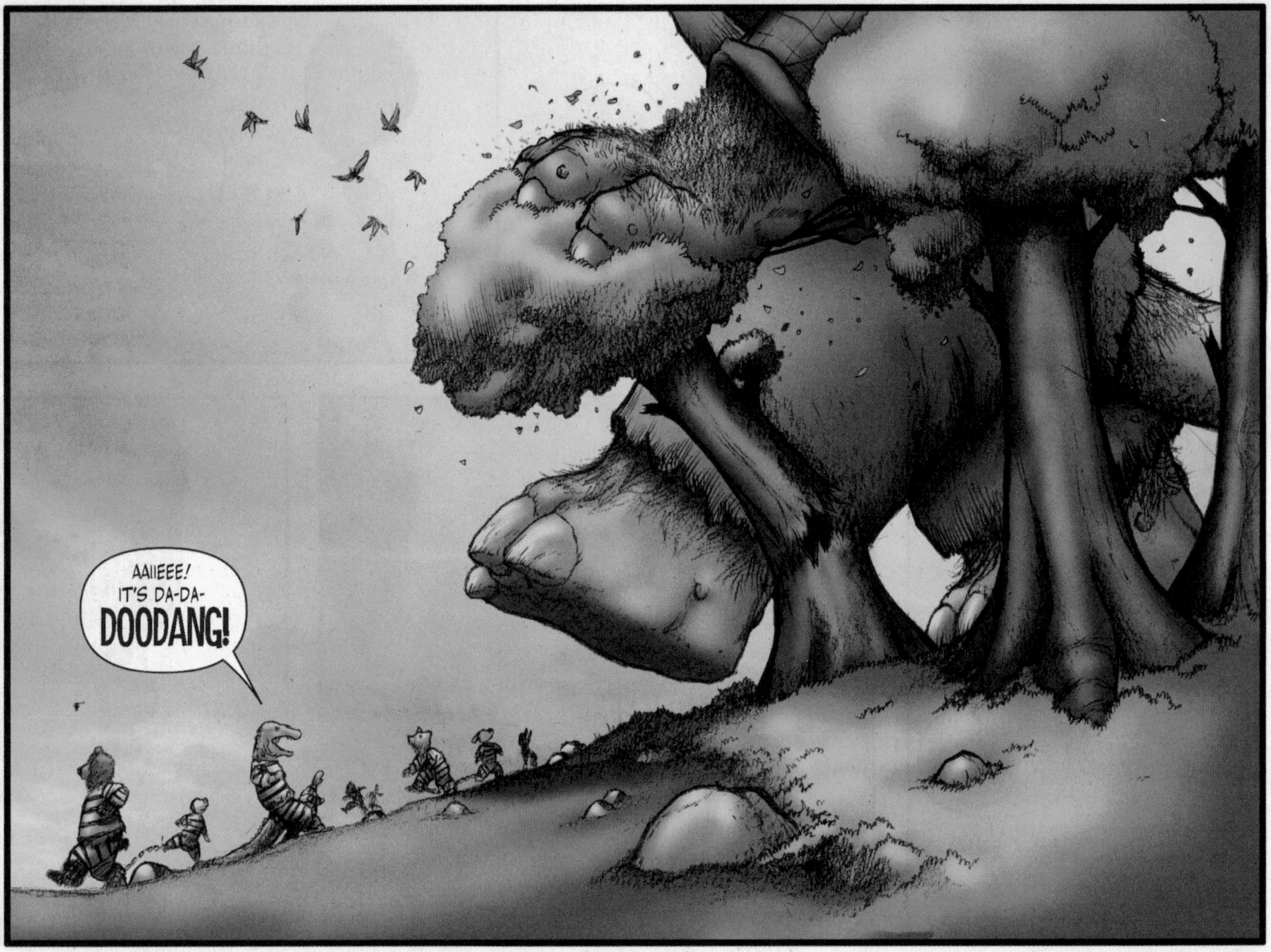
AAIIEEE! IT'S DA-DA- DOODANG!

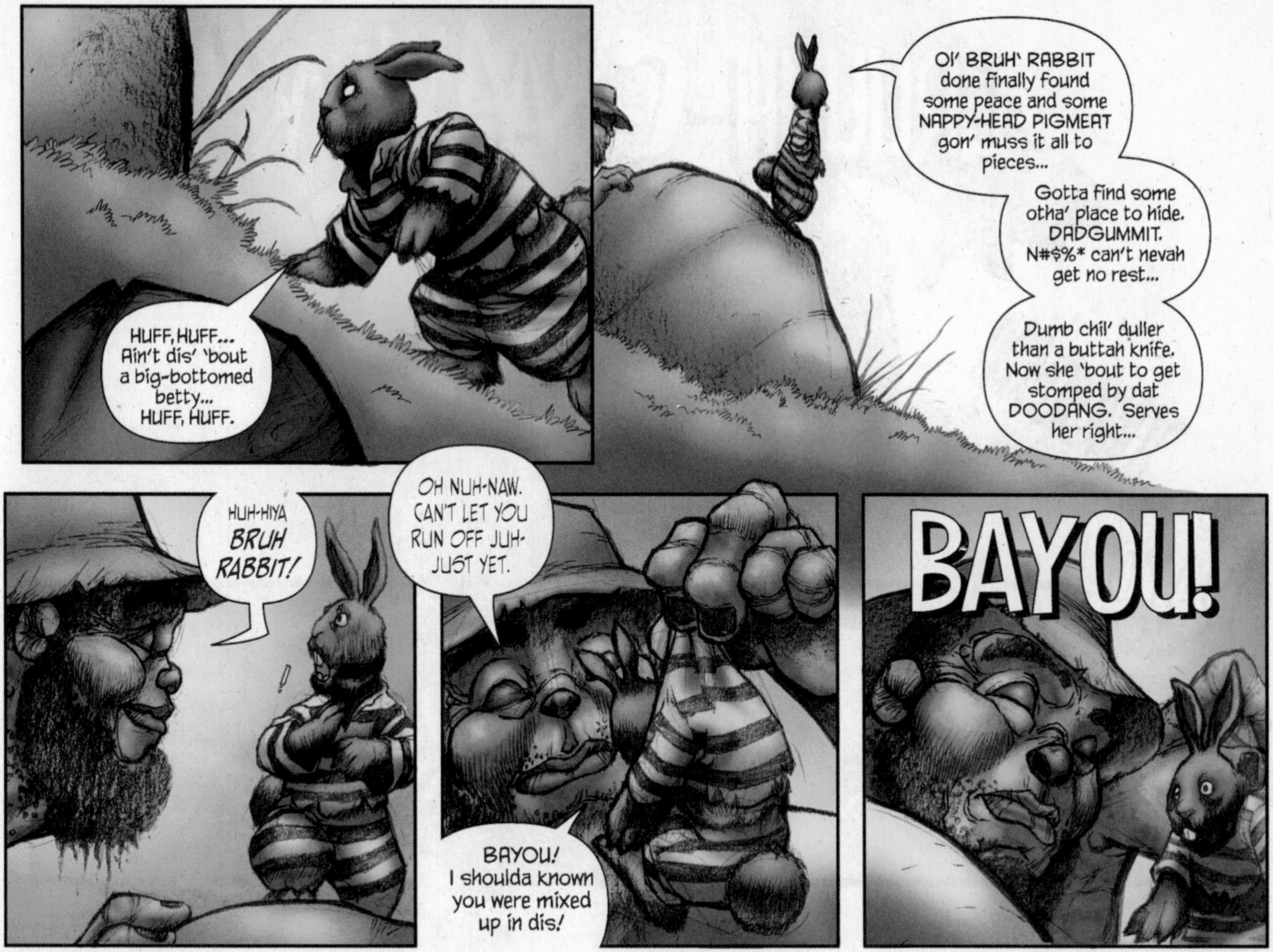
HUFF, HUFF... Ain't dis' 'bout a big-bottomed betty... HUFF, HUFF.
OI' BRUH' RABBIT done finally found some peace and some NAPPY-HEAD PIGMEAT gon' muss it all to pieces...
Gotta find some otha' place to hide. DADGUMMIT. N#$%* can't nevah get no rest...
Dumb chil' duller than a buttah knife. Now she 'bout to get stomped by dat DOODANG. Serves her right...
HUH-HIYA BRUH RABBIT!
!
OH NUH-NAW. CAN'T LET YOU RUN OFF JUH-JUST YET.
BAYOU! I shoulda known you were mixed up in dis!
BAYOU!

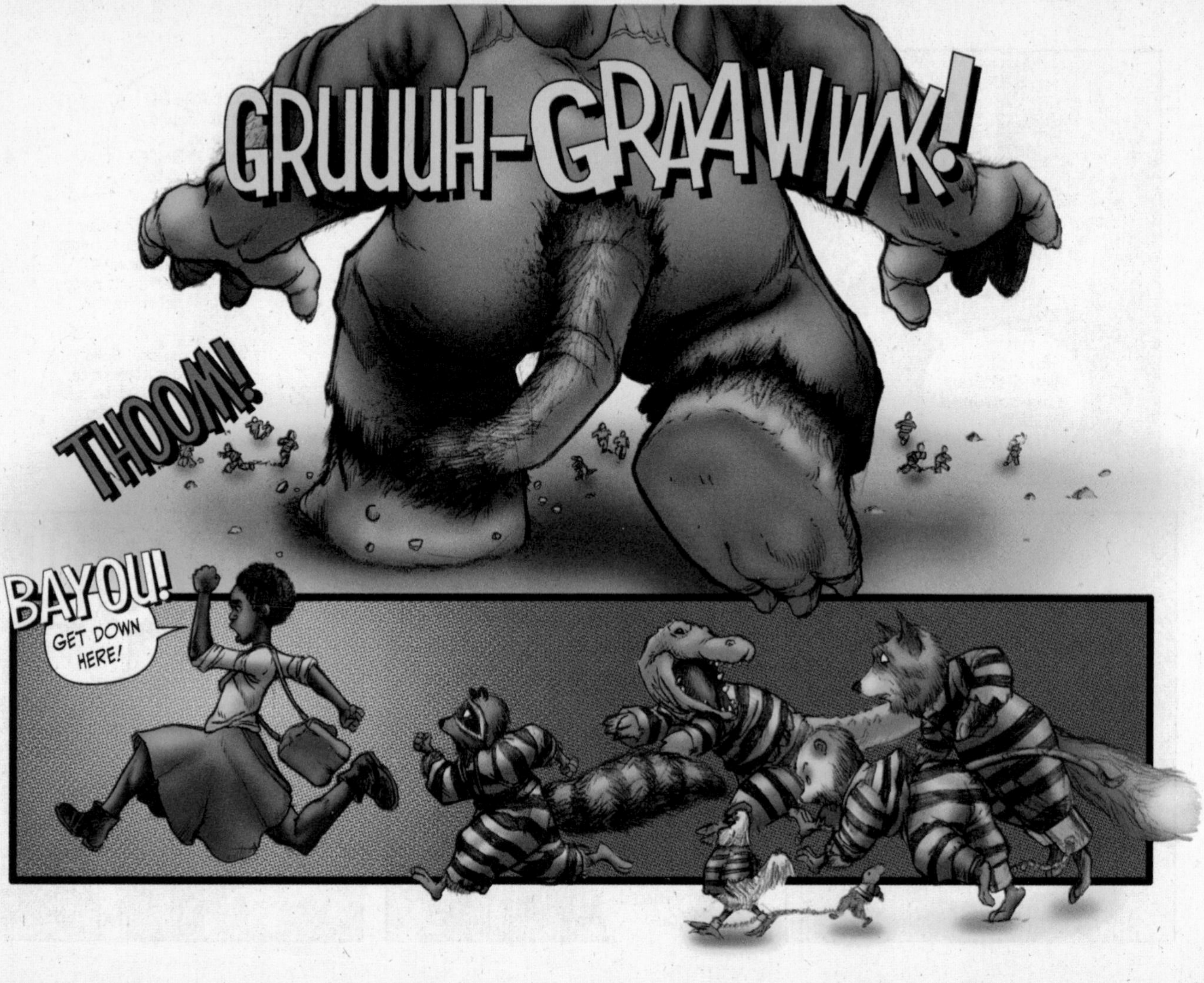
GRUUUH-GRAAWWK!
THOOM!
BAYOU!
GET DOWN HERE!

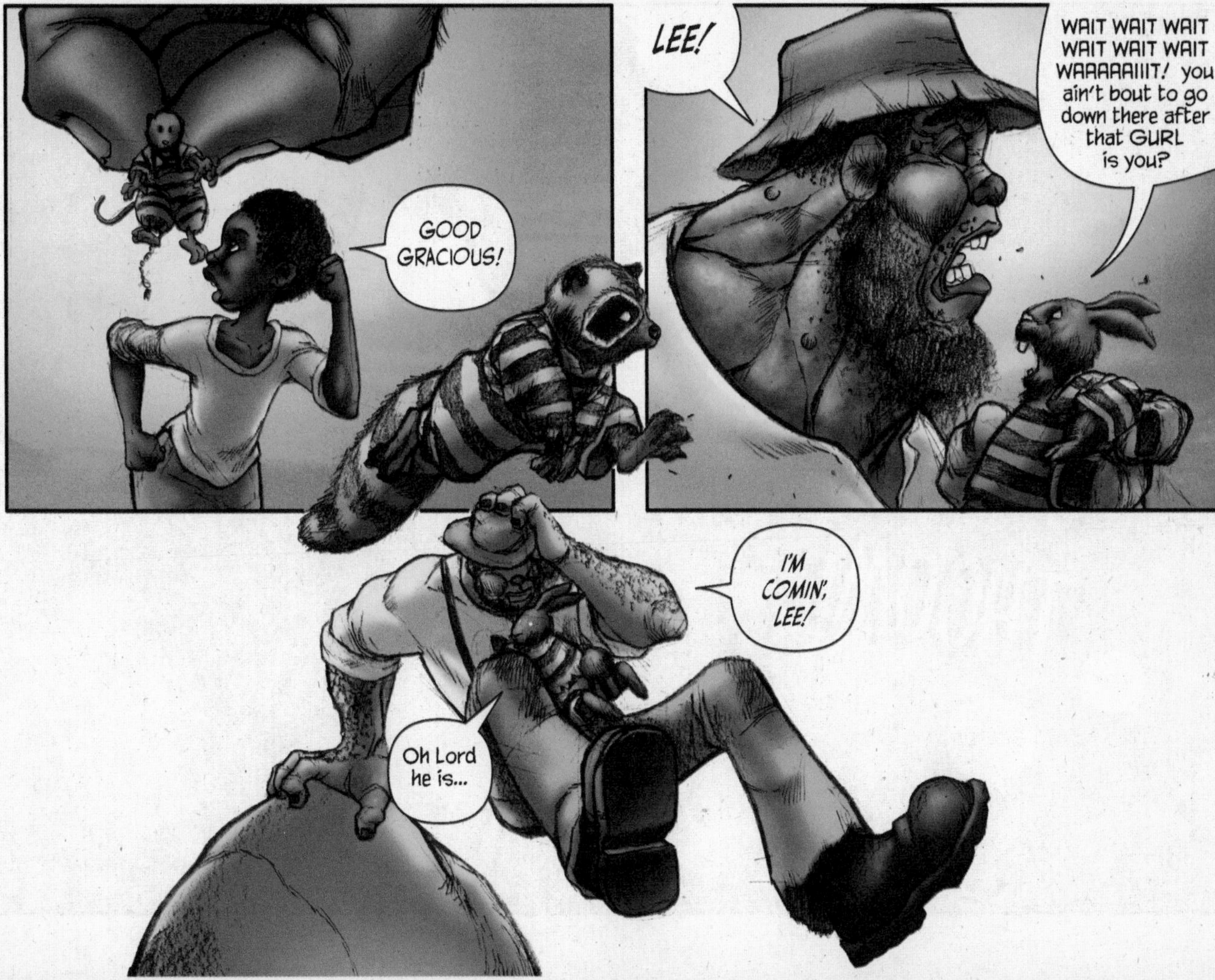
GOOD GRACIOUS!
LEE!
WAIT WAIT WAIT WAIT WAIT WAIT WAAAAAIIIIT! you ain't bout to go down there after that GURL is you?
I'M COMIN', LEE!
Oh Lord he is...

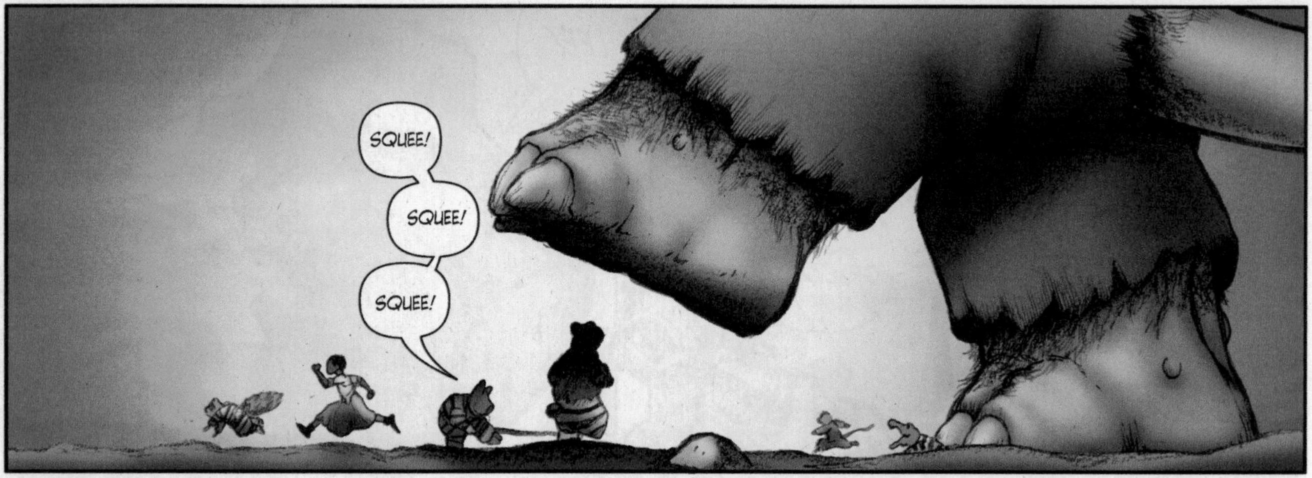
SQUEE!
SQUEE!
SQUEE!

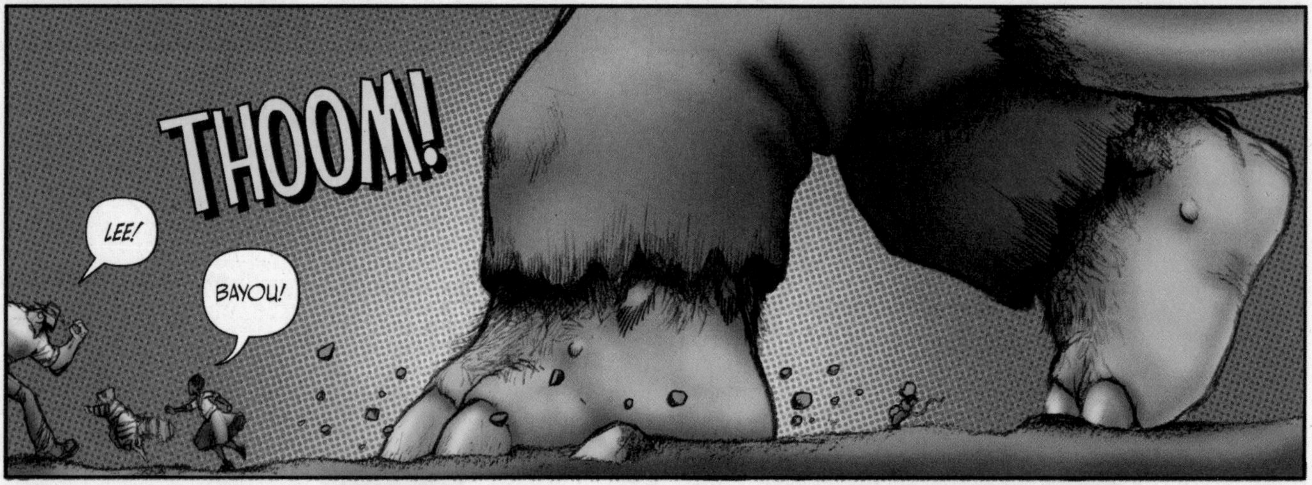
THOOM!
LEE!
BAYOU!

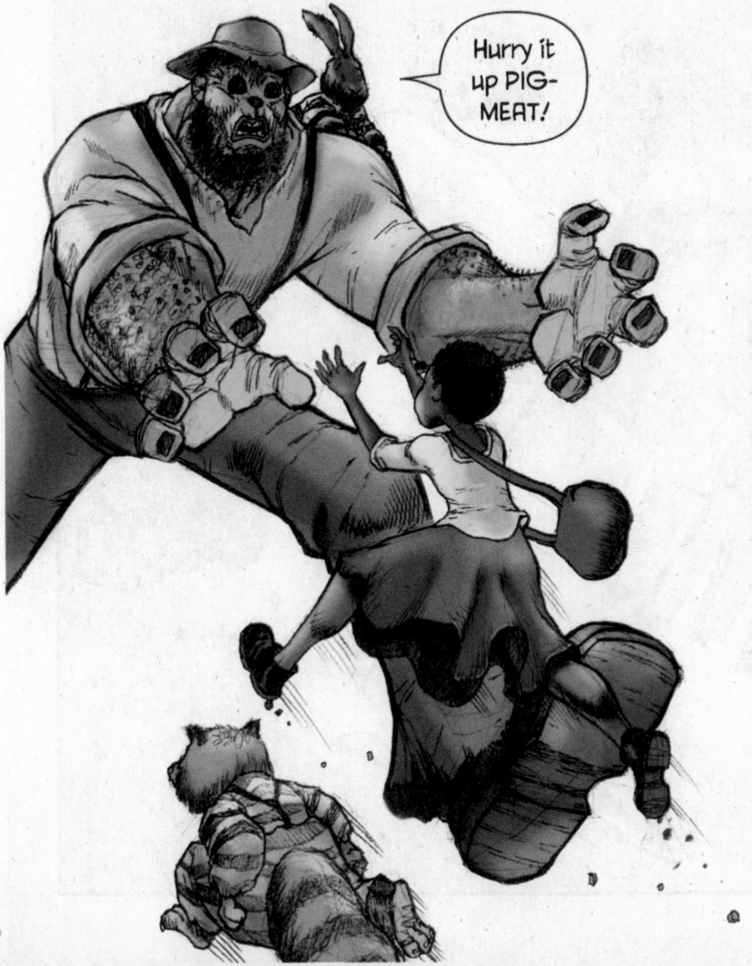
Hurry it up PIG-MEAT!

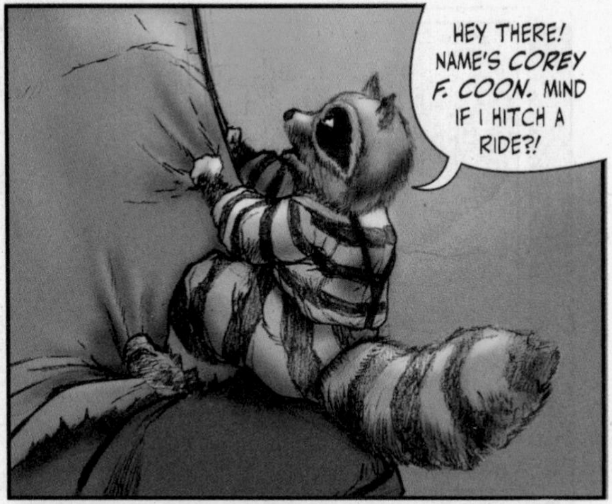
HEY THERE! NAME'S *COREY F. COON.* MIND IF I HITCH A RIDE?!

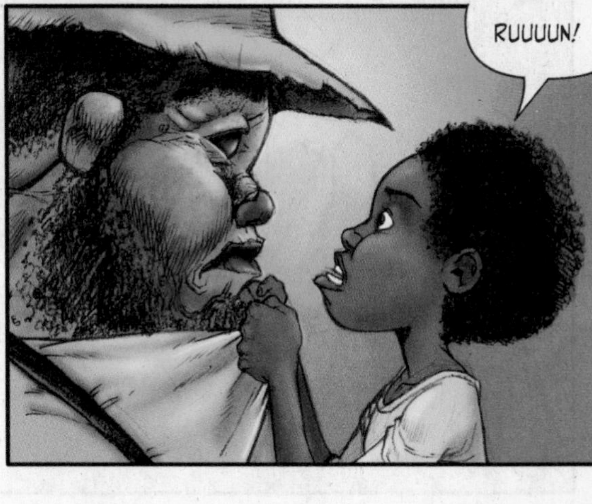
RUUUUN!

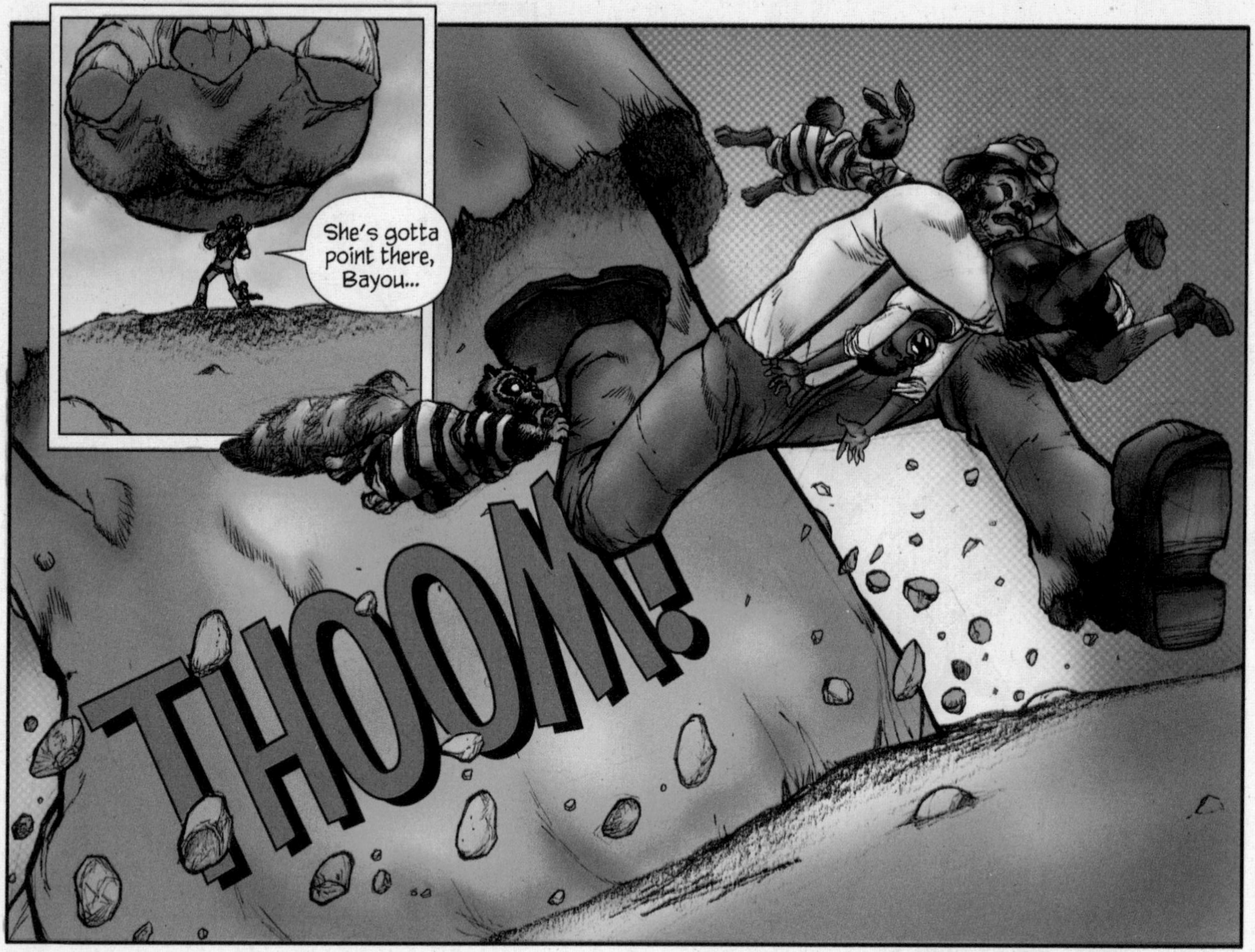
She's gotta point there, Bayou...
THOOM!

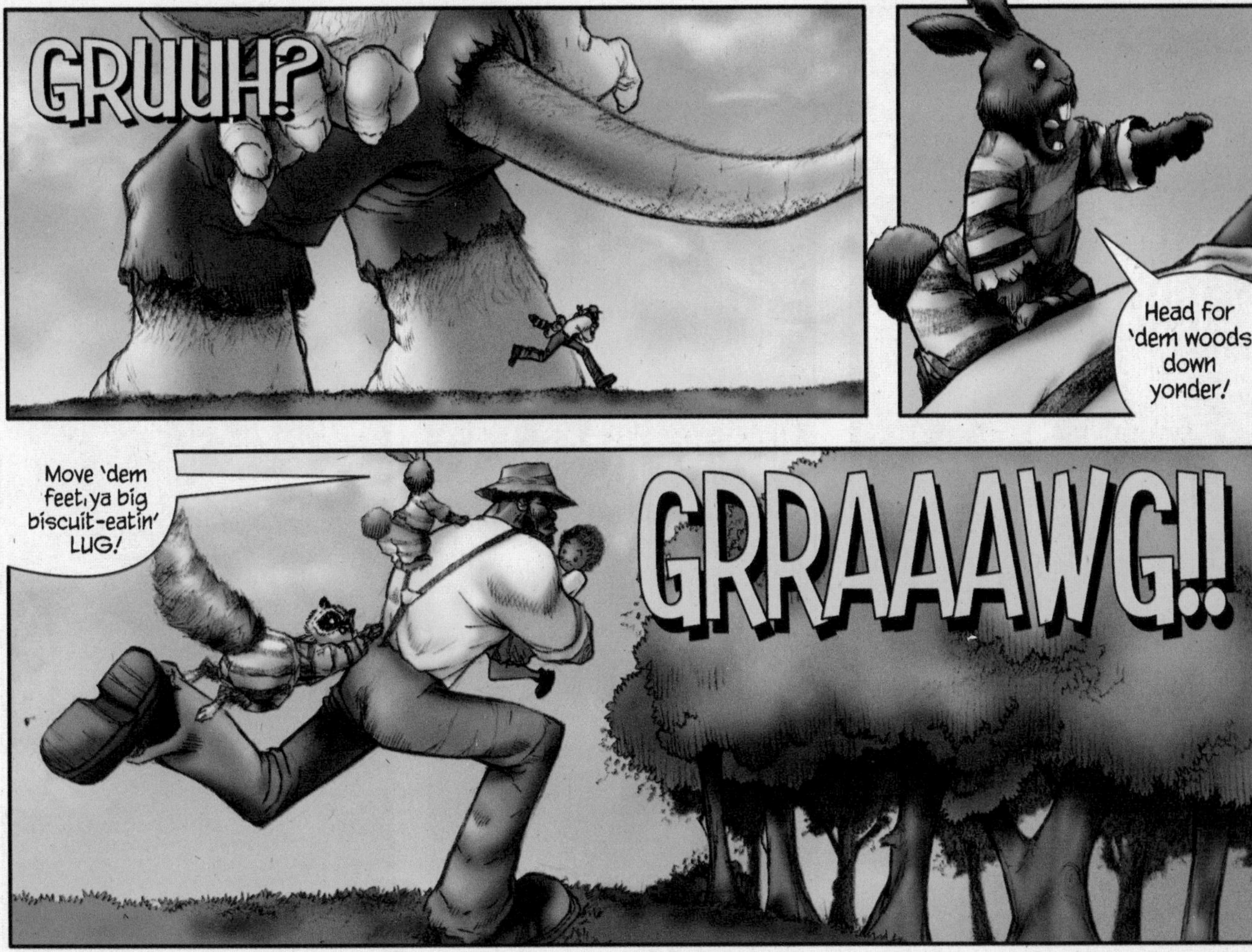
GRUUH?
Head for 'dem woods down yonder!
Move 'dem feet, ya big biscuit-eatin' LUG!
GRRAAAWG!!

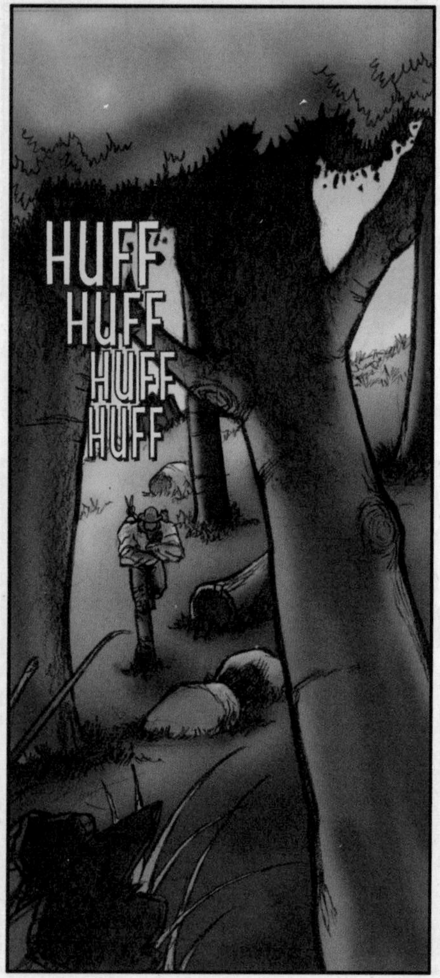
HUFF
HUFF
HUFF
HUFF

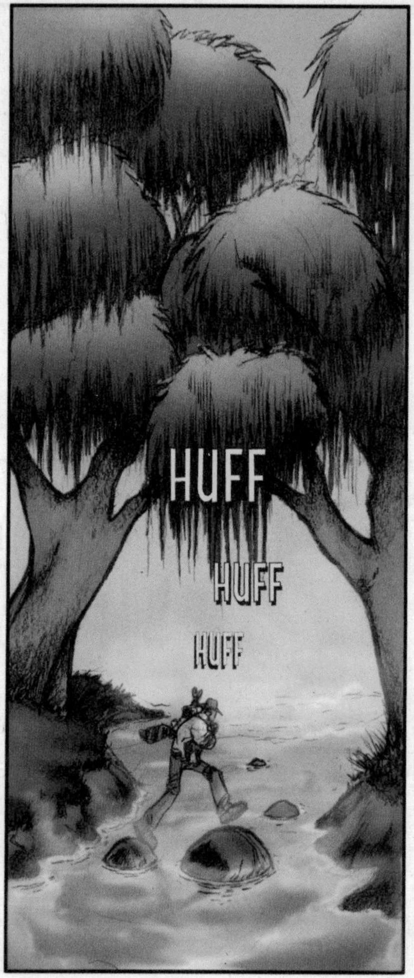
HUFF
HUFF
HUFF

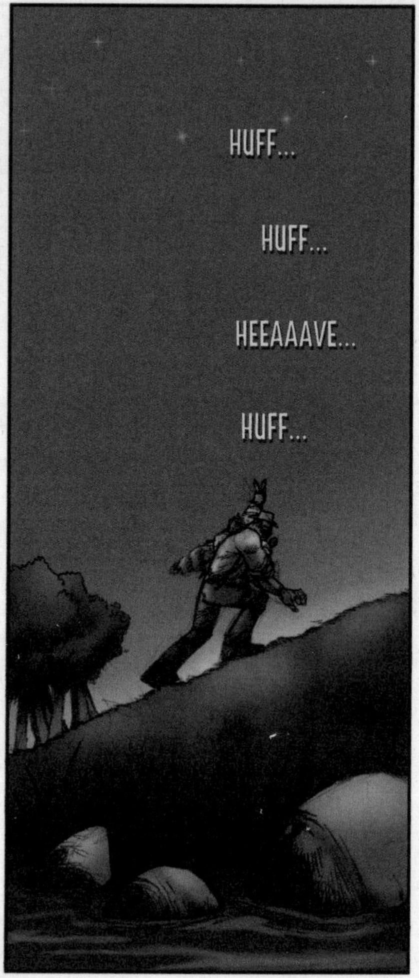
HUFF...
HUFF...
HEEAAAVE...
HUFF...

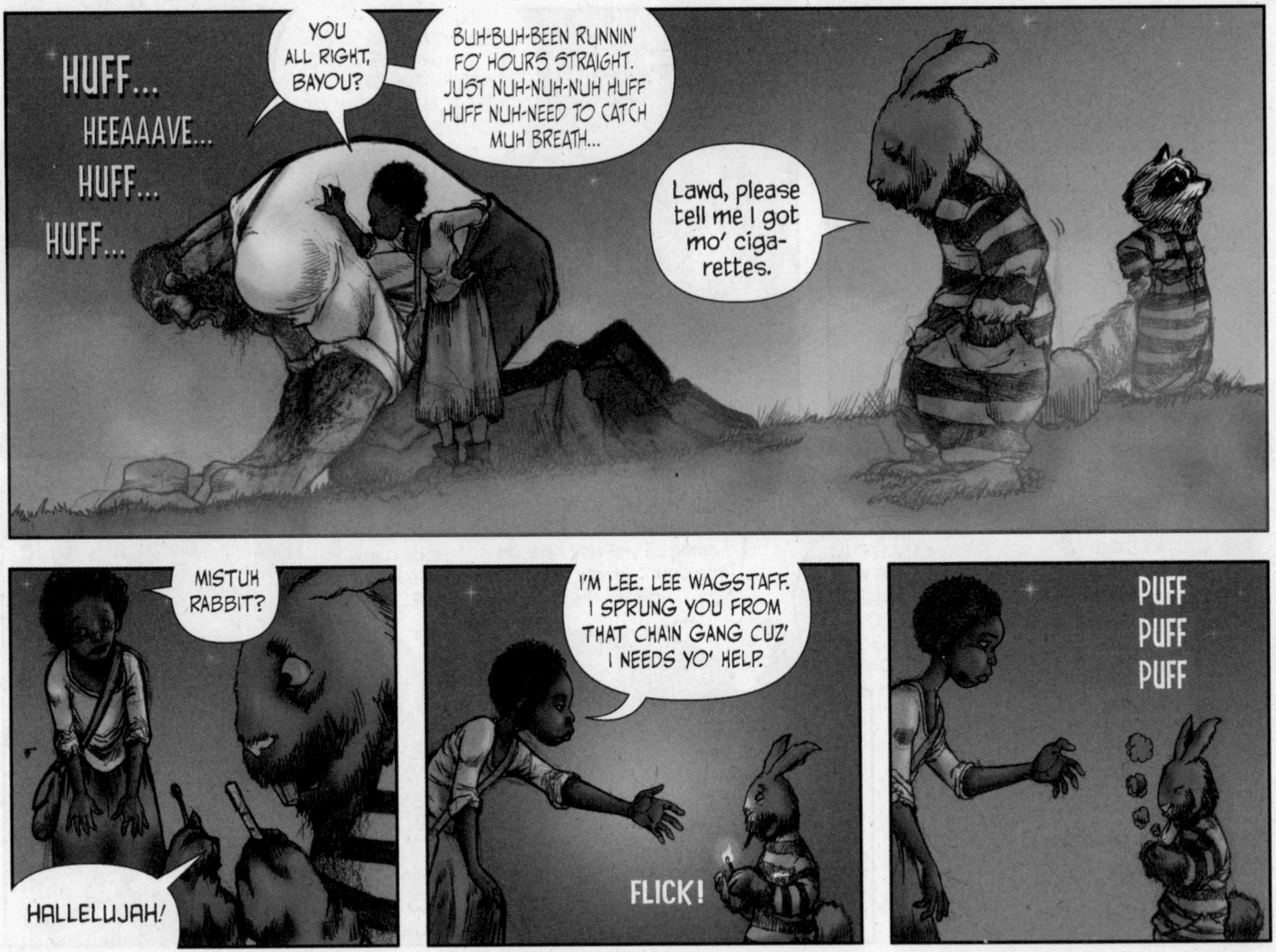
HUFF... HEEAAAVE... HUFF... HUFF...
YOU ALL RIGHT, BAYOU?
BUH-BUH-BEEN RUNNIN' FO' HOURS STRAIGHT. JUST NUH-NUH-NUH HUFF HUFF NUH-NEED TO CATCH MUH BREATH...
Lawd, please tell me I got mo' cigarettes.
MISTUH RABBIT?
HALLELUJAH!
I'M LEE. LEE WAGSTAFF. I SPRUNG YOU FROM THAT CHAIN GANG CUZ' I NEEDS YO' HELP.
FLICK!
PUFF PUFF PUFF

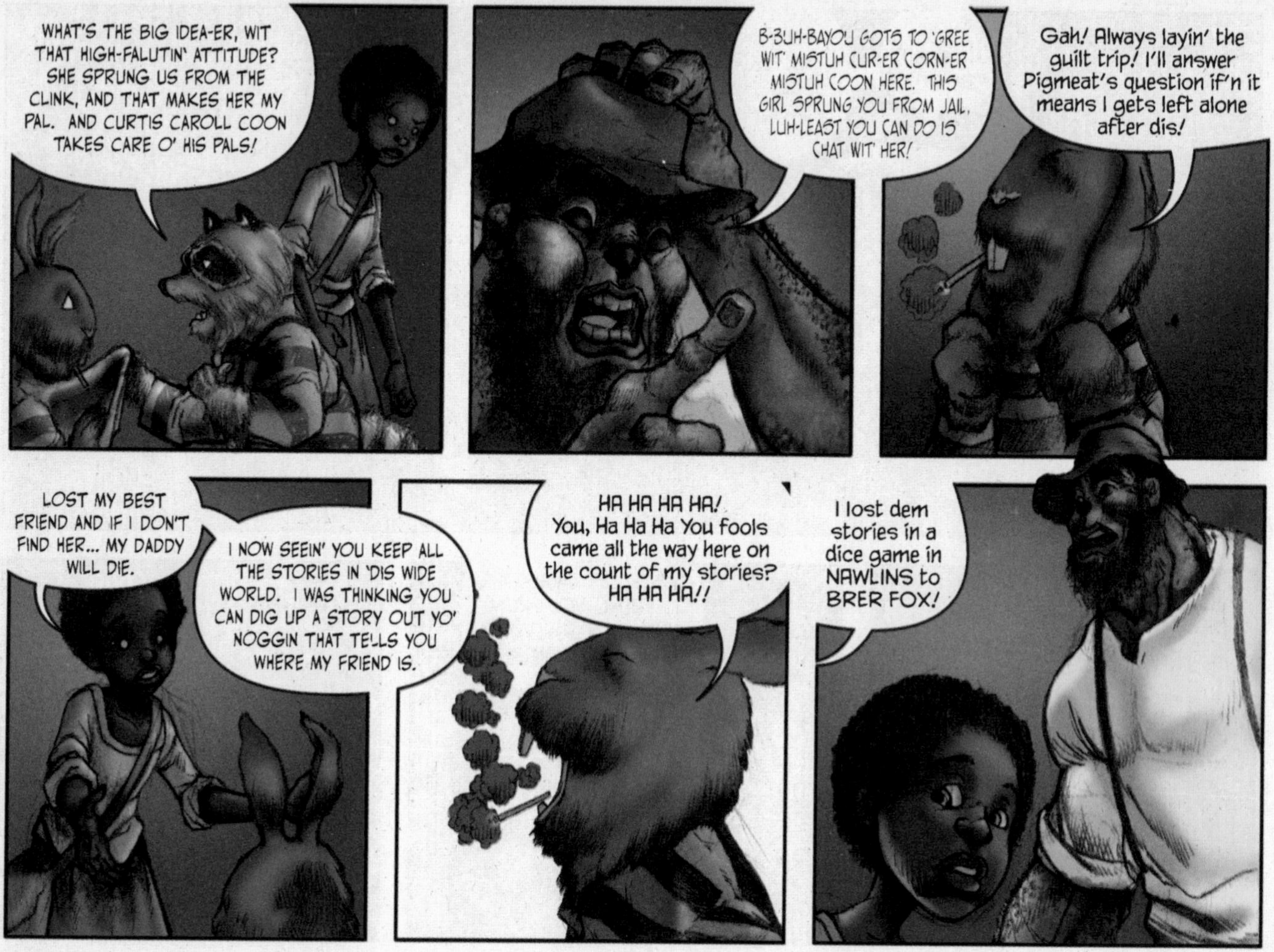
WHAT'S THE BIG IDEA-ER, WIT THAT HIGH-FALUTIN' ATTITUDE? SHE SPRUNG US FROM THE CLINK, AND THAT MAKES HER MY PAL. AND CURTIS CAROLL COON TAKES CARE O' HIS PALS!
B-BUH-BAYOU GOTS TO 'GREE WIT' MISTUH CUR-ER CORN-ER MISTUH COON HERE. THIS GIRL SPRUNG YOU FROM JAIL. LUH-LEAST YOU CAN DO IS CHAT WIT' HER!
Gah! Always layin' the guilt trip! I'll answer Pigmeat's question if'n it means I gets left alone after dis!
LOST MY BEST FRIEND AND IF I DON'T FIND HER... MY DADDY WILL DIE.
I NOW SEEIN' YOU KEEP ALL THE STORIES IN 'DIS WIDE WORLD. I WAS THINKING YOU CAN DIG UP A STORY OUT YO' NOGGIN THAT TELLS YOU WHERE MY FRIEND IS.
HA HA HA HA! You, Ha Ha Ha You fools came all the way here on the count of my stories? HA HA HA!!
I lost dem stories in a dice game in NAWLINS to BRER FOX!

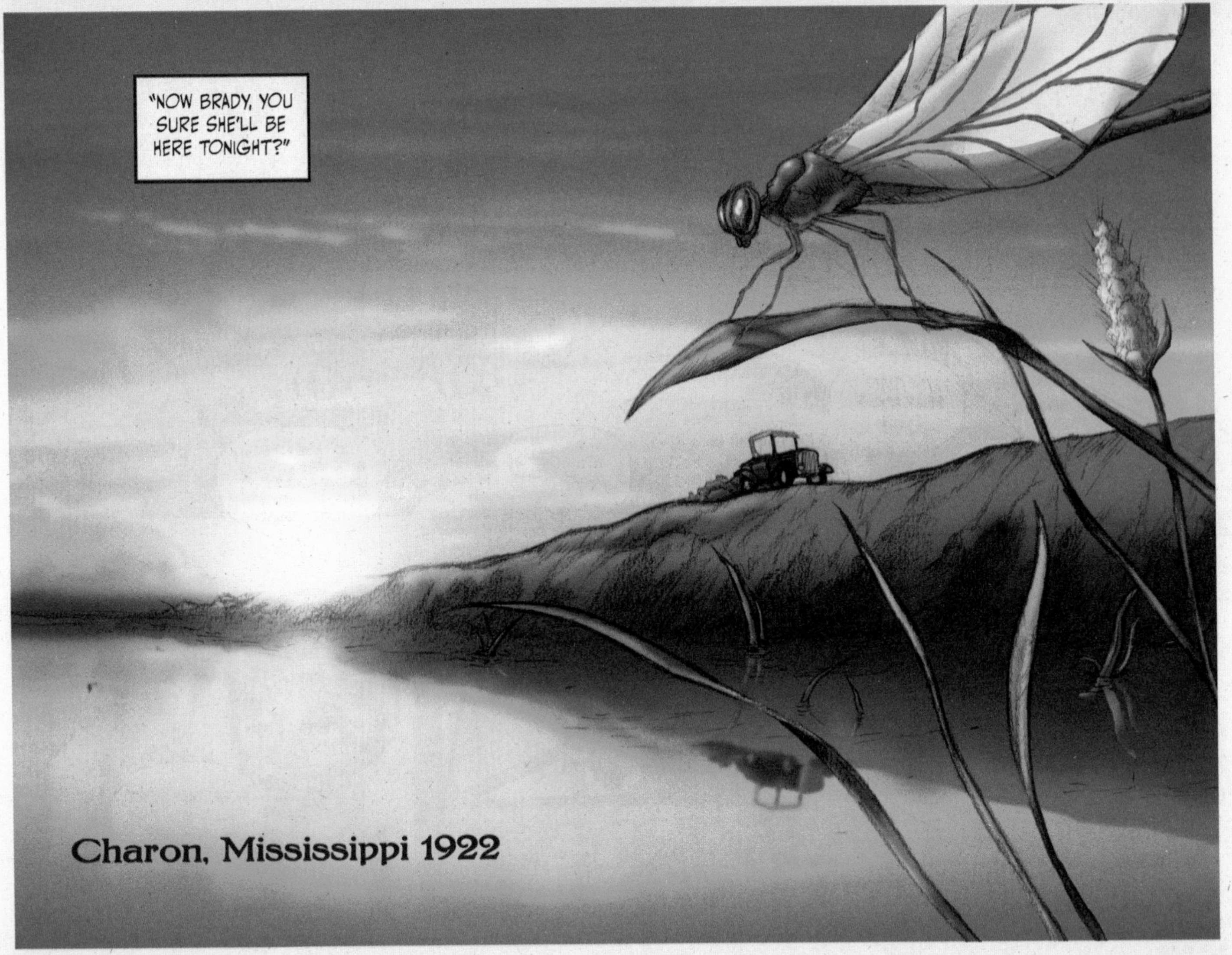
"NOW BRADY, YOU SURE SHE'LL BE HERE TONIGHT?"
Charon, Mississippi 1922

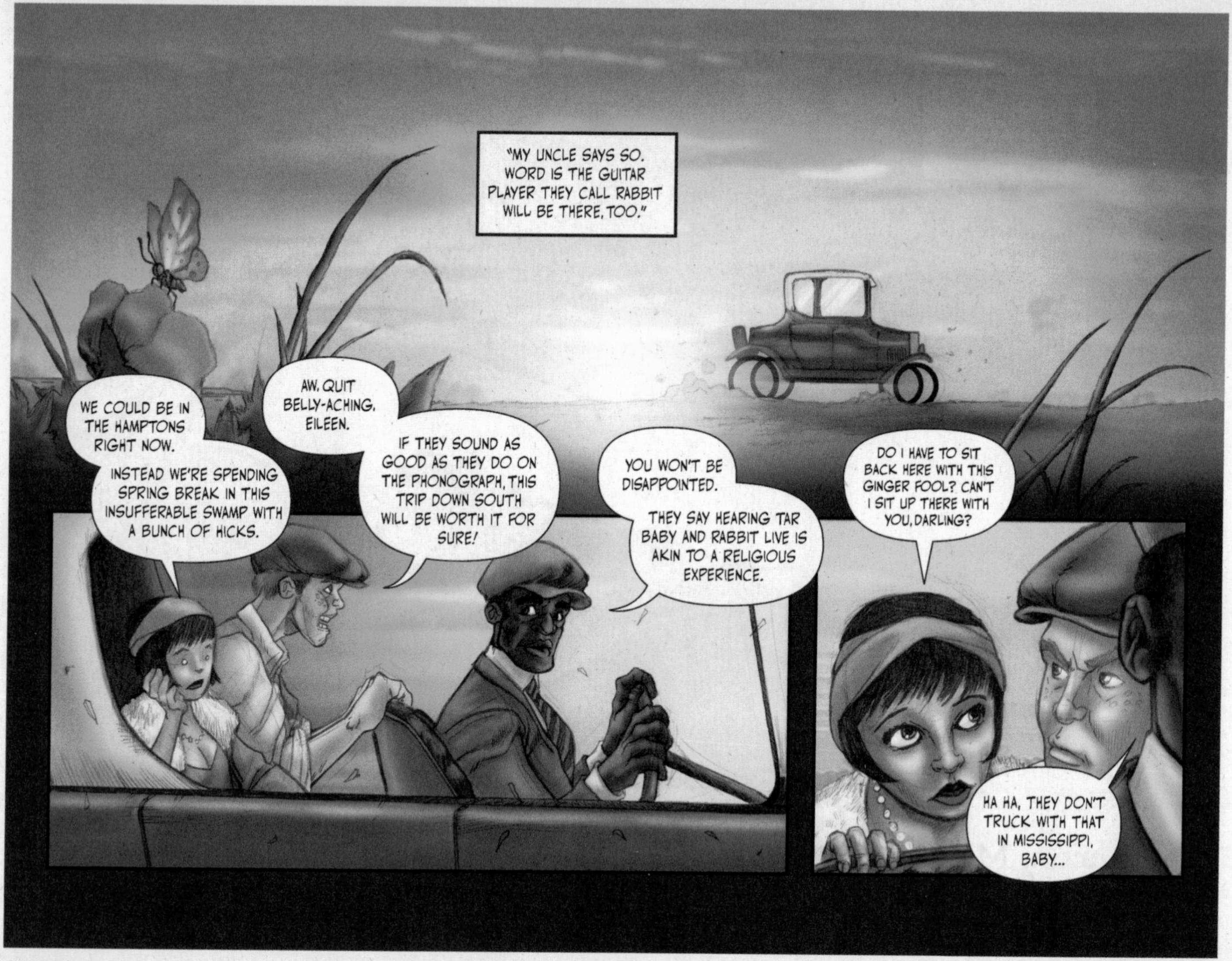
"MY UNCLE SAYS SO. WORD IS THE GUITAR PLAYER THEY CALL RABBIT WILL BE THERE, TOO."
WE COULD BE IN THE HAMPTONS RIGHT NOW.
INSTEAD WE'RE SPENDING SPRING BREAK IN THIS INSUFFERABLE SWAMP WITH A BUNCH OF HICKS.
AW, QUIT BELLY-ACHING, EILEEN.
IF THEY SOUND AS GOOD AS THEY DO ON THE PHONOGRAPH, THIS TRIP DOWN SOUTH WILL BE WORTH IT FOR SURE!
YOU WON'T BE DISAPPOINTED.
THEY SAY HEARING TAR BABY AND RABBIT LIVE IS AKIN TO A RELIGIOUS EXPERIENCE.
DO I HAVE TO SIT BACK HERE WITH THIS GINGER FOOL? CAN'T I SIT UP THERE WITH YOU, DARLING?
HA HA, THEY DON'T TRUCK WITH THAT IN MISSISSIPPI, BABY...

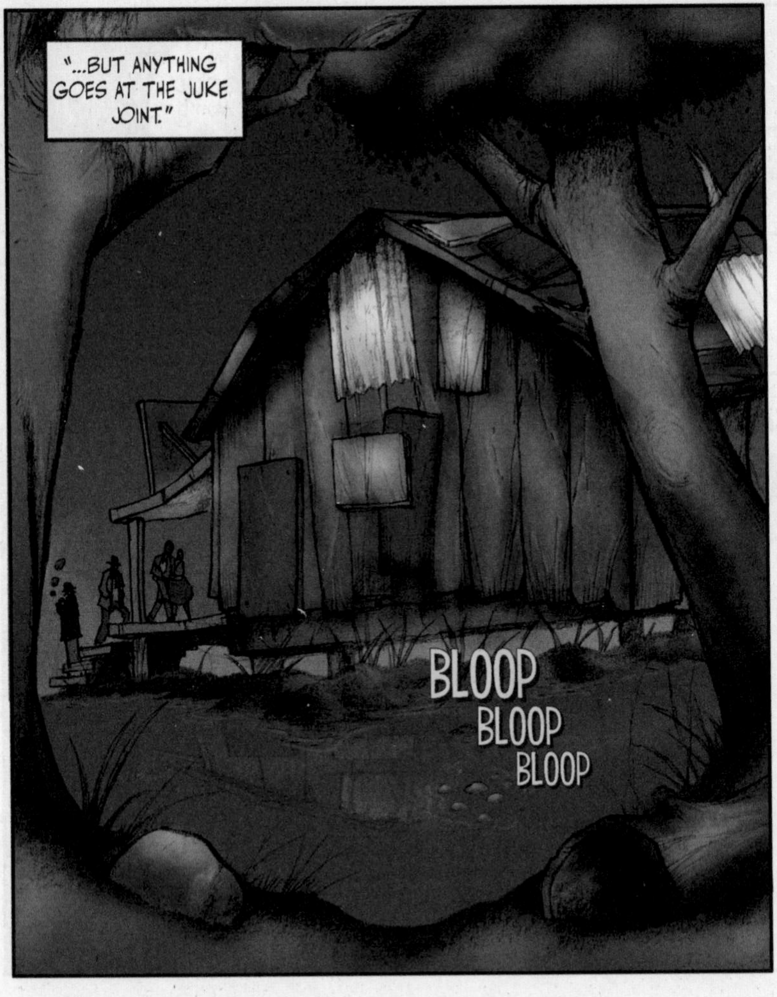
"...BUT ANYTHING GOES AT THE JUKE JOINT."
BLOOP
BLOOP
BLOOP

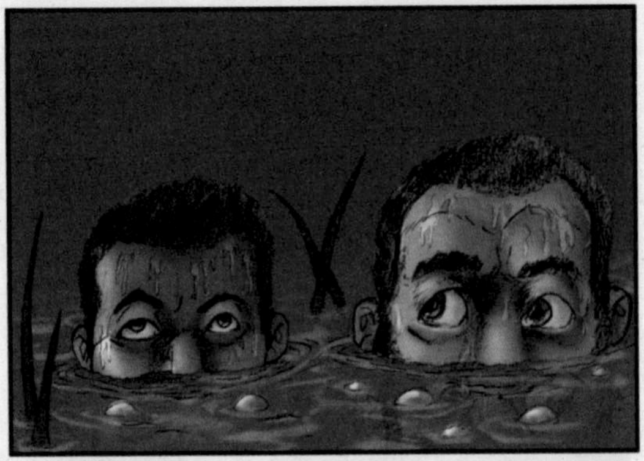

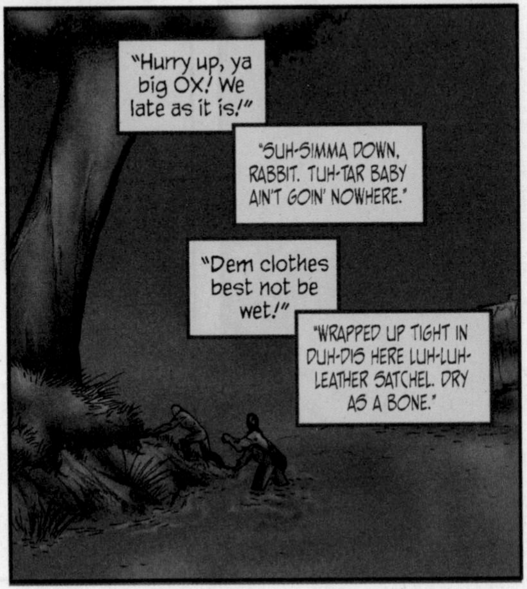
"Hurry up, ya big OX! We late as it is!"
"SUH-SIMMA DOWN, RABBIT. TUH-TAR BABY AIN'T GOIN' NOWHERE."
"Dem clothes best not be wet!"
"WRAPPED UP TIGHT IN DUH-DIS HERE LUH-LUH-LEATHER SATCHEL. DRY AS A BONE."

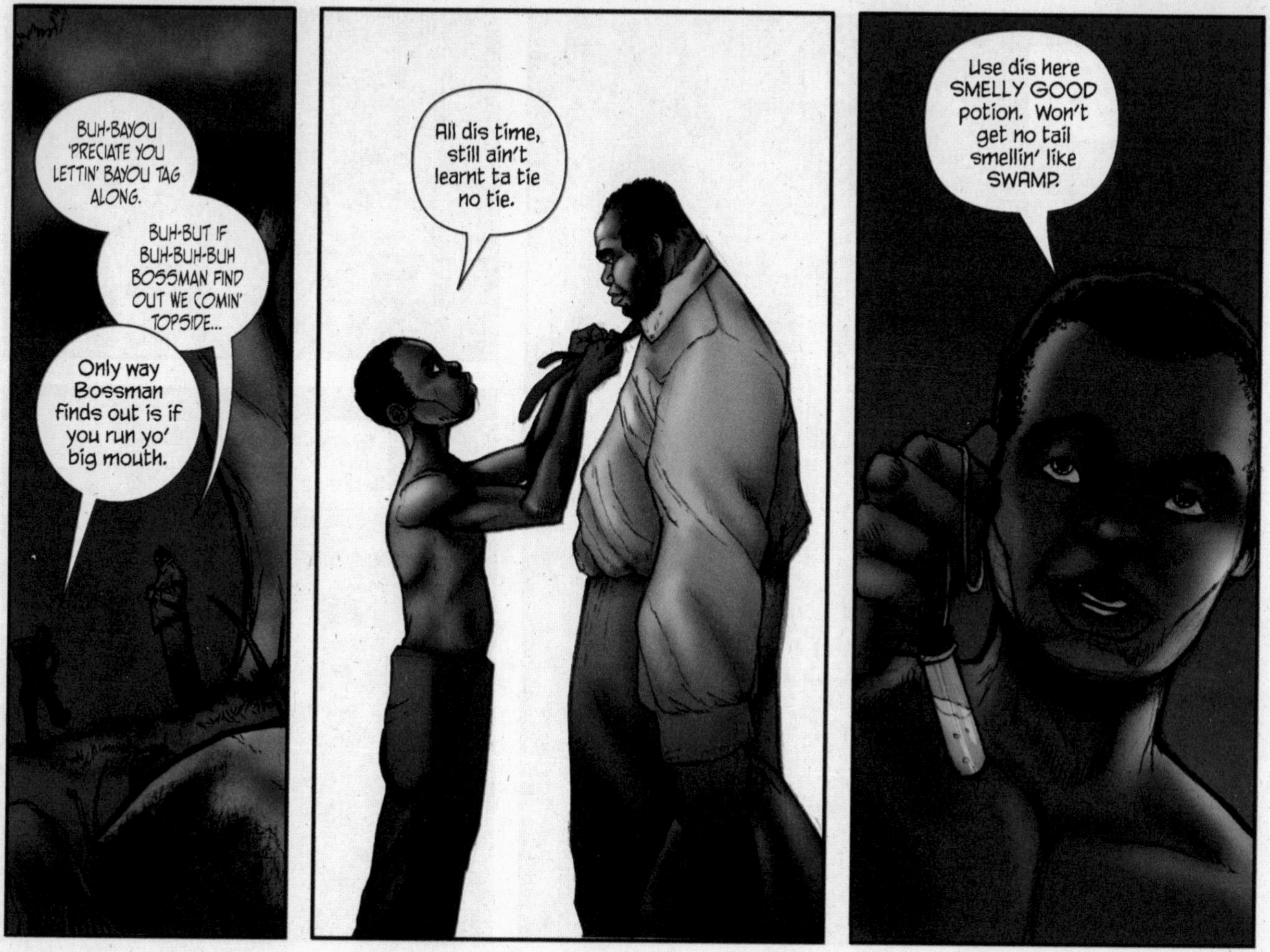

BUH-BAYOU 'PRECIATE YOU LETTIN' BAYOU TAG ALONG.
BUH-BUT IF BUH-BUH-BUH BOSSMAN FIND OUT WE COMIN' TOPSIDE...
Only way Bossman finds out is if you run yo' big mouth.
All dis time, still ain't learnt ta tie no tie.
Use dis here SMELLY GOOD potion. Won't get no tail smellin' like SWAMP.

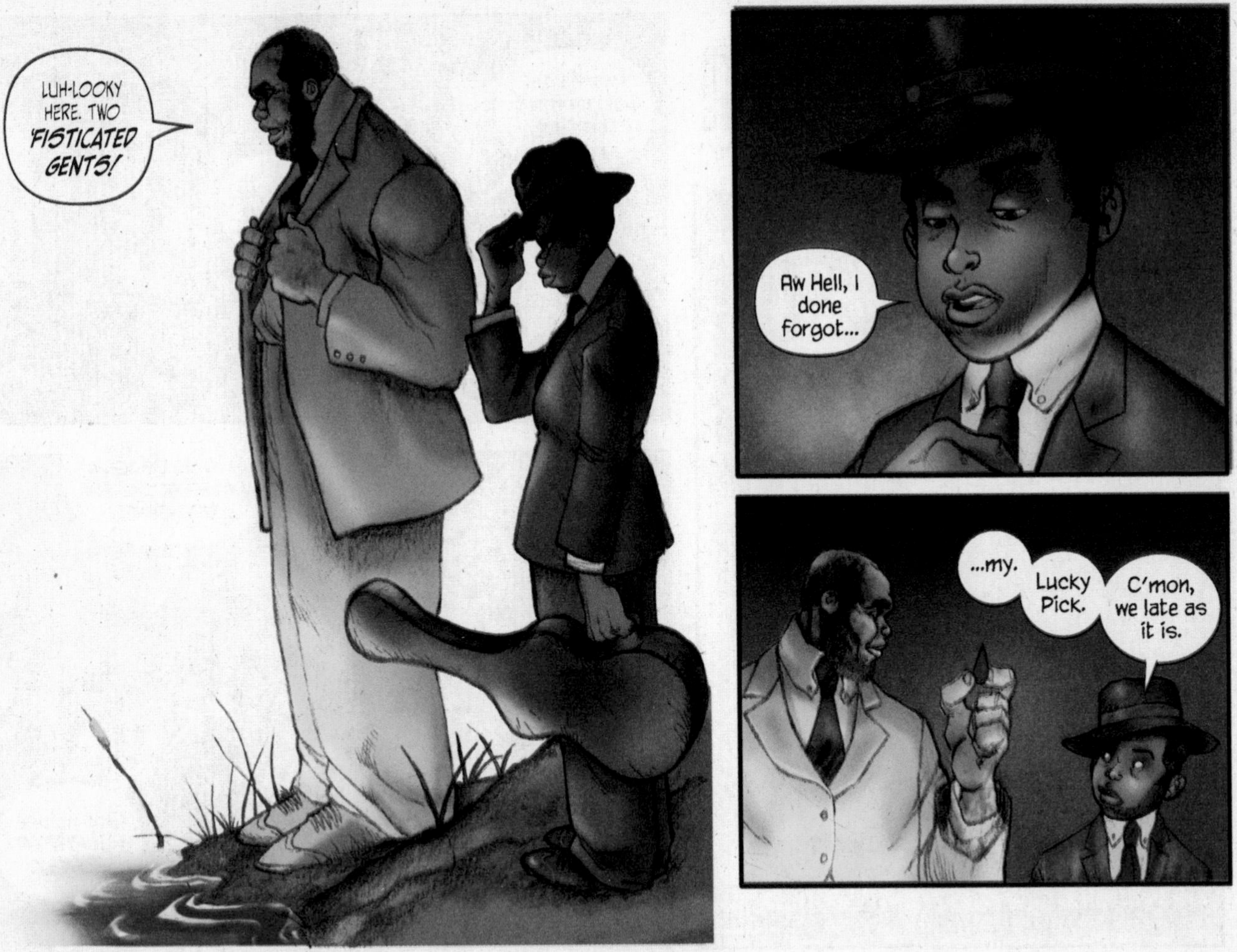
LUH-LOOKY HERE. TWO 'FISTICATED GENTS!
Aw Hell, I done forgot...
...my.
Lucky Pick.
C'mon, we late as it is.

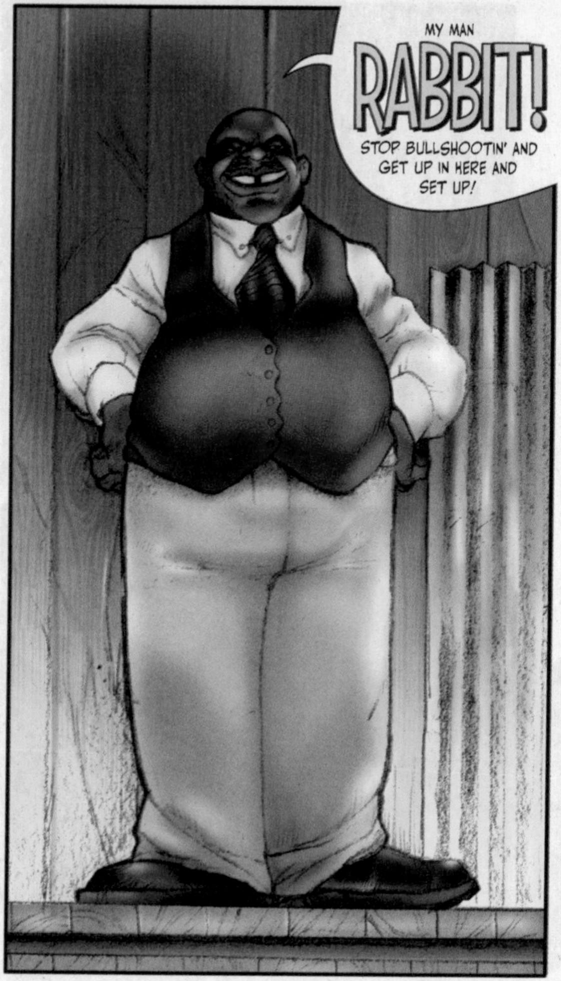
MY MAN RABBIT! STOP BULLSHOOTIN' AND GET UP IN HERE AND SET UP!

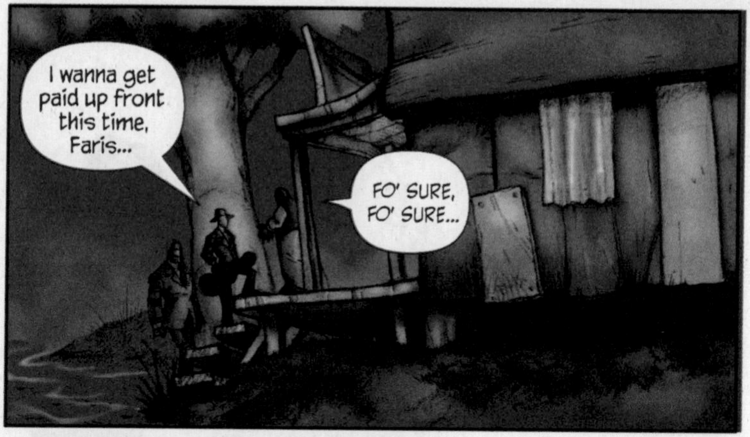
I wanna get paid up front this time, Faris...
FO' SURE, FO' SURE...

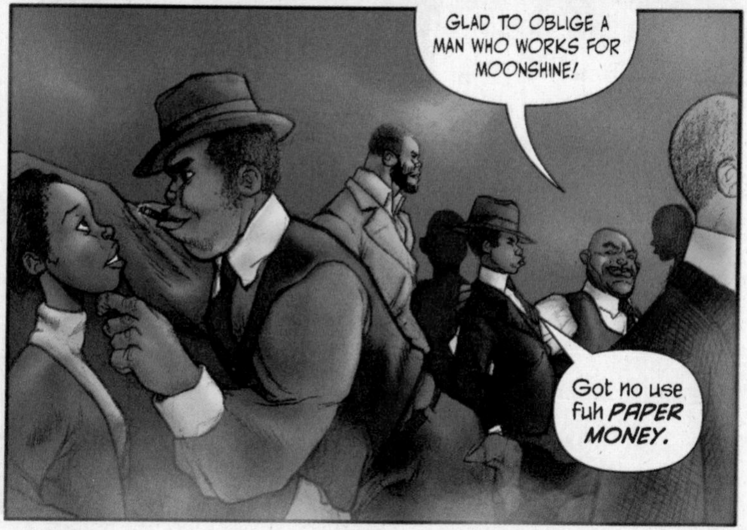
GLAD TO OBLIGE A MAN WHO WORKS FOR MOONSHINE!
Got no use fuh *PAPER MONEY.*

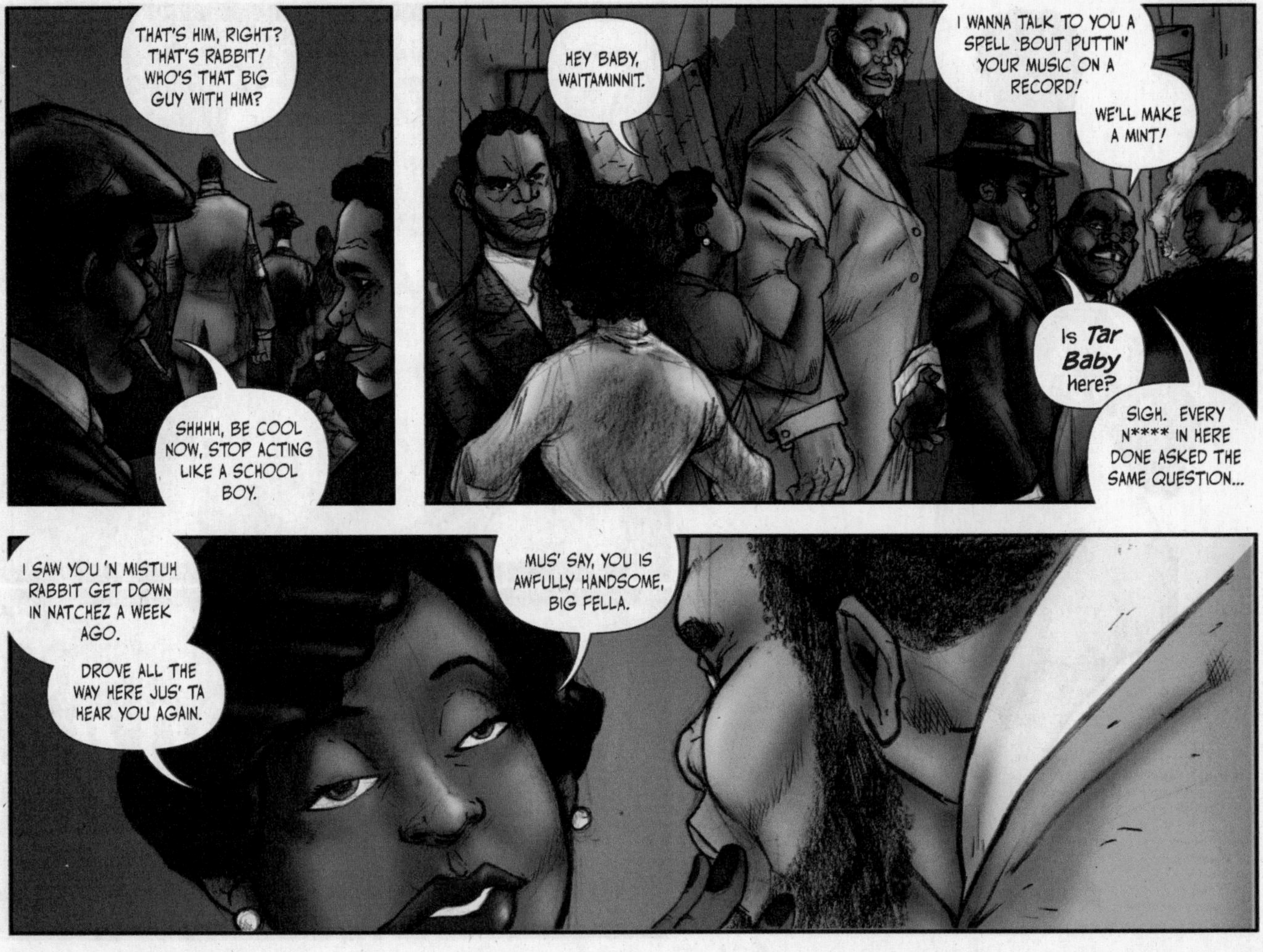
THAT'S HIM, RIGHT? THAT'S RABBIT! WHO'S THAT BIG GUY WITH HIM?
SHHHH, BE COOL NOW, STOP ACTING LIKE A SCHOOL BOY.
HEY BABY, WAITAMINNIT.
I WANNA TALK TO YOU A SPELL 'BOUT PUTTIN' YOUR MUSIC ON A RECORD!
WE'LL MAKE A MINT!
Is *Tar Baby* here?
SIGH. EVERY N**** IN HERE DONE ASKED THE SAME QUESTION...
I SAW YOU 'N MISTUH RABBIT GET DOWN IN NATCHEZ A WEEK AGO.
DROVE ALL THE WAY HERE JUS' TA HEAR YOU AGAIN.
MUS' SAY, YOU IS AWFULLY HANDSOME, BIG FELLA.

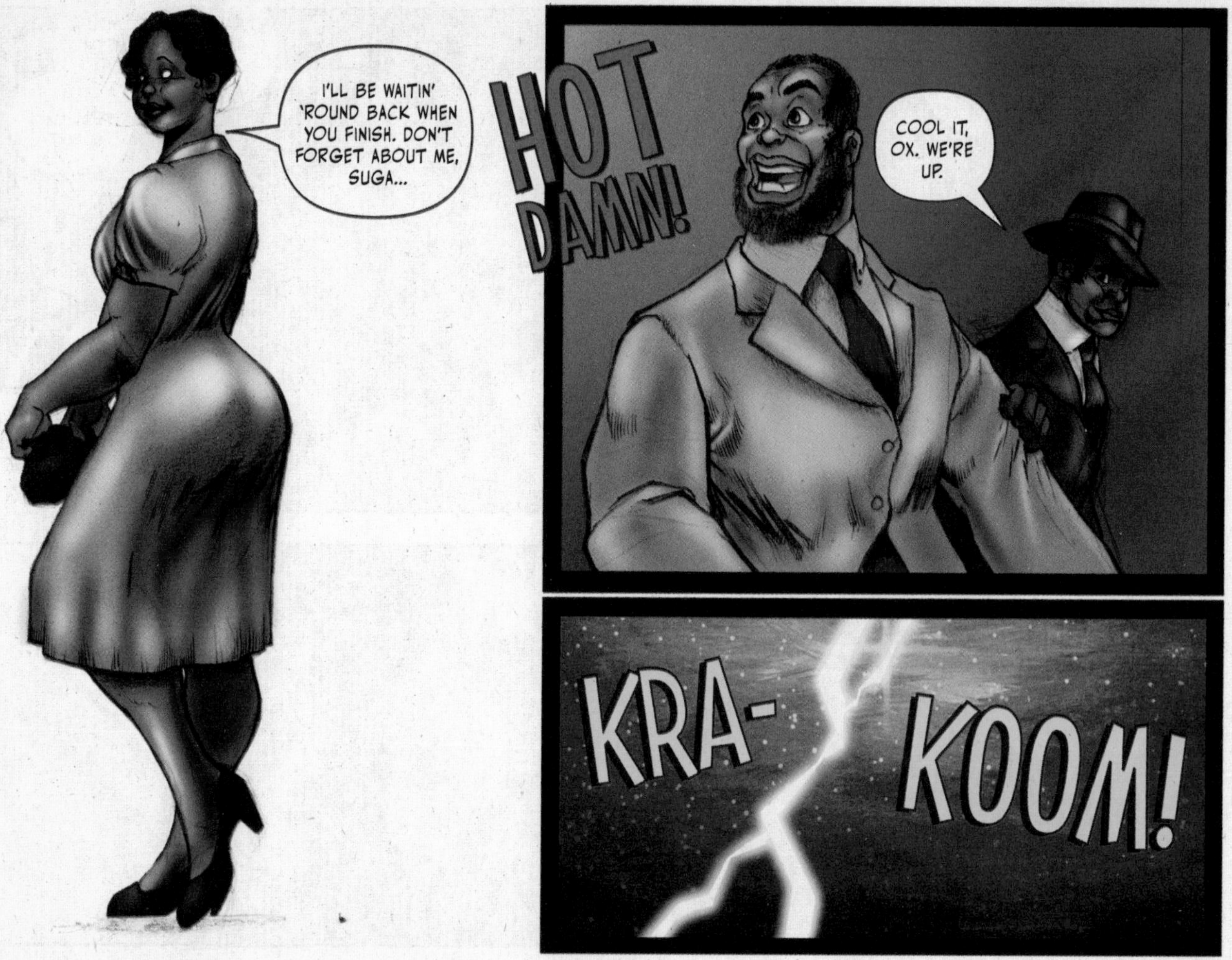
I'LL BE WAITIN' 'ROUND BACK WHEN YOU FINISH. DON'T FORGET ABOUT ME, SUGA...
HOT DAMN!
COOL IT, OX. WE'RE UP.
KRA- KOOM!

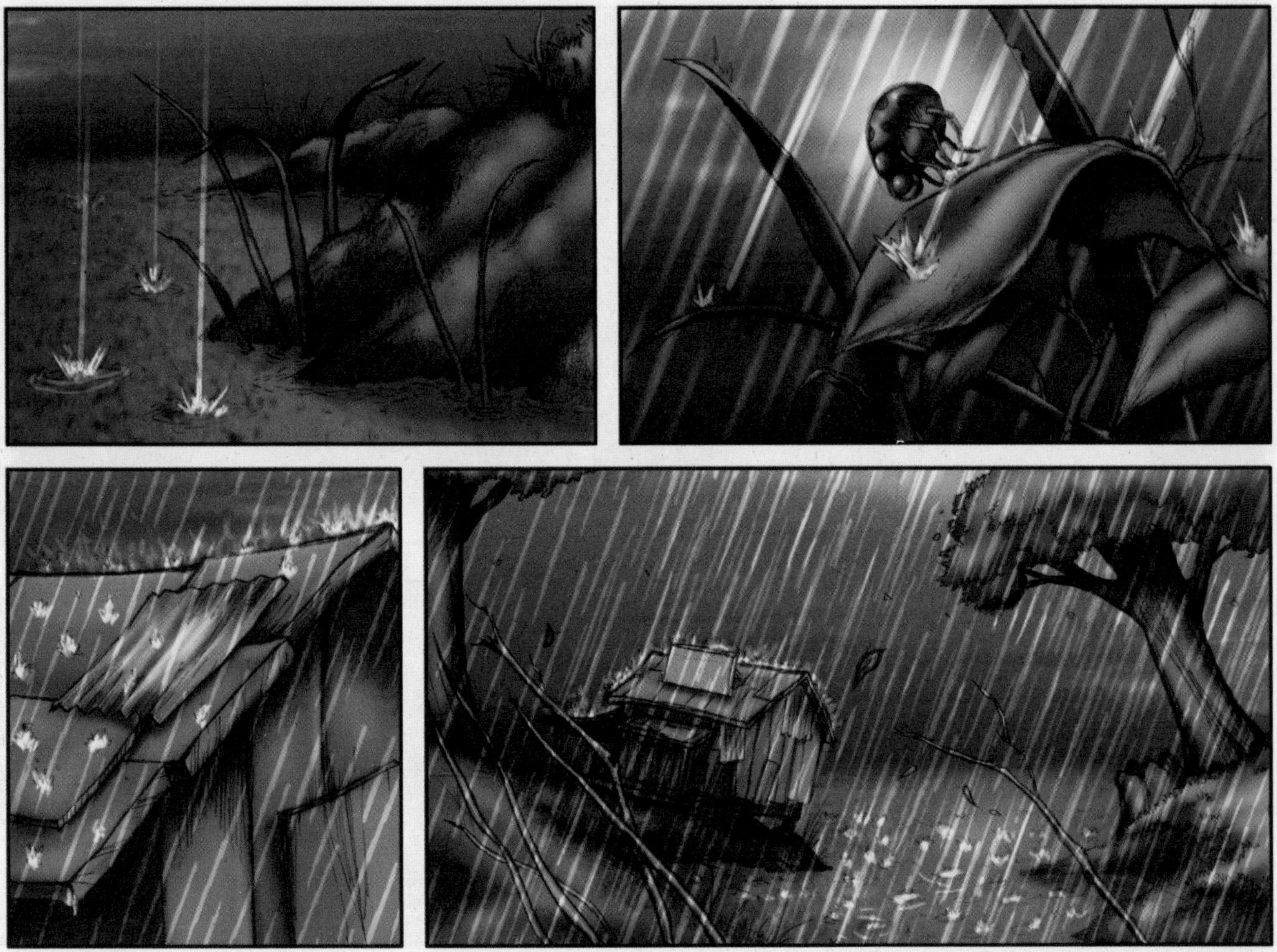

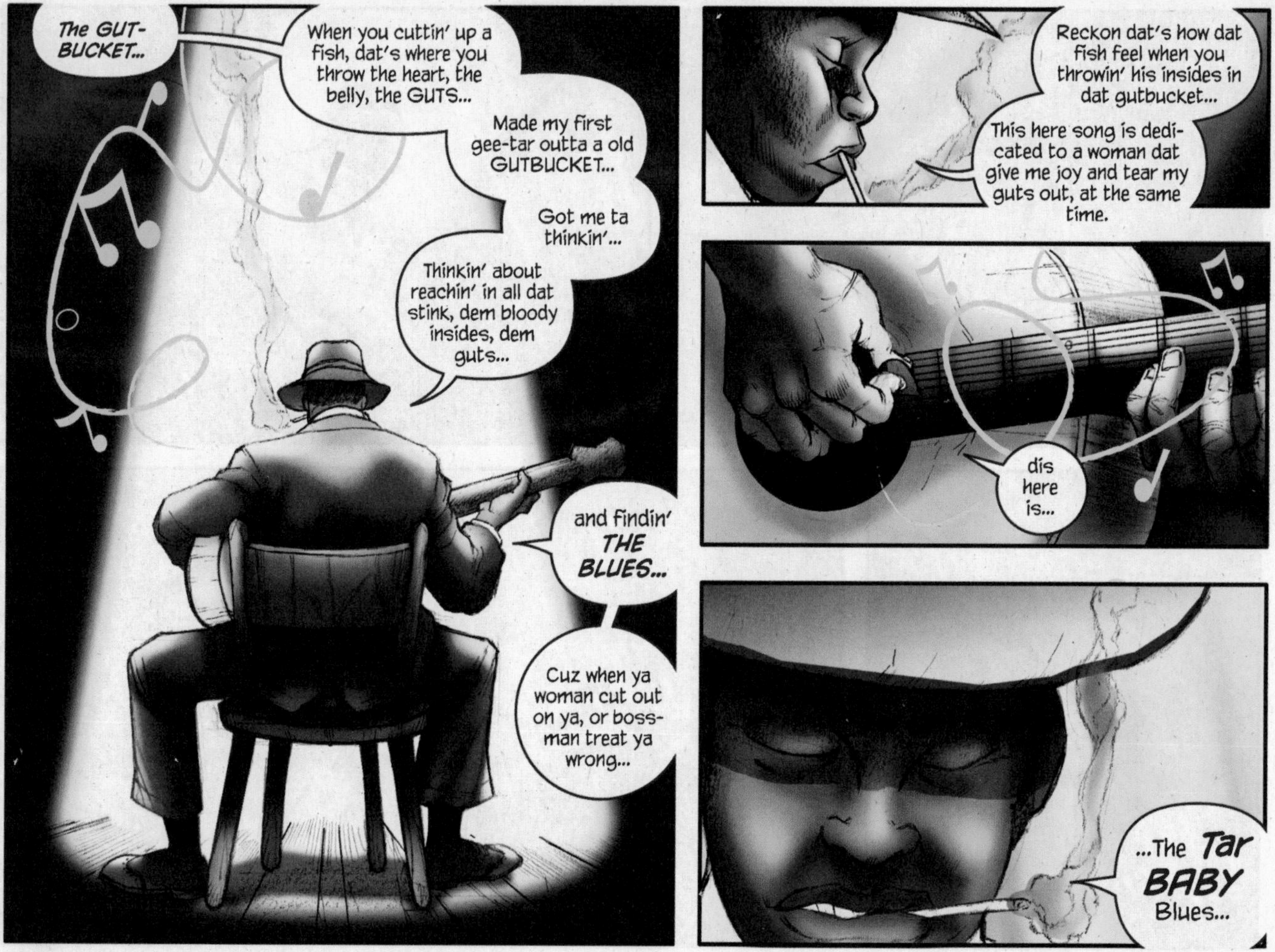

The GUT-BUCKET...
When you cuttin' up a fish, dat's where you throw the heart, the belly, the GUTS...
Made my first gee-tar outta a old GUTBUCKET...
Got me ta thinkin'...
Thinkin' about reachin' in all dat stink, dem bloody insides, dem guts...
and findin' THE BLUES...
Cuz when ya woman cut out on ya, or boss-man treat ya wrong...
Reckon dat's how dat fish feel when you throwin' his insides in dat gutbucket...
This here song is dedi-cated to a woman dat give me joy and tear my guts out, at the same time.
dis here is...
...The Tar BABY Blues...

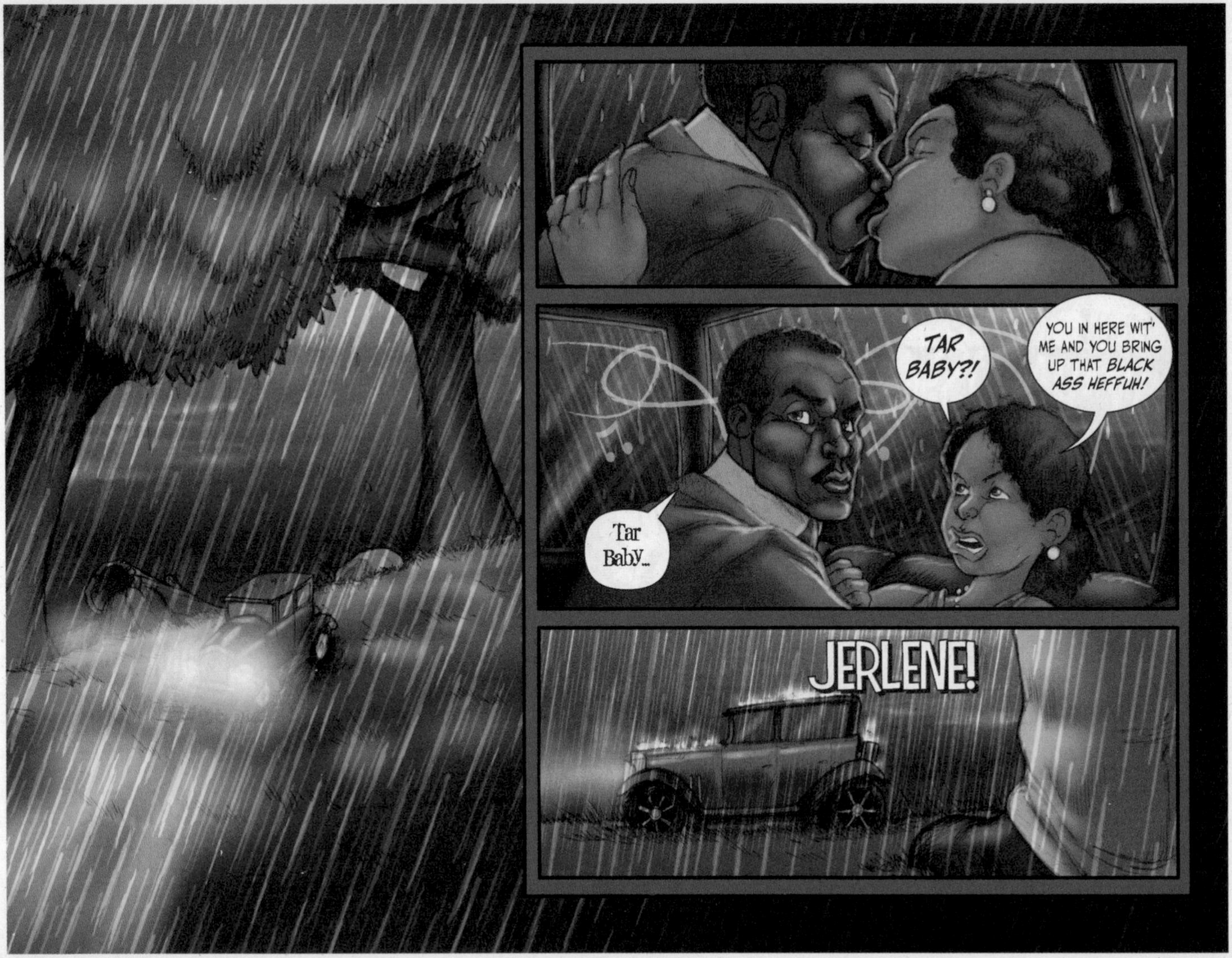
Tar Baby...
TAR BABY?!
YOU IN HERE WIT' ME AND YOU BRING UP THAT BLACK ASS HEFFUH!
JERLENE!

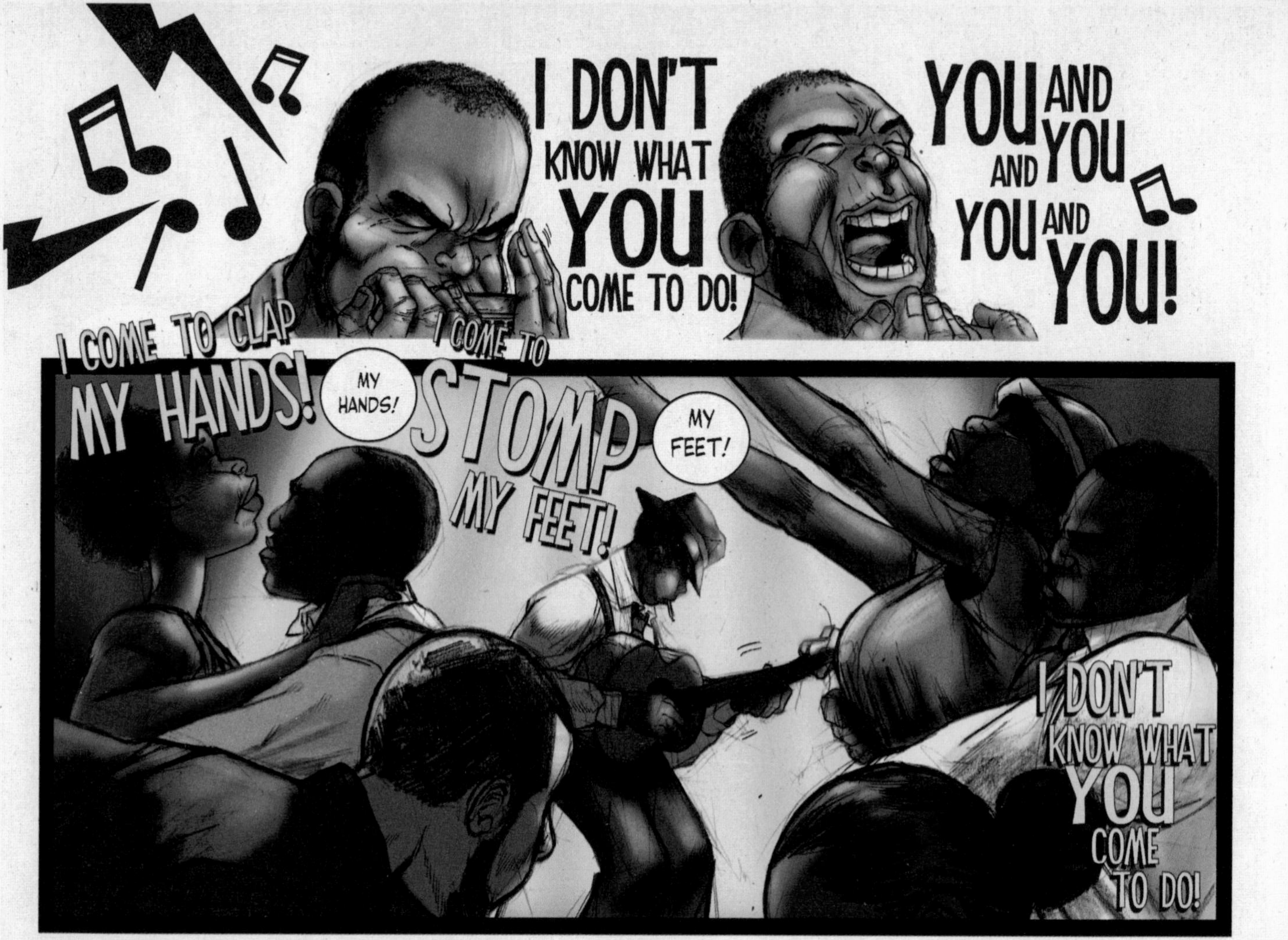

I DON'T KNOW WHAT YOU COME TO DO!
YOU AND YOU AND YOU AND YOU AND YOU!
I COME TO CLAP MY HANDS!
MY HANDS!
I COME TO STOMP MY FEET!
MY FEET!
I DON'T KNOW WHAT YOU COME TO DO!

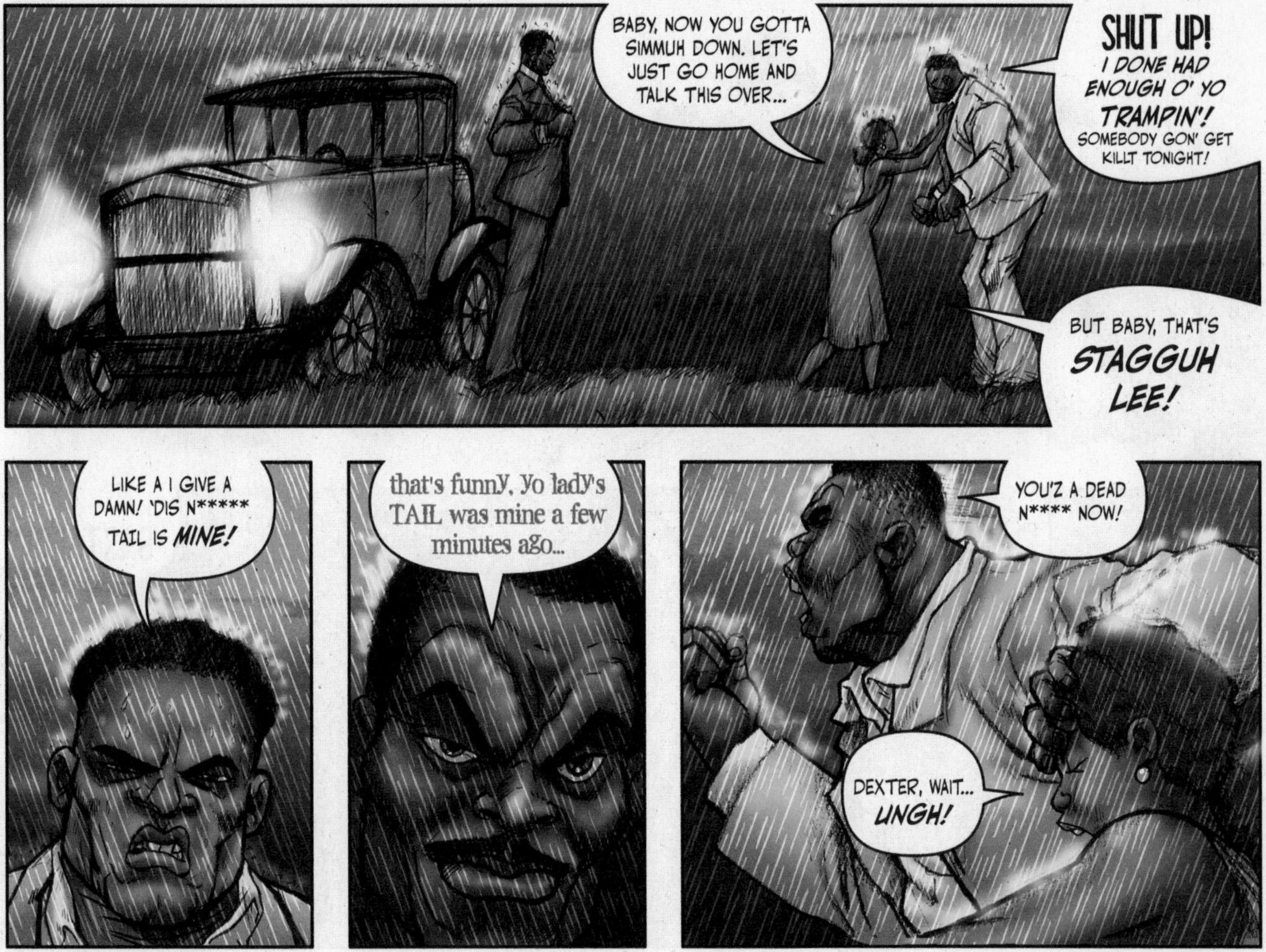
BABY, NOW YOU GOTTA SIMMUH DOWN. LET'S JUST GO HOME AND TALK THIS OVER...
SHUT UP! I DONE HAD ENOUGH O' YO TRAMPIN'! SOMEBODY GON' GET KILLT TONIGHT!
BUT BABY, THAT'S STAGGUH LEE!
LIKE A I GIVE A DAMN! 'DIS N***** TAIL IS MINE!
that's funny. Yo lady's TAIL was mine a few minutes ago...
YOU'Z A DEAD N**** NOW!
DEXTER, WAIT... UNGH!

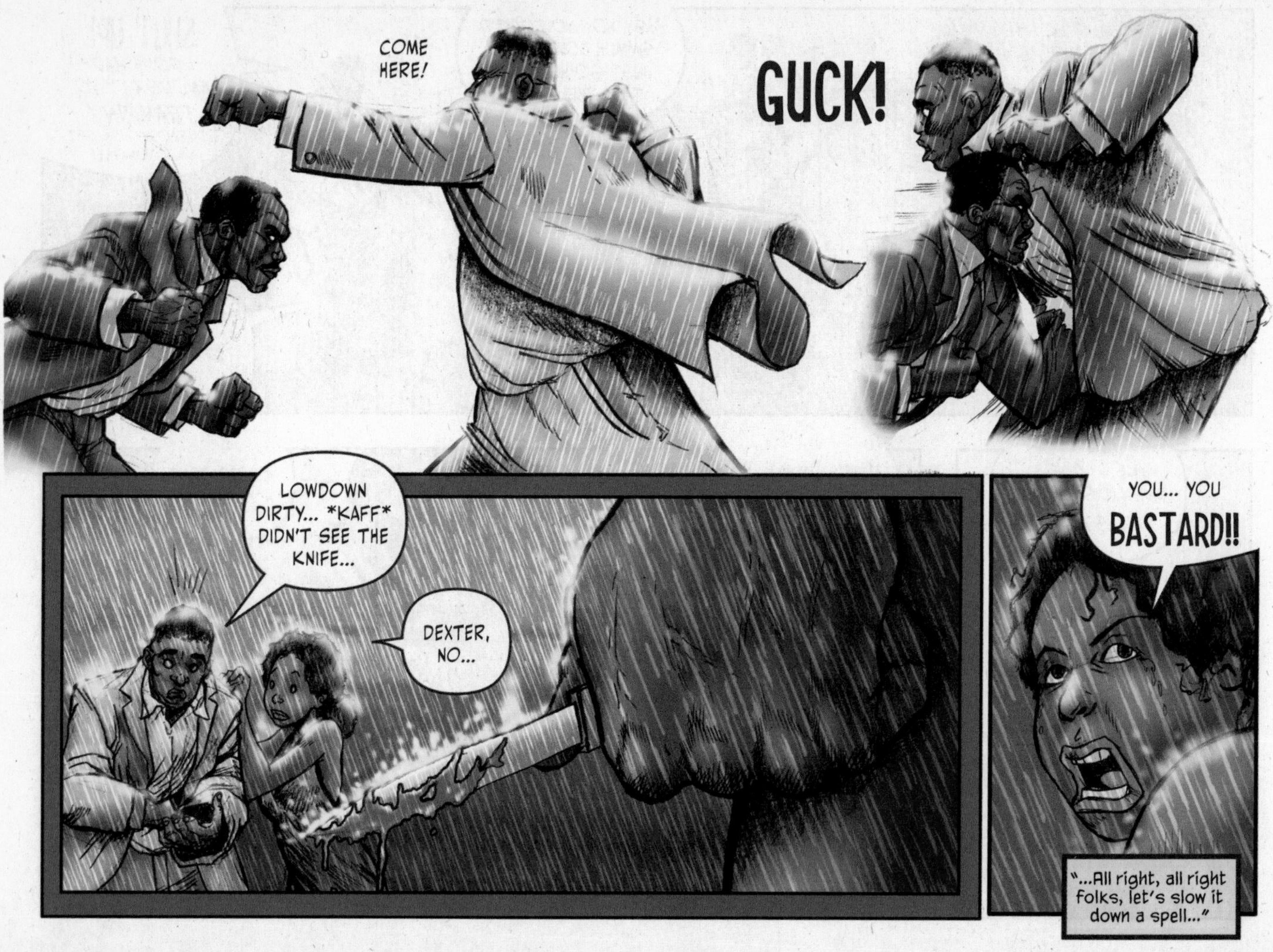
COME HERE!
GUCK!
LOWDOWN DIRTY... *KAFF* DIDN'T SEE THE KNIFE...
DEXTER, NO...
YOU... YOU BASTARD!!
"...All right, all right folks, let's slow it down a spell..."

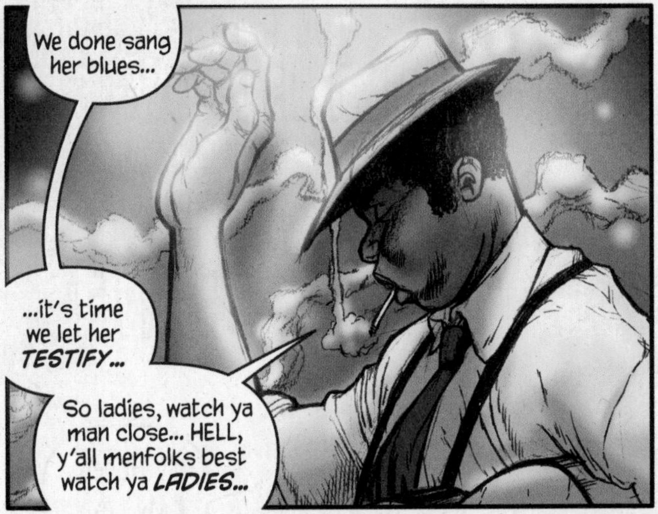
We done sang her blues...
...it's time we let her TESTIFY...
So ladies, watch ya man close... HELL, y'all menfolks best watch ya LADIES...

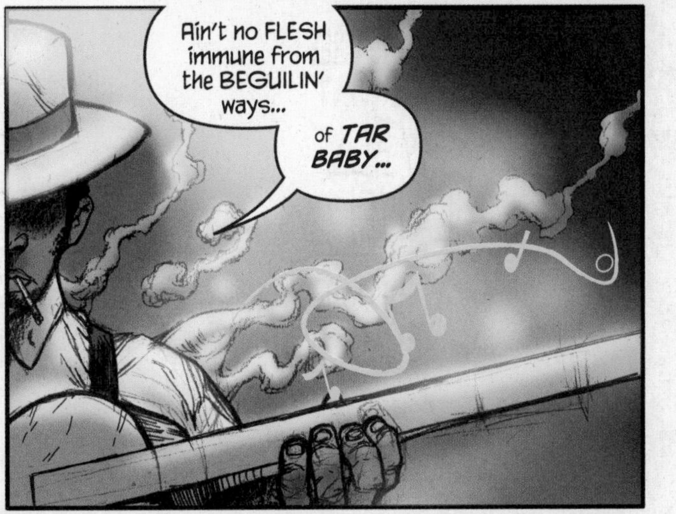
Ain't no FLESH immune from the BEGUILIN' ways...
of TAR BABY...

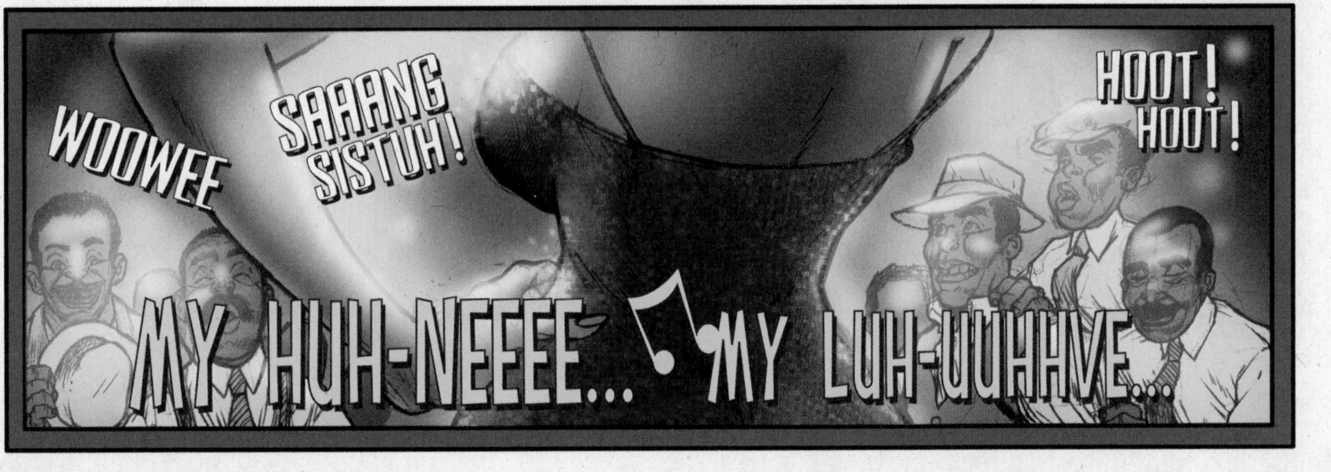
WOOWEE
SAAAANG SISTUH!
HOOT! HOOT!
MY HUH-NEEEE... MY LUH-UUHHVE...

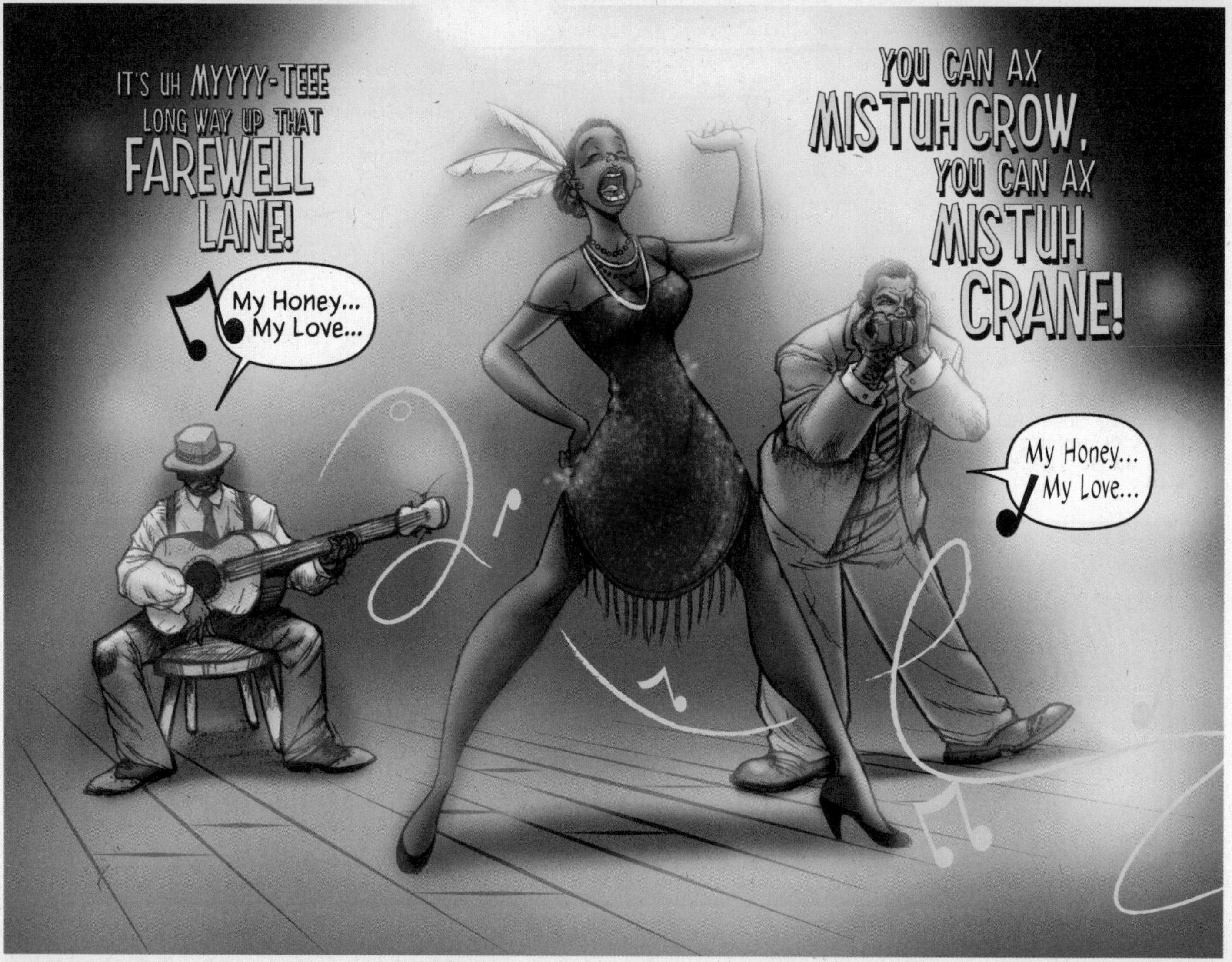
IT'S UH MYYYY-TEEE LONG WAY UP THAT FAREWELL LANE!
YOU CAN AX MISTUH CROW, YOU CAN AX MISTUH CRANE!
My Honey... My Love...
My Honey... My Love...

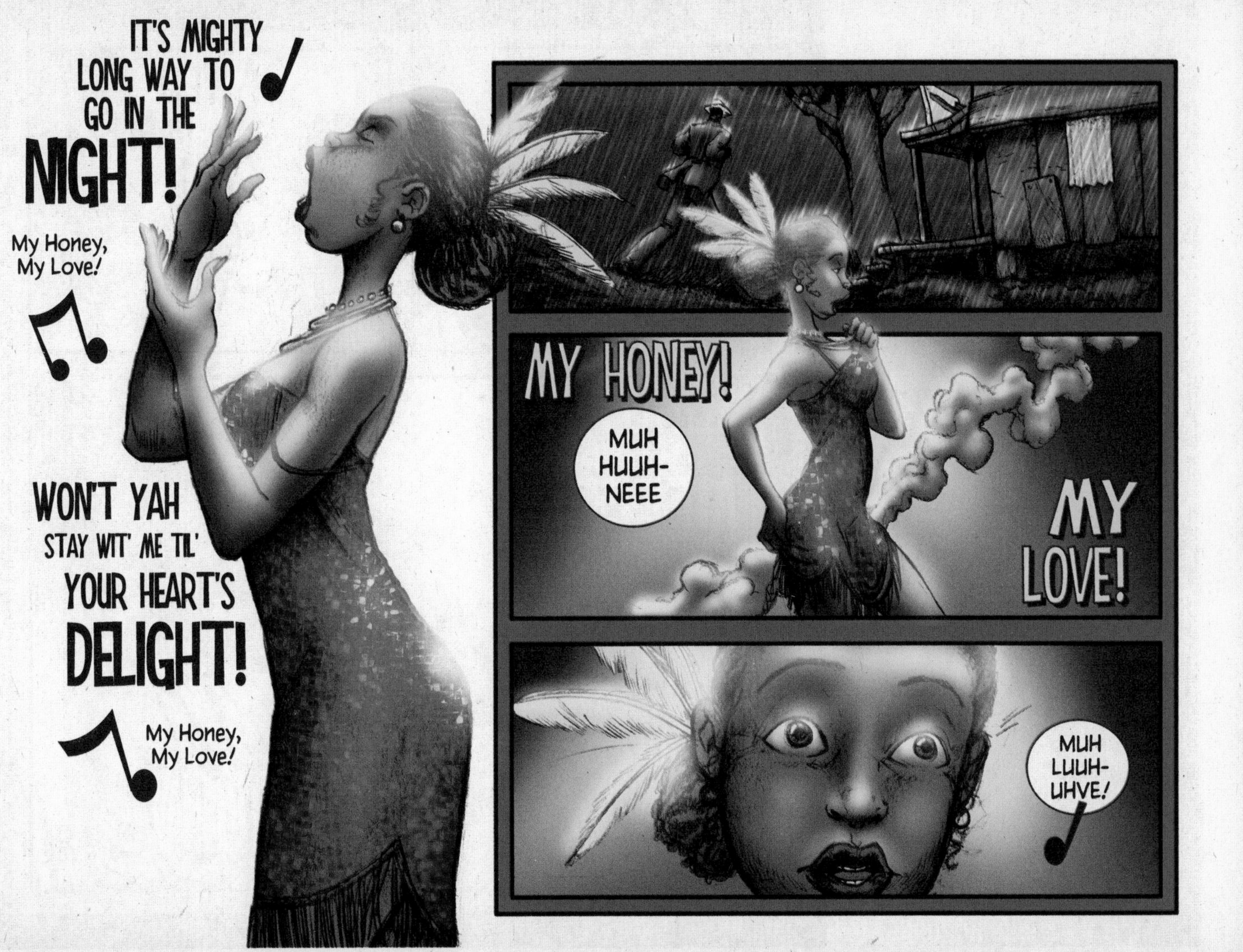

IT'S MIGHTY LONG WAY TO GO IN THE NIGHT!
My Honey, My Love!
WON'T YAH STAY WIT' ME TIL' YOUR HEART'S DELIGHT!
My Honey, My Love!
MY HONEY!
MUH HUUH-NEEE
MY LOVE!
MUH LUUH-UHVE!

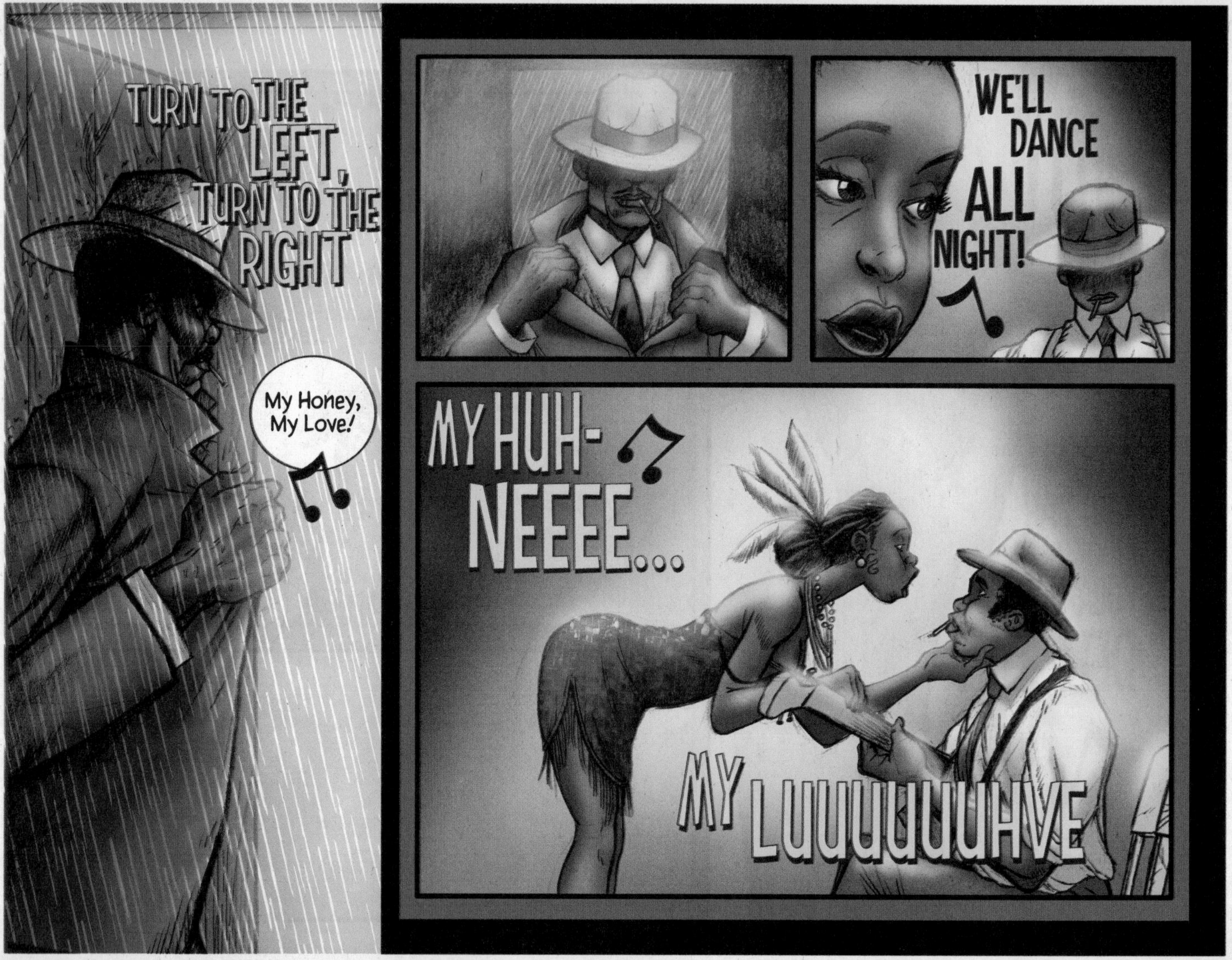
TURN TO THE LEFT, TURN TO THE RIGHT
My Honey, My Love!
WE'LL DANCE ALL NIGHT!
MY HUH-NEEEE...
MY LUUUUUUHVE

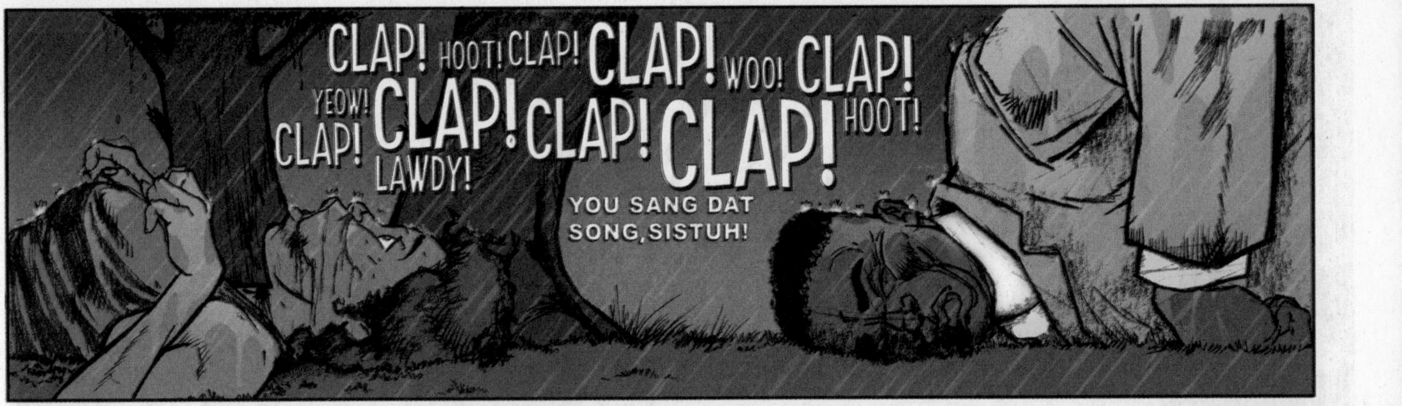
CLAP! HOOT! CLAP! CLAP! WOO! CLAP!
YEOW! CLAP! CLAP! CLAP! HOOT!
CLAP!
LAWDY!
YOU SANG DAT SONG, SISTUH!

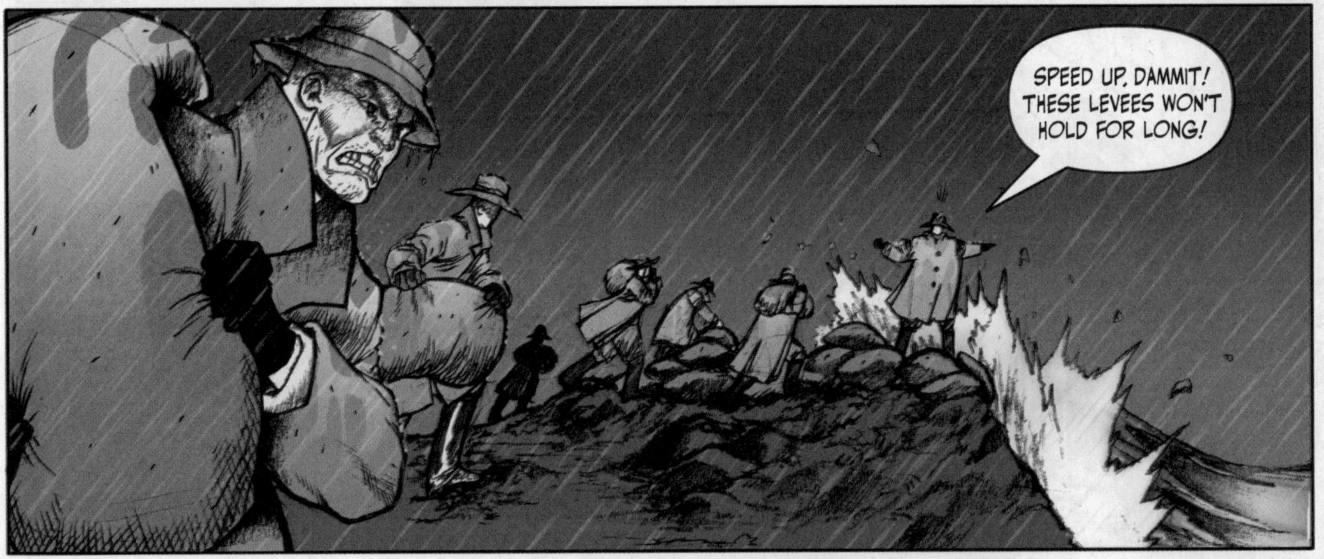
SPEED UP, DAMMIT! THESE LEVEES WON'T HOLD FOR LONG!

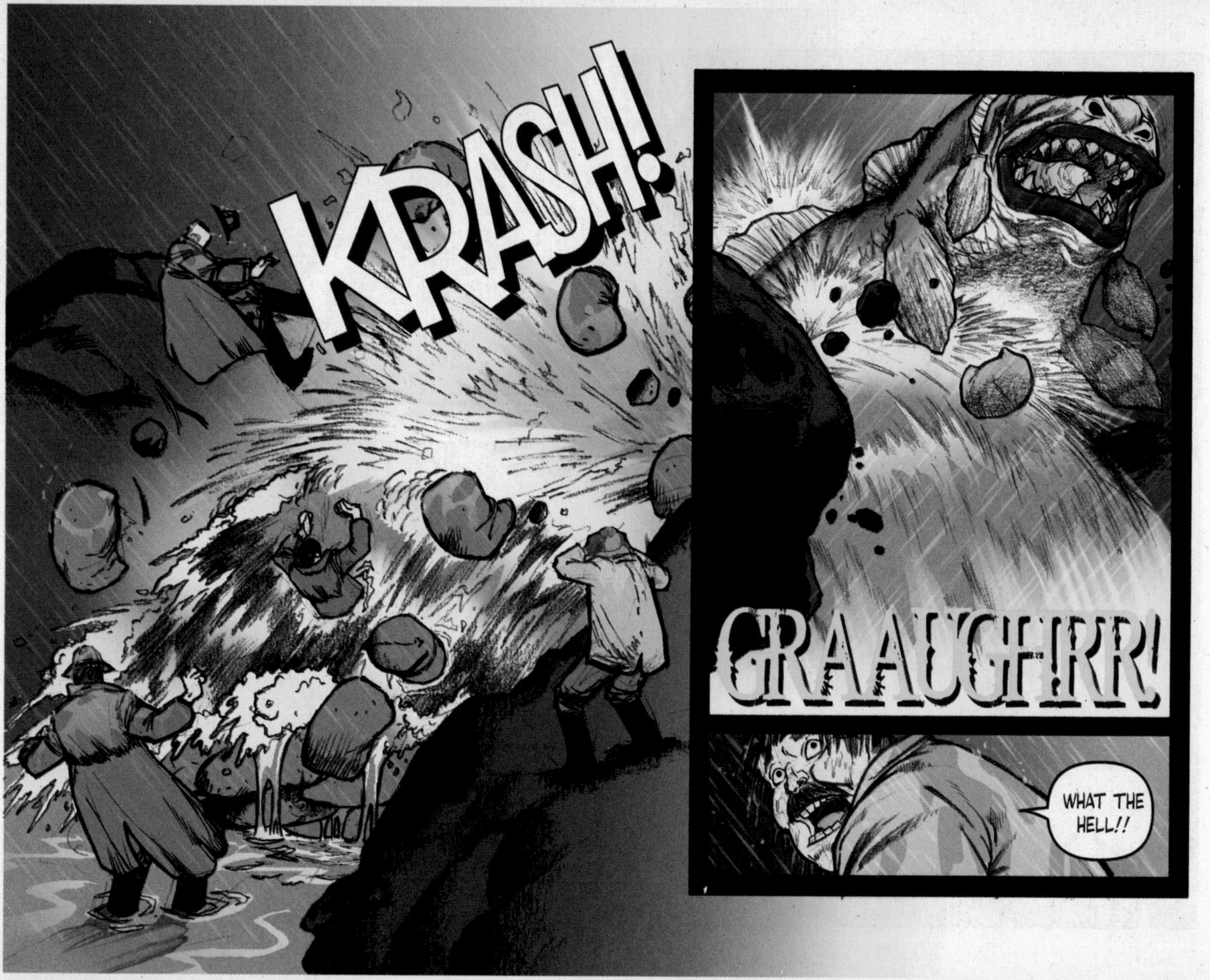
KRASH!
GRAAUGHRR!
WHAT THE HELL!!

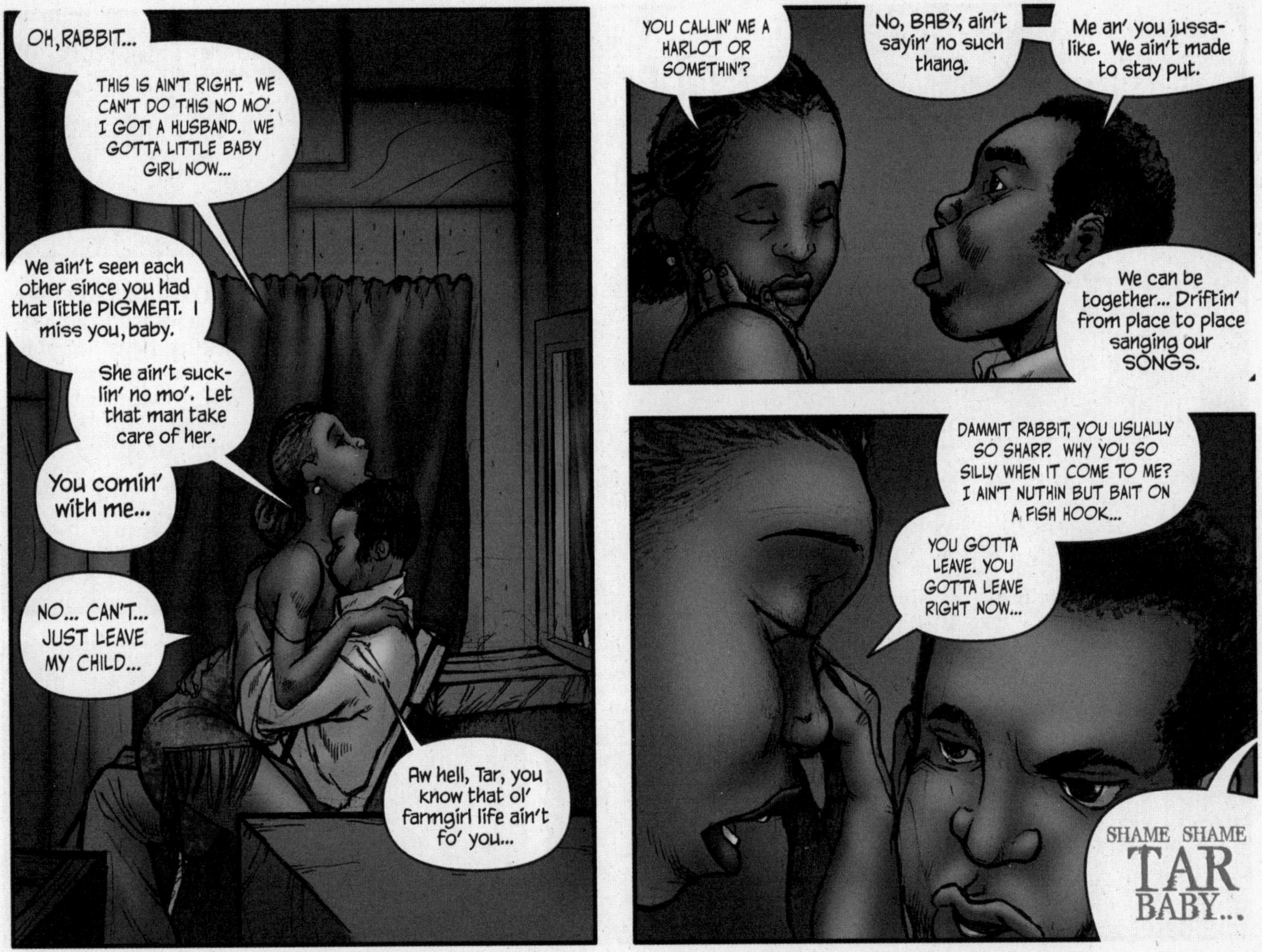
OH, RABBIT...
THIS IS AIN'T RIGHT. WE CAN'T DO THIS NO MO'. I GOT A HUSBAND. WE GOTTA LITTLE BABY GIRL NOW...
We ain't seen each other since you had that little PIGMEAT. I miss you, baby.
She ain't suck-lin' no mo'. Let that man take care of her.
You comin' with me...
NO... CAN'T... JUST LEAVE MY CHILD...
Aw hell, Tar, you know that ol' farmgirl life ain't fo' you...
YOU CALLIN' ME A HARLOT OR SOMETHIN'?
No, BABY, ain't sayin' no such thang.
Me an' you jussa-like. We ain't made to stay put.
We can be together... Driftin' from place to place sanging our SONGS.
DAMMIT RABBIT, YOU USUALLY SO SHARP. WHY YOU SO SILLY WHEN IT COME TO ME? I AIN'T NUTHIN BUT BAIT ON A FISH HOOK...
YOU GOTTA LEAVE. YOU GOTTA LEAVE RIGHT NOW...
SHAME SHAME TAR BABY...

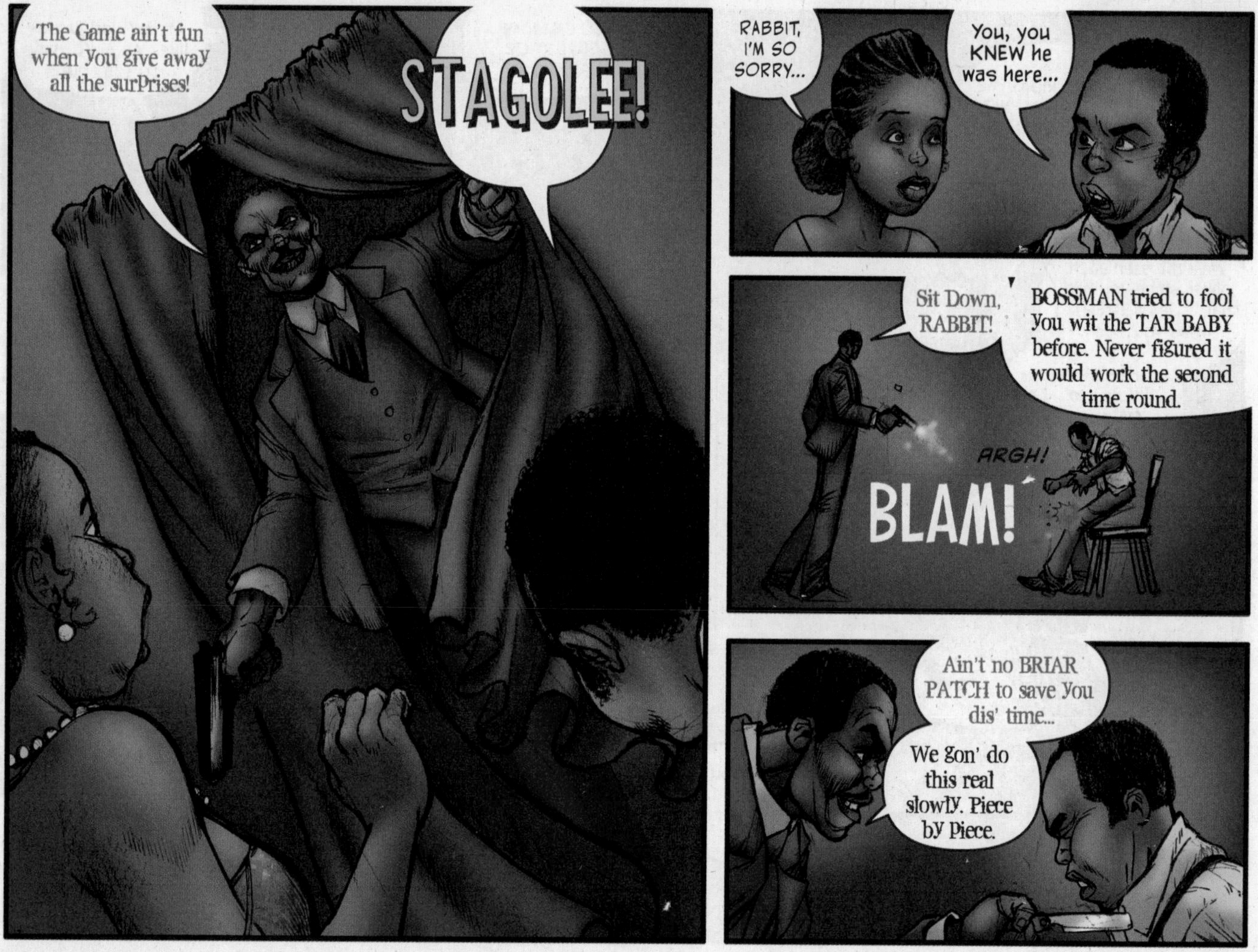
The Game ain't fun when You give away all the surPrises!
STAGOLEE!
RABBIT, I'M SO SORRY...
You, you KNEW he was here...
Sit Down, RABBIT!
BOSSMAN tried to fool You wit the TAR BABY before. Never figured it would work the second time round.
ARGH!
BLAM!
Ain't no BRIAR PATCH to save You dis' time...
We gon' do this real slowly. Piece by Piece.

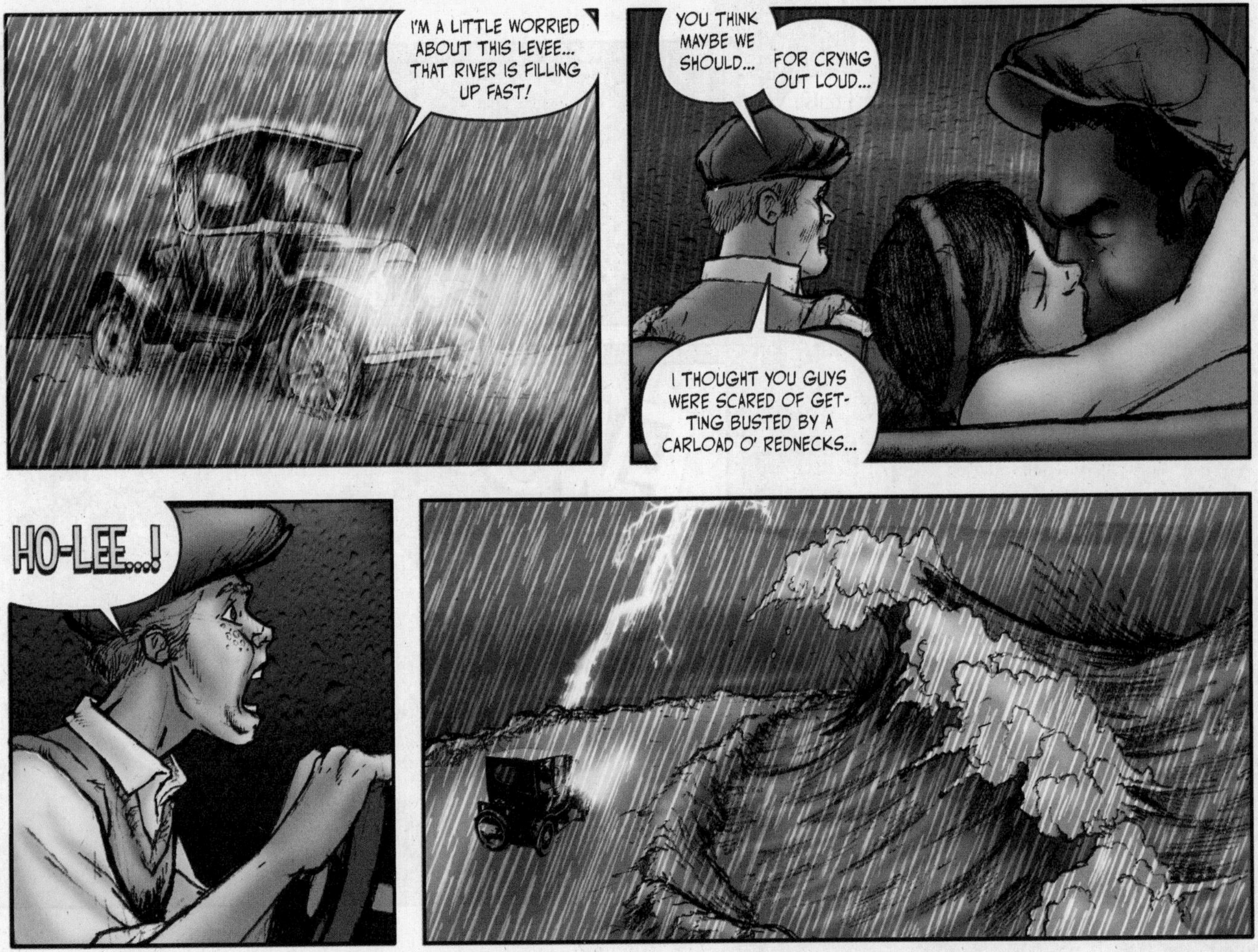
I'M A LITTLE WORRIED ABOUT THIS LEVEE... THAT RIVER IS FILLING UP FAST!
YOU THINK MAYBE WE SHOULD...
FOR CRYING OUT LOUD...
I THOUGHT YOU GUYS WERE SCARED OF GET-TING BUSTED BY A CARLOAD O' REDNECKS...
HO-LEE...!

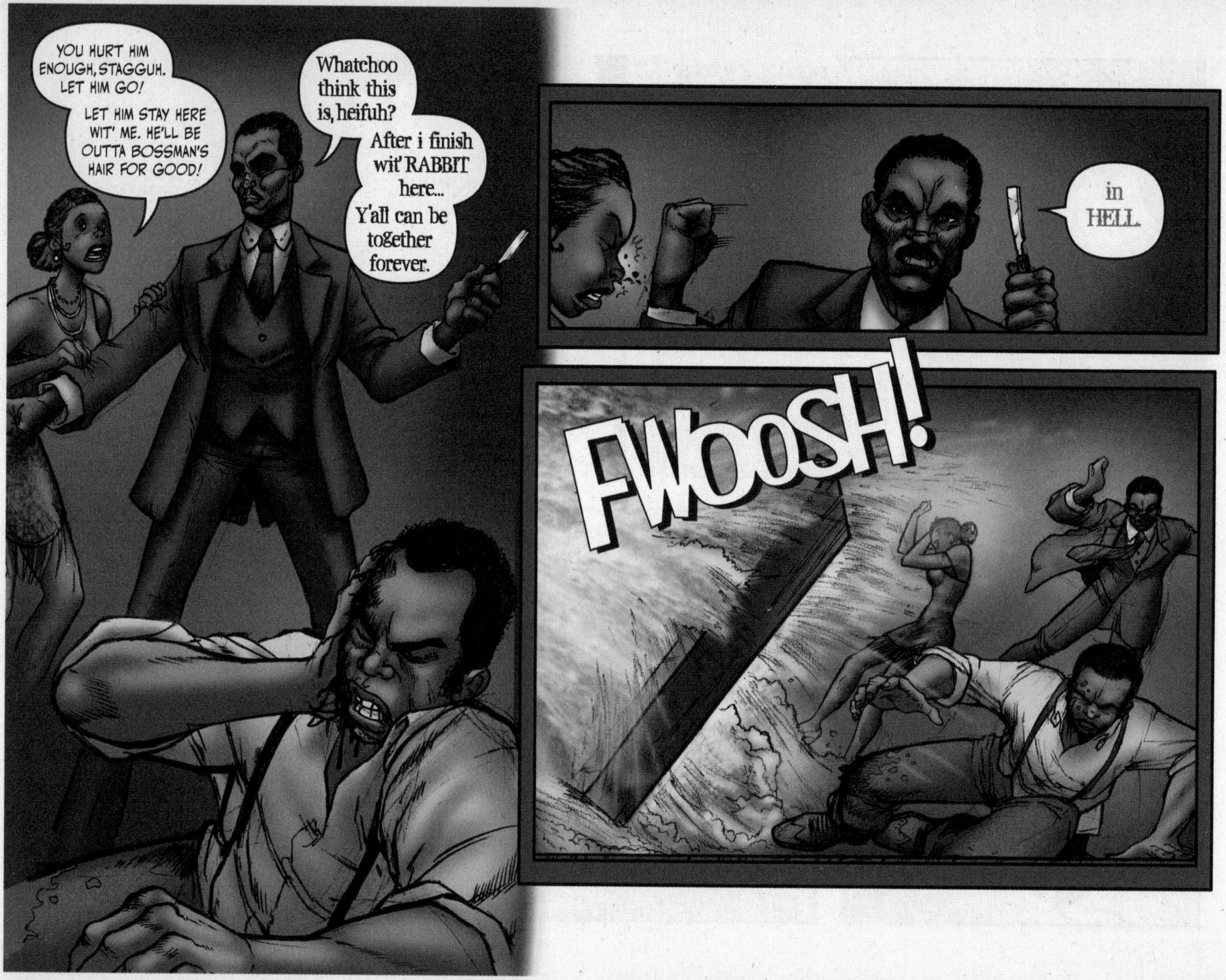
YOU HURT HIM ENOUGH, STAGGUH. LET HIM GO!
LET HIM STAY HERE WIT' ME. HE'LL BE OUTTA BOSSMAN'S HAIR FOR GOOD!
Whatchoo think this is, heifuh?
After i finish wit' RABBIT here... Y'all can be together forever.
in HELL.
FWOOSH!

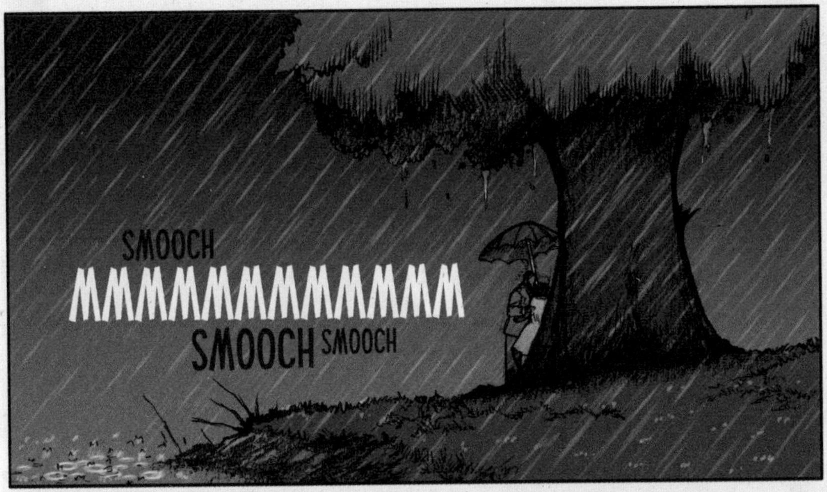
SMOOCH
MMMMMMMMMMMMM
SMOOCH SMOOCH

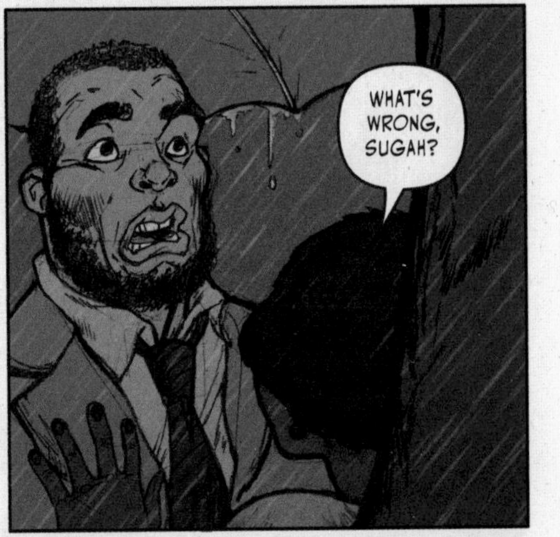
WHAT'S WRONG, SUGAH?

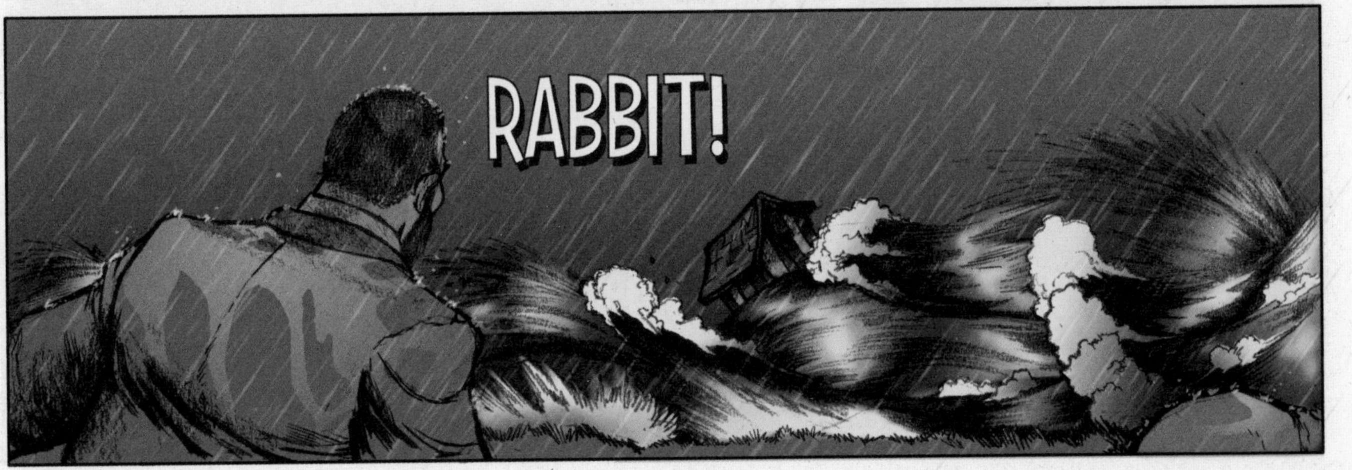
RABBIT!

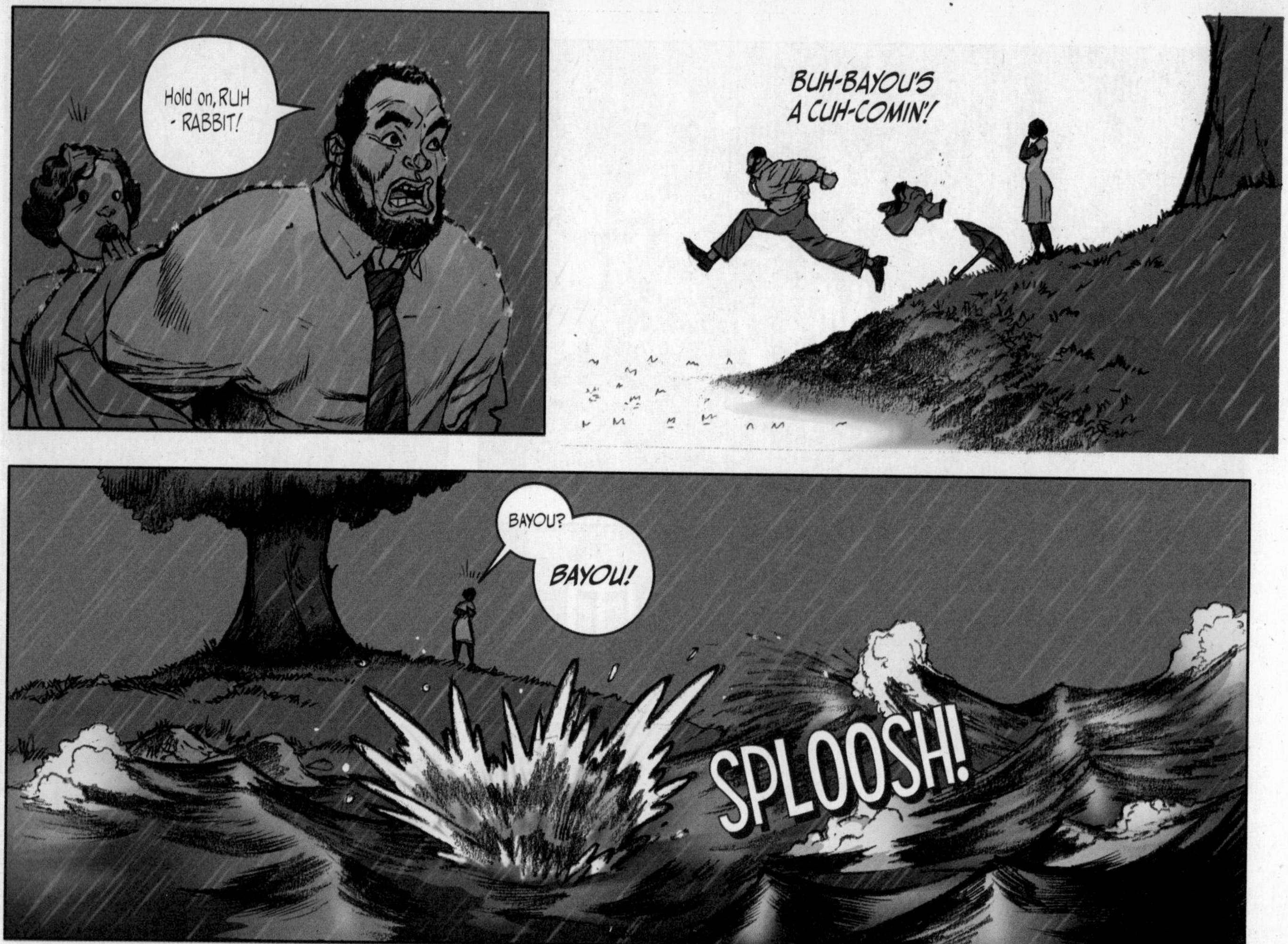
Hold on, RUH - RABBIT!
BUH-BAYOU'S A CUH-COMIN'!
BAYOU?
BAYOU!
SPLOOSH!

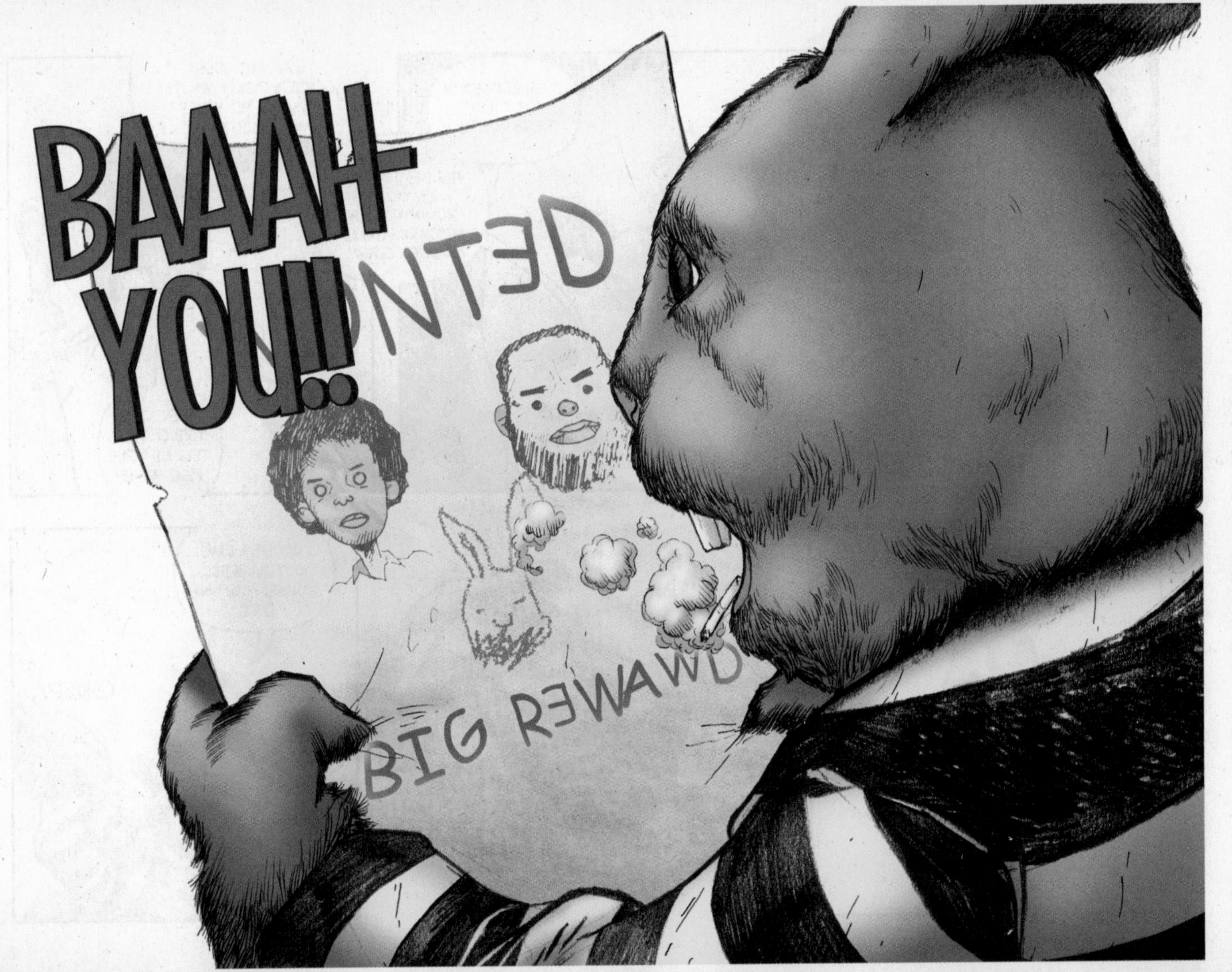
BAAAH-YOU!!!
ONT3D
BIG R3WAWD

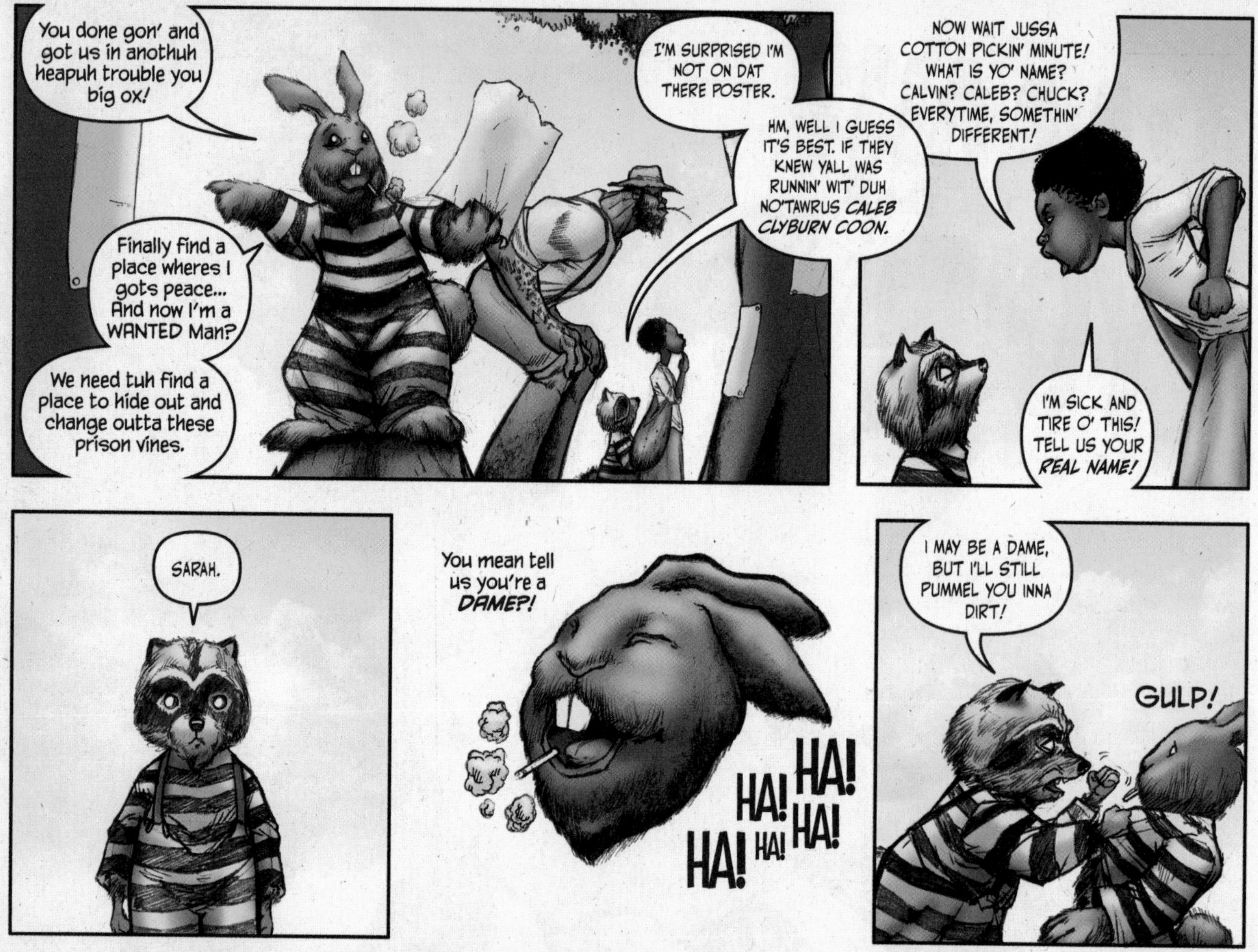
You done gon' and got us in anothuh heapuh trouble you big ox!
Finally find a place wheres I gots peace... And now I'm a WANTED Man?
We need tuh find a place to hide out and change outta these prison vines.
I'M SURPRISED I'M NOT ON DAT THERE POSTER.
HM, WELL I GUESS IT'S BEST. IF THEY KNEW YALL WAS RUNNIN' WIT' DUH NO'TAWRUS CALEB CLYBURN COON.
NOW WAIT JUSSA COTTON PICKIN' MINUTE! WHAT IS YO' NAME? CALVIN? CALEB? CHUCK? EVERYTIME, SOMETHIN' DIFFERENT!
I'M SICK AND TIRE O' THIS! TELL US YOUR REAL NAME!
SARAH.
You mean tell us you're a DAME?!
HA! HA! HA! HA! HA!
I MAY BE A DAME, BUT I'LL STILL PUMMEL YOU INNA DIRT!
GULP!

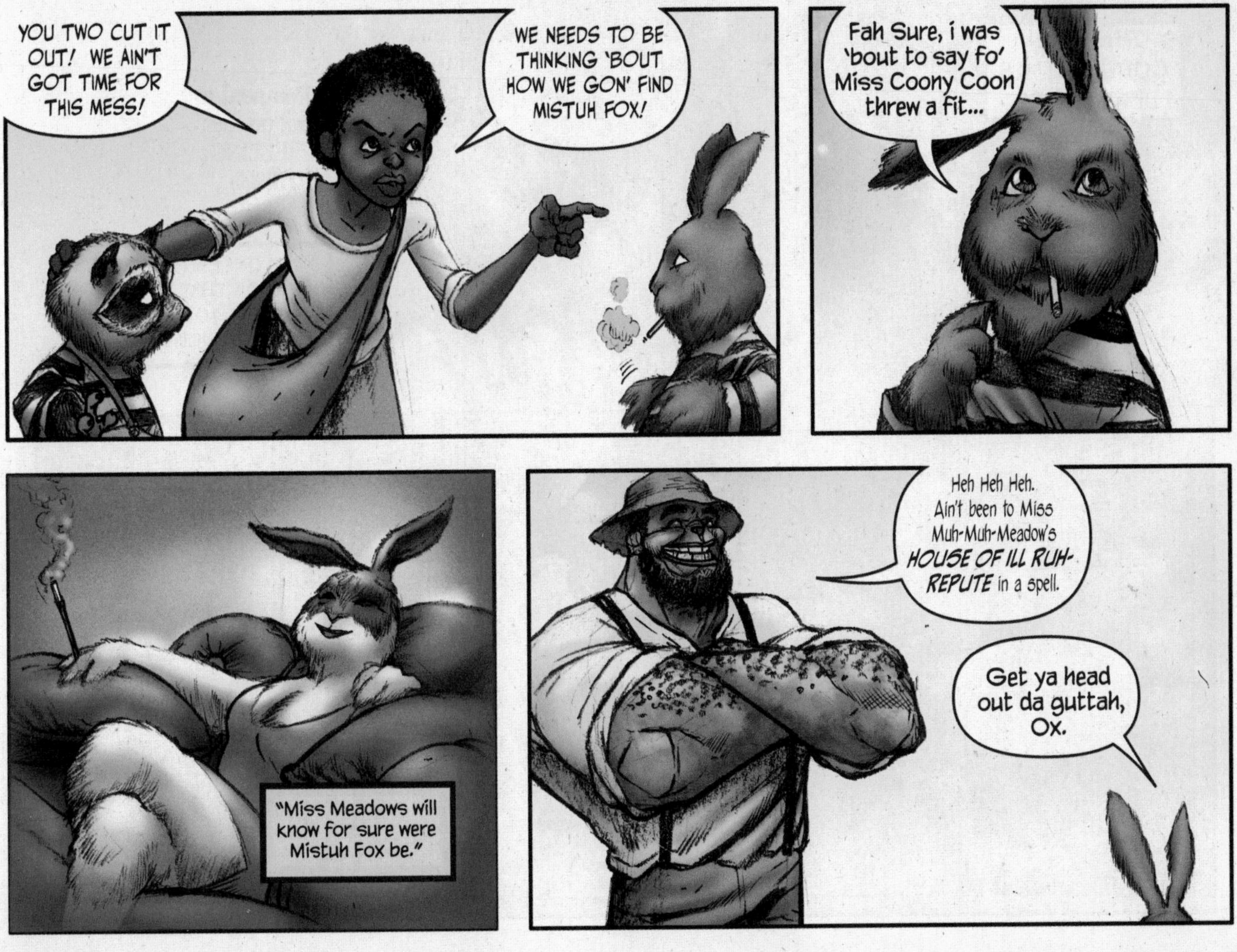
YOU TWO CUT IT OUT! WE AIN'T GOT TIME FOR THIS MESS!
WE NEEDS TO BE THINKING 'BOUT HOW WE GON' FIND MISTUH FOX!
Fah Sure, i was 'bout to say fo' Miss Coony Coon threw a fit...
"Miss Meadows will know for sure were Mistuh Fox be."
Heh Heh Heh. Ain't been to Miss Muh-Muh-Meadow's HOUSE OF ILL RUH-REPUTE in a spell.
Get ya head out da guttah, Ox.

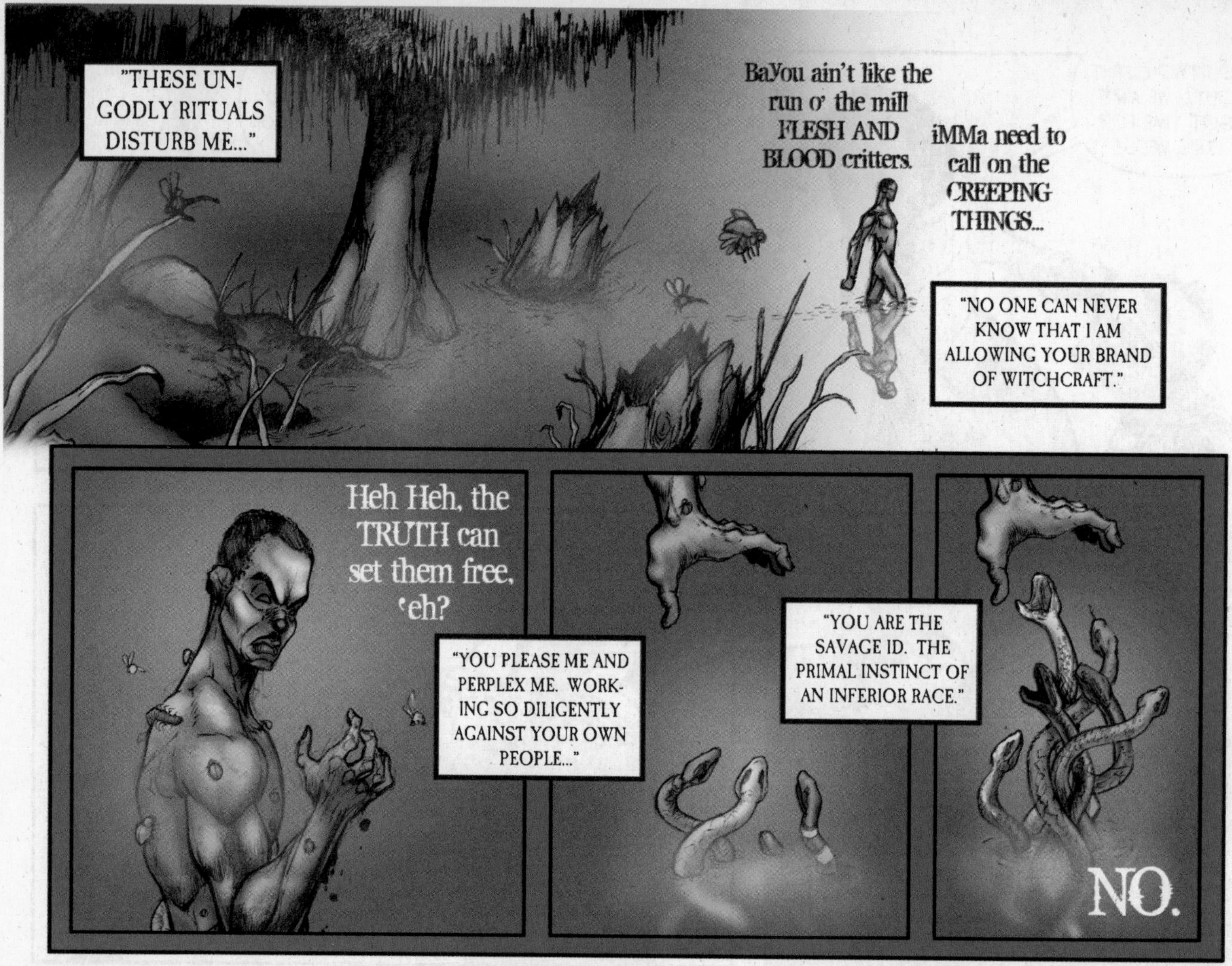
"THESE UN-GODLY RITUALS DISTURB ME..."
BaYou ain't like the run o' the mill FLESH AND BLOOD critters.
iMMa need to call on the CREEPING THINGS...
"NO ONE CAN NEVER KNOW THAT I AM ALLOWING YOUR BRAND OF WITCHCRAFT."
Heh Heh, the TRUTH can set them free, 'eh?
"YOU PLEASE ME AND PERPLEX ME. WORK-ING SO DILIGENTLY AGAINST YOUR OWN PEOPLE..."
"YOU ARE THE SAVAGE ID. THE PRIMAL INSTINCT OF AN INFERIOR RACE."
NO.

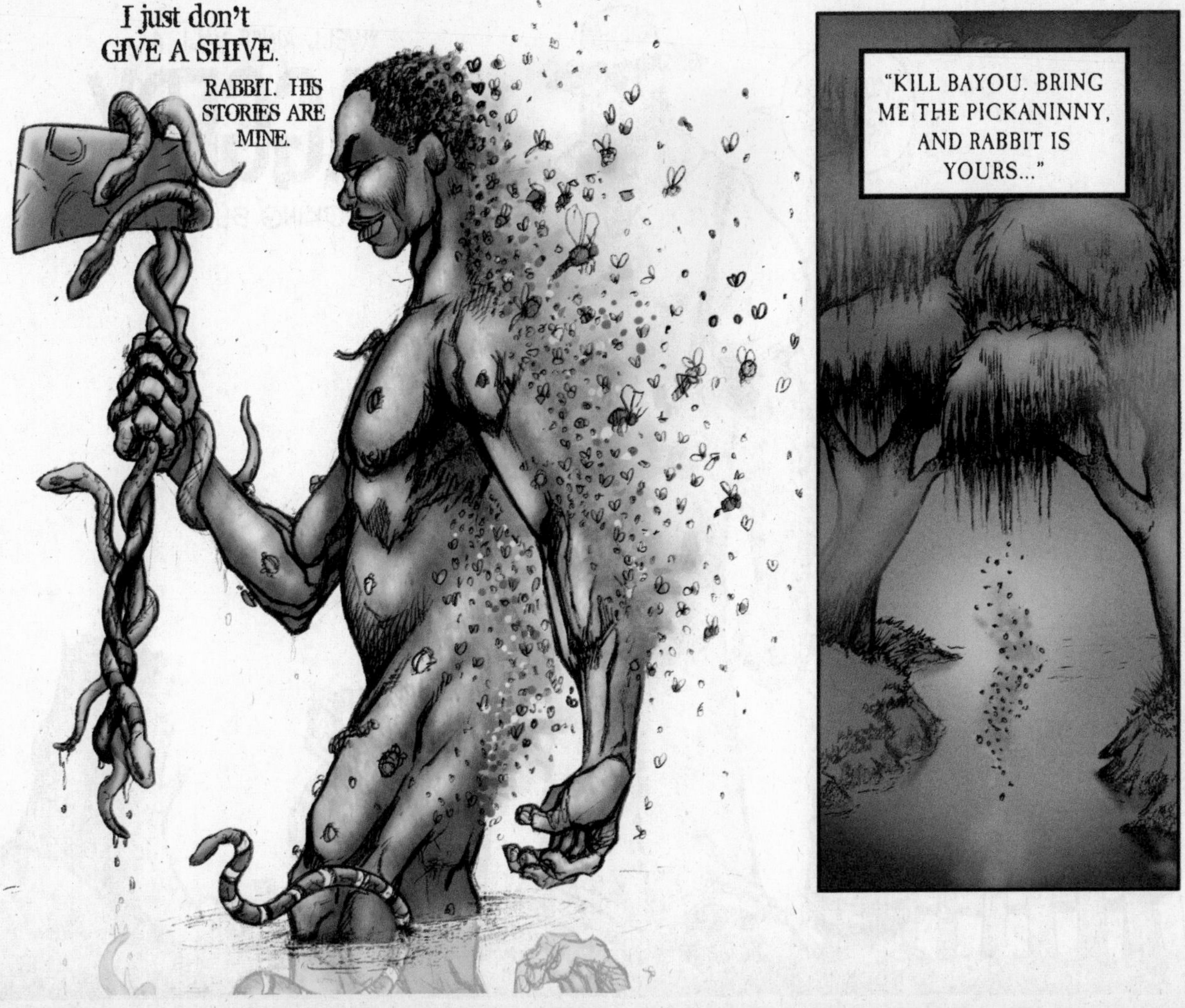
I just don't GIVE A SHIVE.
RABBIT. HIS STORIES ARE MINE.
"KILL BAYOU. BRING ME THE PICKANINNY, AND RABBIT IS YOURS..."

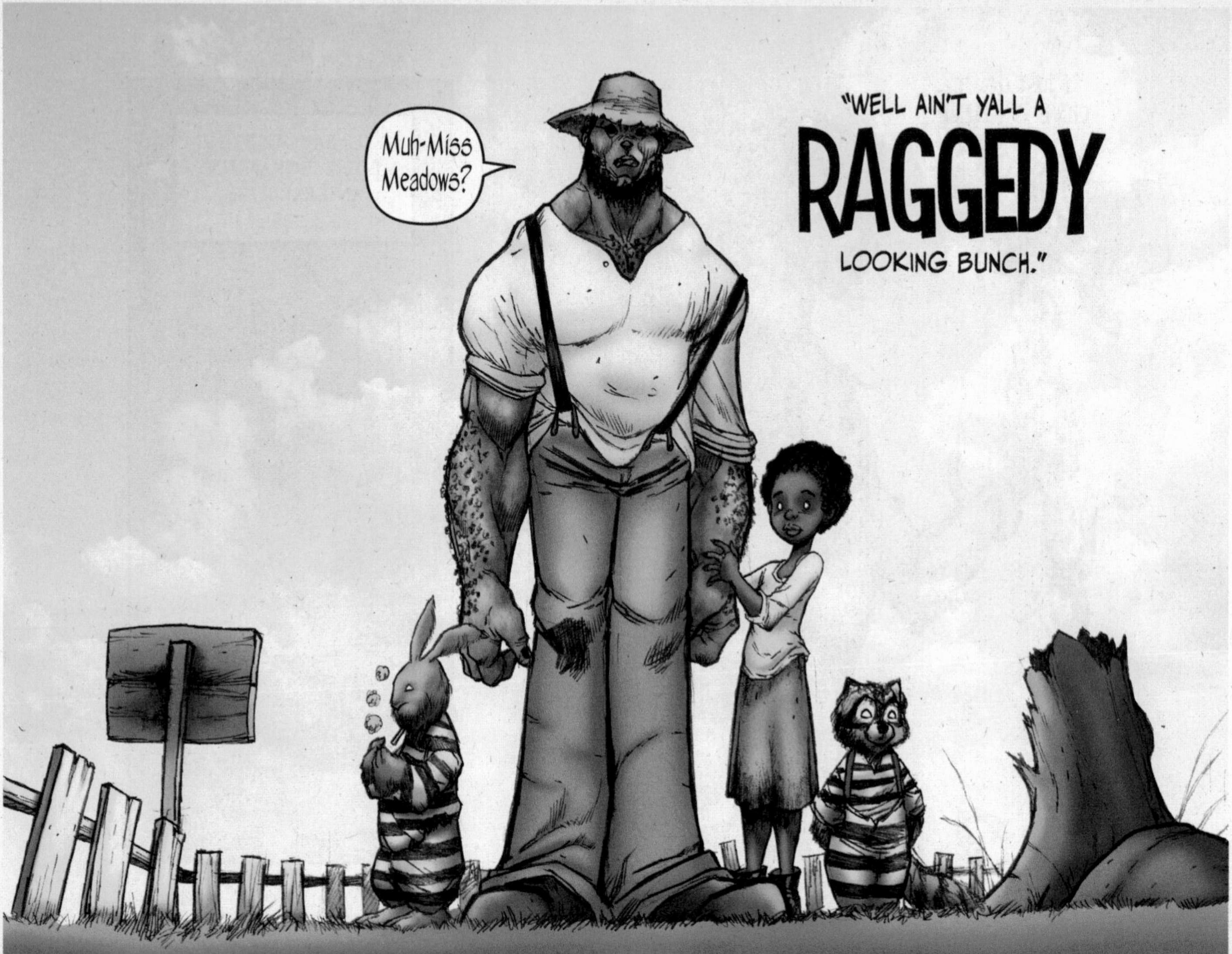
Muh-Miss Meadows?
"WELL AIN'T YALL A RAGGEDY LOOKING BUNCH."

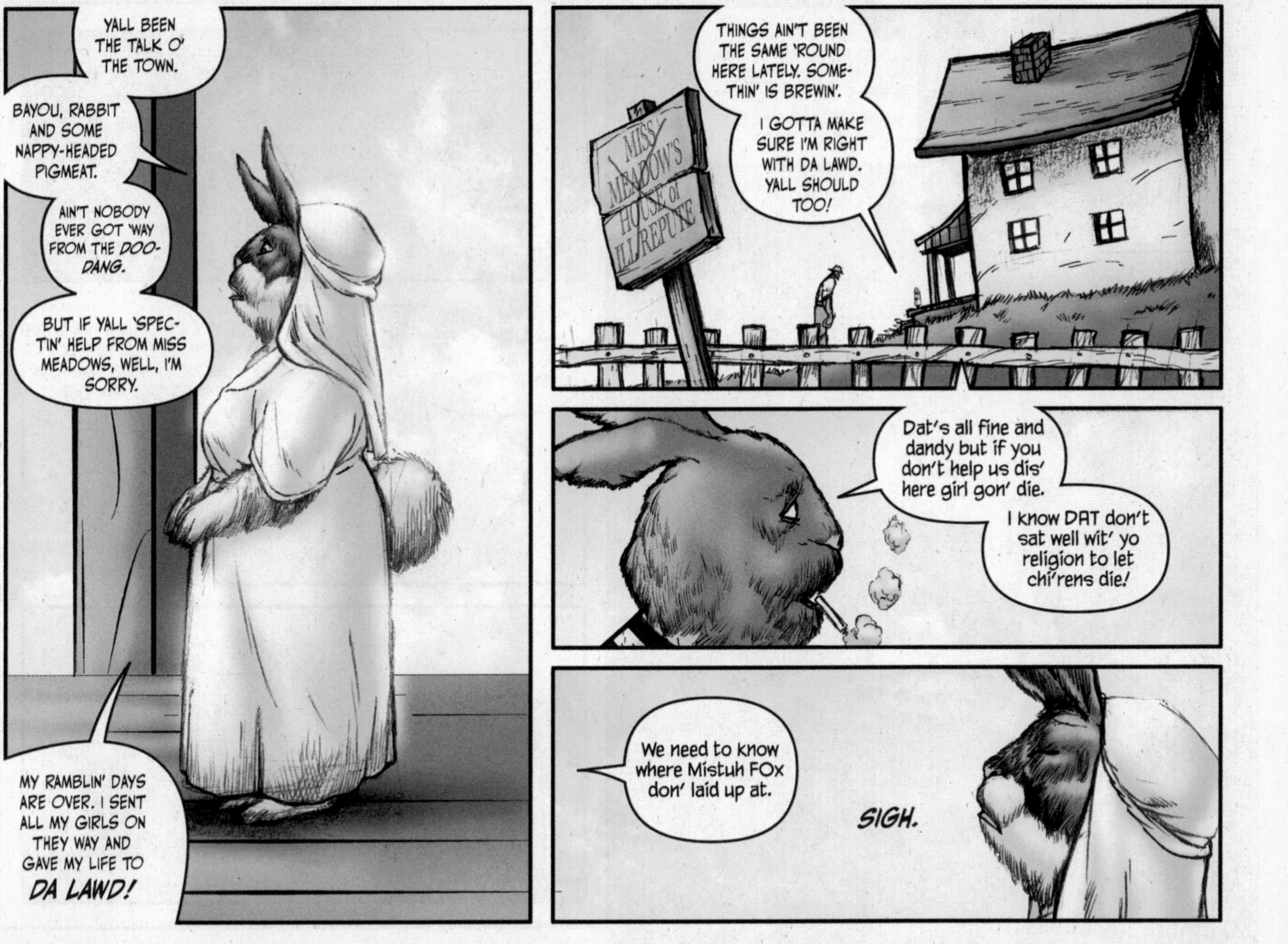
YALL BEEN THE TALK O' THE TOWN.
BAYOU, RABBIT AND SOME NAPPY-HEADED PIGMEAT.
AIN'T NOBODY EVER GOT 'WAY FROM THE DOO-DANG.
BUT IF YALL 'SPEC-TIN' HELP FROM MISS MEADOWS, WELL, I'M SORRY.
MY RAMBLIN' DAYS ARE OVER. I SENT ALL MY GIRLS ON THEY WAY AND GAVE MY LIFE TO DA LAWD!
MISS MEADOW'S HOUSE of ILL REPUTE
THINGS AIN'T BEEN THE SAME 'ROUND HERE LATELY. SOME-THIN' IS BREWIN'.
I GOTTA MAKE SURE I'M RIGHT WITH DA LAWD. YALL SHOULD TOO!
Dat's all fine and dandy but if you don't help us dis' here girl gon' die.
I know DAT don't sat well wit' yo religion to let chi'rens die!
We need to know where Mistuh FOx don' laid up at.
SIGH.

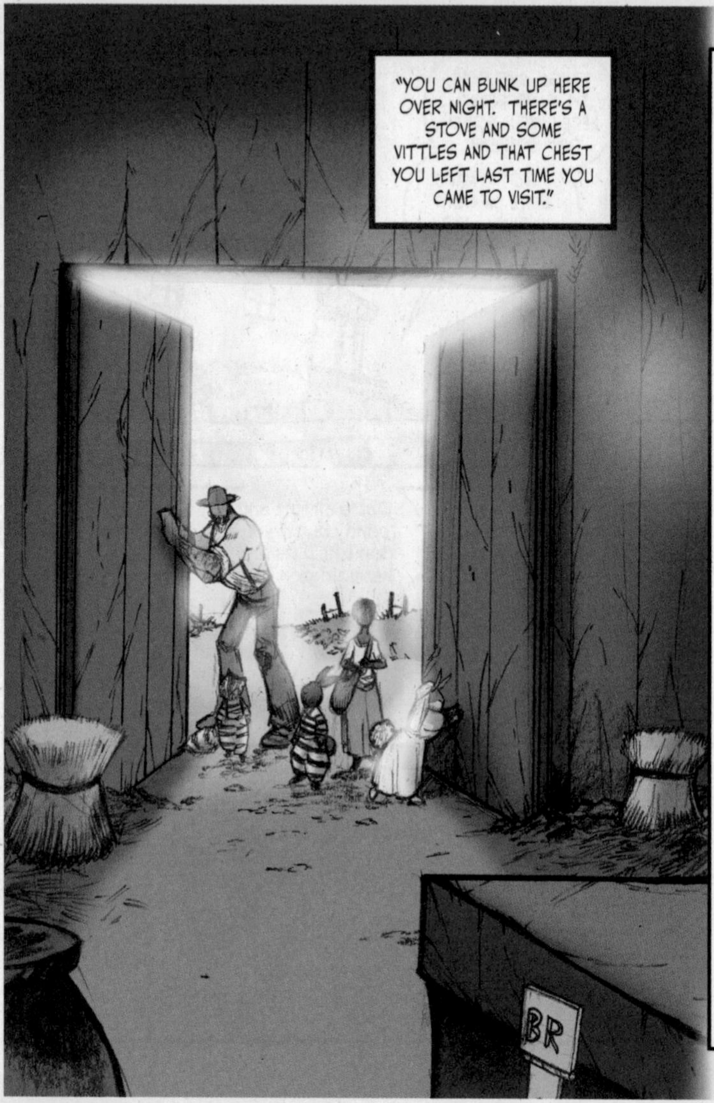
"YOU CAN BUNK UP HERE OVER NIGHT. THERE'S A STOVE AND SOME VITTLES AND THAT CHEST YOU LEFT LAST TIME YOU CAME TO VISIT."
BR

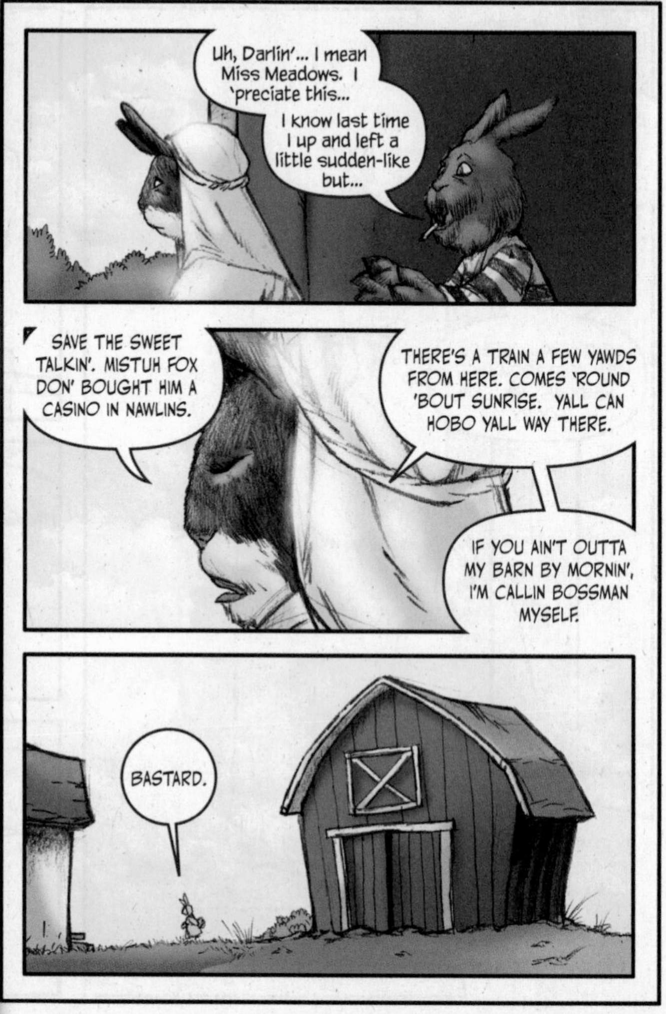
Uh, Darlin'... I mean Miss Meadows. I 'preciate this...
I know last time I up and left a little sudden-like but...
SAVE THE SWEET TALKIN'. MISTUH FOX DON' BOUGHT HIM A CASINO IN NAWLINS.
THERE'S A TRAIN A FEW YAWDS FROM HERE. COMES 'ROUND 'BOUT SUNRISE. YALL CAN HOBO YALL WAY THERE.
IF YOU AIN'T OUTTA MY BARN BY MORNIN', I'M CALLIN BOSSMAN MYSELF.
BASTARD.

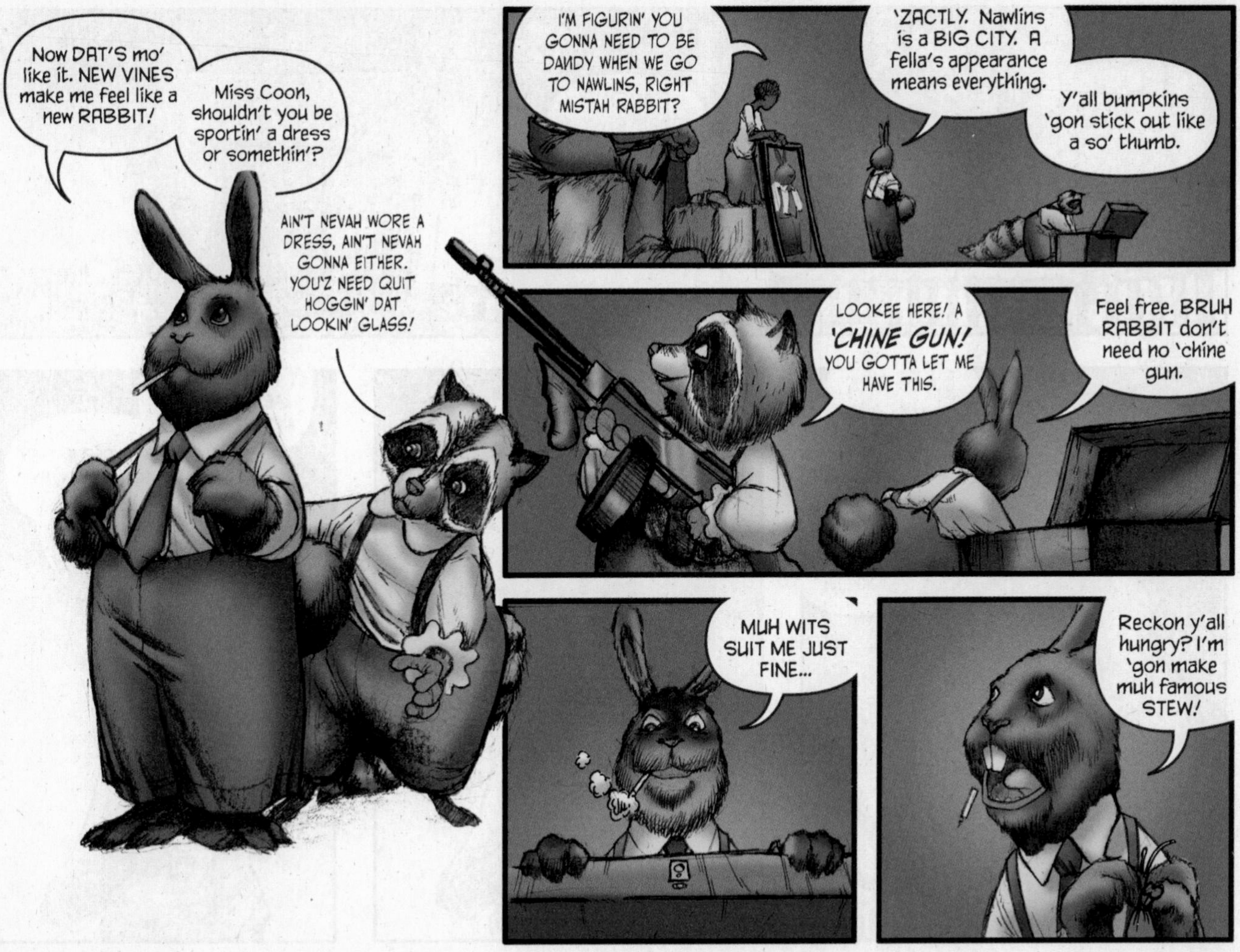
Now DAT'S mo' like it. NEW VINES make me feel like a new RABBIT!
Miss Coon, shouldn't you be sportin' a dress or somethin'?
AIN'T NEVAH WORE A DRESS, AIN'T NEVAH GONNA EITHER. YOU'Z NEED QUIT HOGGIN' DAT LOOKIN' GLASS!
I'M FIGURIN' YOU GONNA NEED TO BE DANDY WHEN WE GO TO NAWLINS, RIGHT MISTAH RABBIT?
'ZACTLY. Nawlins is a BIG CITY. A fella's appearance means everything.
Y'all bumpkins 'gon stick out like a so' thumb.
LOOKEE HERE! A 'CHINE GUN! YOU GOTTA LET ME HAVE THIS.
Feel free. BRUH RABBIT don't need no 'chine gun.
MUH WITS SUIT ME JUST FINE...
Reckon y'all hungry? I'm 'gon make muh famous STEW!

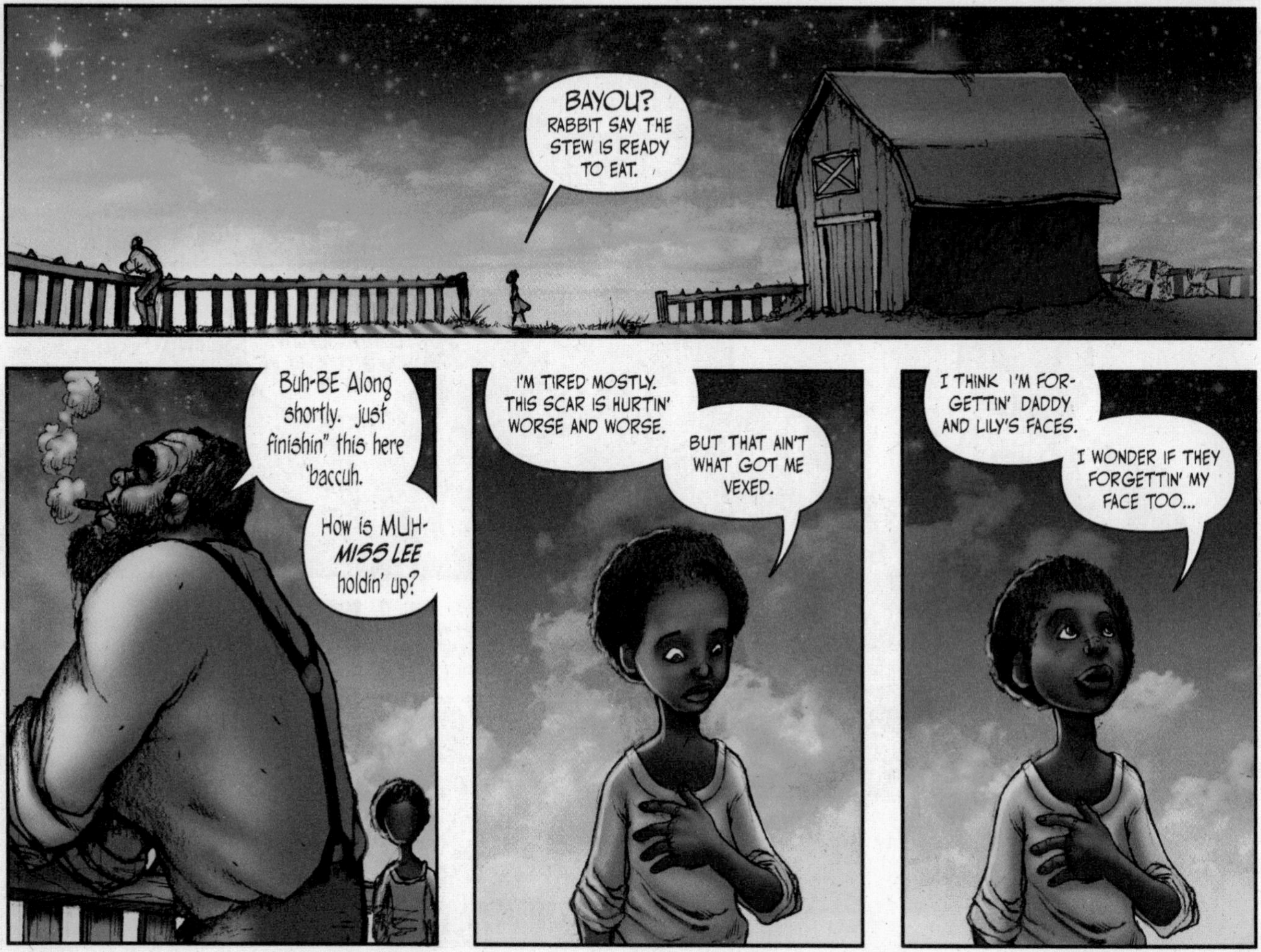
BAYOU? RABBIT SAY THE STEW IS READY TO EAT.
Buh-BE Along shortly. just finishin" this here 'baccuh.
How is MUH- *MISS LEE* holdin' up?
I'M TIRED MOSTLY. THIS SCAR IS HURTIN' WORSE AND WORSE.
BUT THAT AIN'T WHAT GOT ME VEXED.
I THINK I'M FOR-GETTIN' DADDY AND LILY'S FACES.
I WONDER IF THEY FORGETTIN' MY FACE TOO...

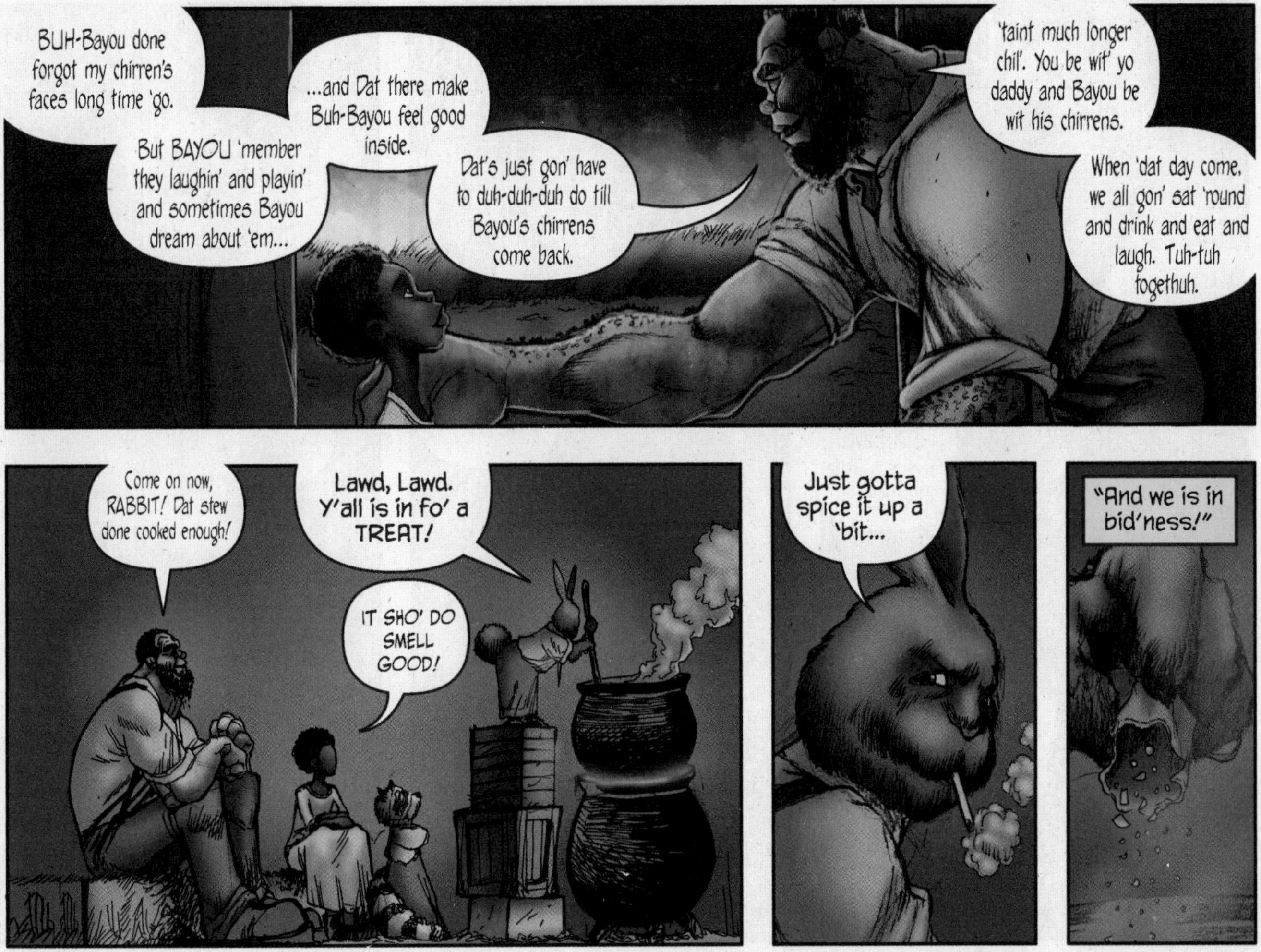
BUH-Bayou done forgot my chirren's faces long time 'go.
But BAYOU 'member they laughin' and playin' and sometimes Bayou dream about 'em...
...and Dat there make Buh-Bayou feel good inside.
Dat's just gon' have to duh-duh-duh do till Bayou's chirrens come back.
'taint much longer chil'. You be wit' yo daddy and Bayou be wit his chirrens.
When 'dat day come, we all gon' sat 'round and drink and eat and laugh. Tuh-tuh togethuh.
Come on now, RABBIT! Dat stew done cooked enough!
Lawd, Lawd. Y'all is in fo' a TREAT!
IT SHO' DO SMELL GOOD!
Just gotta spice it up a 'bit...
"And we is in bid'ness!"

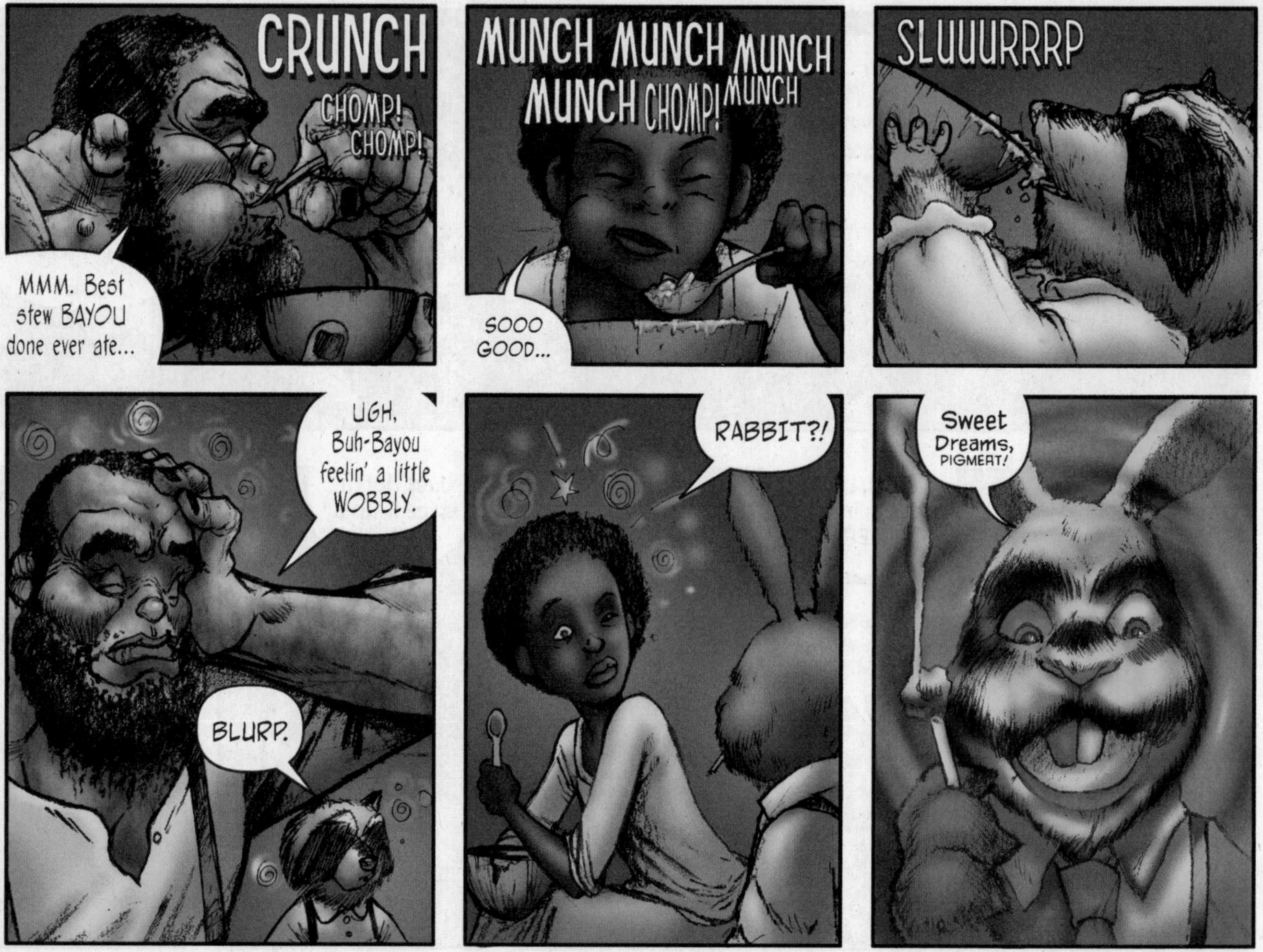
CRUNCH
CHOMP! CHOMP!
MMM. Best stew BAYOU done ever ate...
MUNCH MUNCH MUNCH MUNCH CHOMP! MUNCH
SOOO GOOD...
SLUUURRRP
UGH, Buh-Bayou feelin' a little WOBBLY.
BLURP.
RABBIT?!
Sweet Dreams, PIGMEAT!

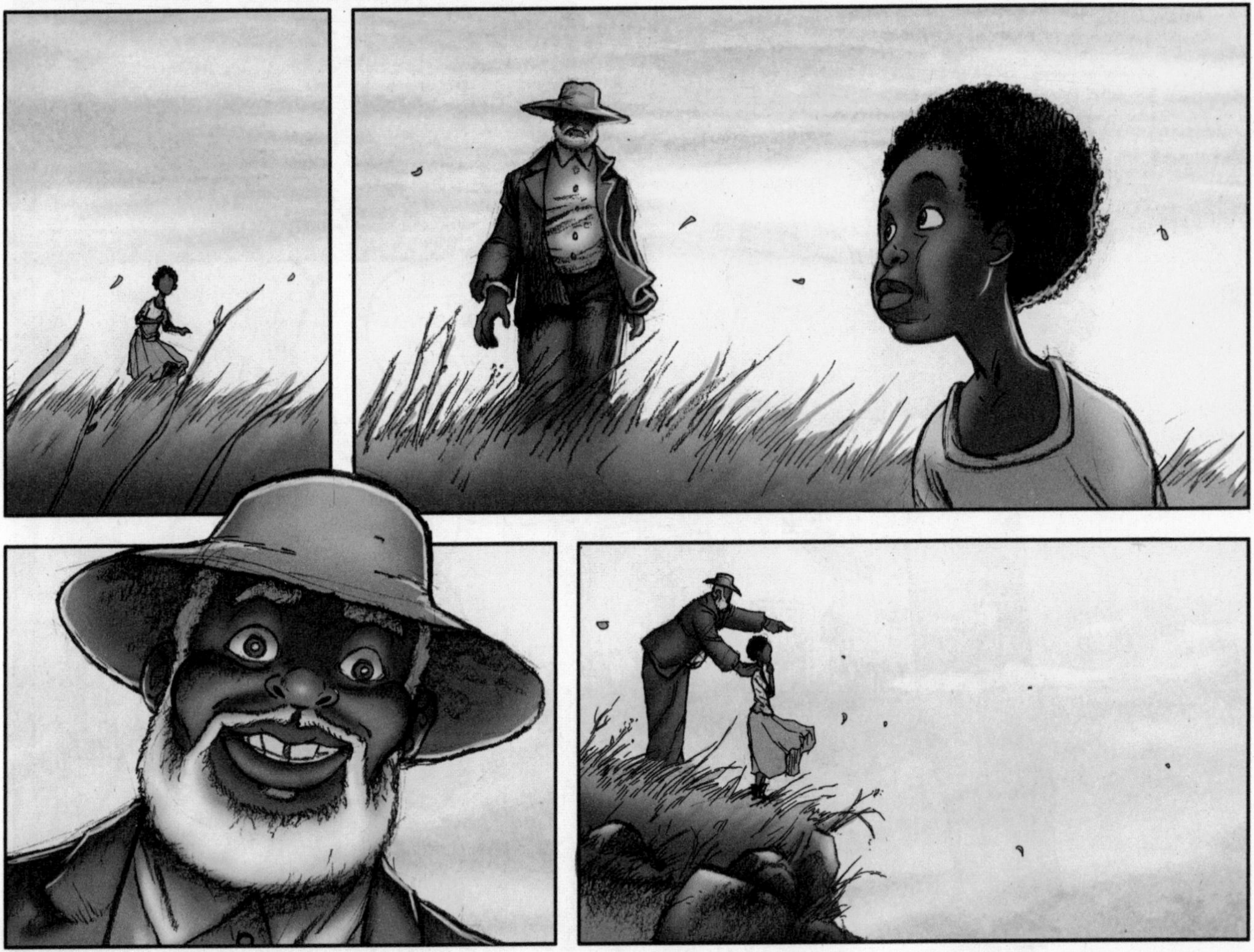

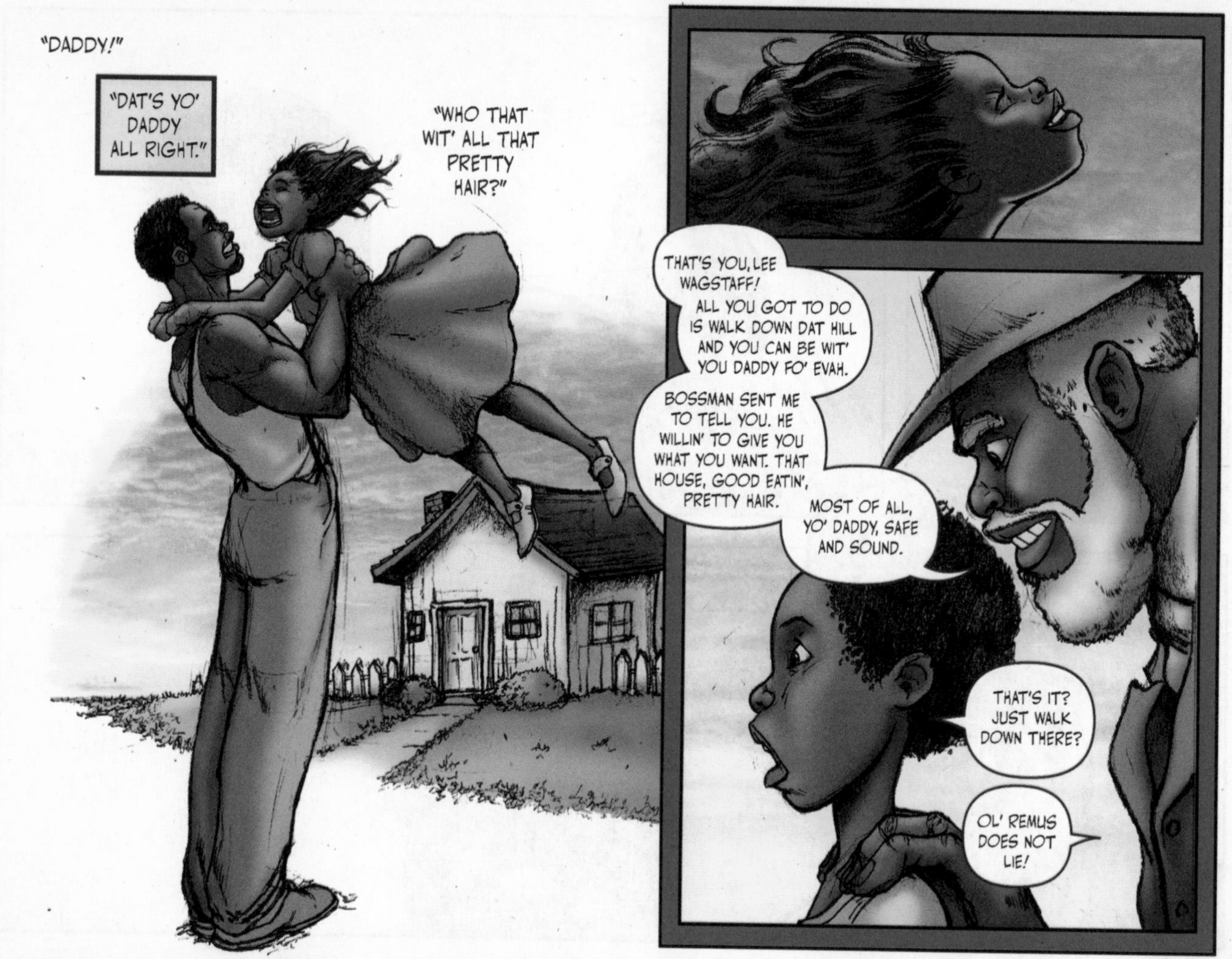

"DADDY!"
"DAT'S YO' DADDY ALL RIGHT."
"WHO THAT WIT' ALL THAT PRETTY HAIR?"
THAT'S YOU, LEE WAGSTAFF!
ALL YOU GOT TO DO IS WALK DOWN DAT HILL AND YOU CAN BE WIT' YOU DADDY FO' EVAH.
BOSSMAN SENT ME TO TELL YOU. HE WILLIN' TO GIVE YOU WHAT YOU WANT. THAT HOUSE, GOOD EATIN', PRETTY HAIR.
MOST OF ALL, YO' DADDY, SAFE AND SOUND.
THAT'S IT? JUST WALK DOWN THERE?
OL' REMUS DOES NOT LIE!

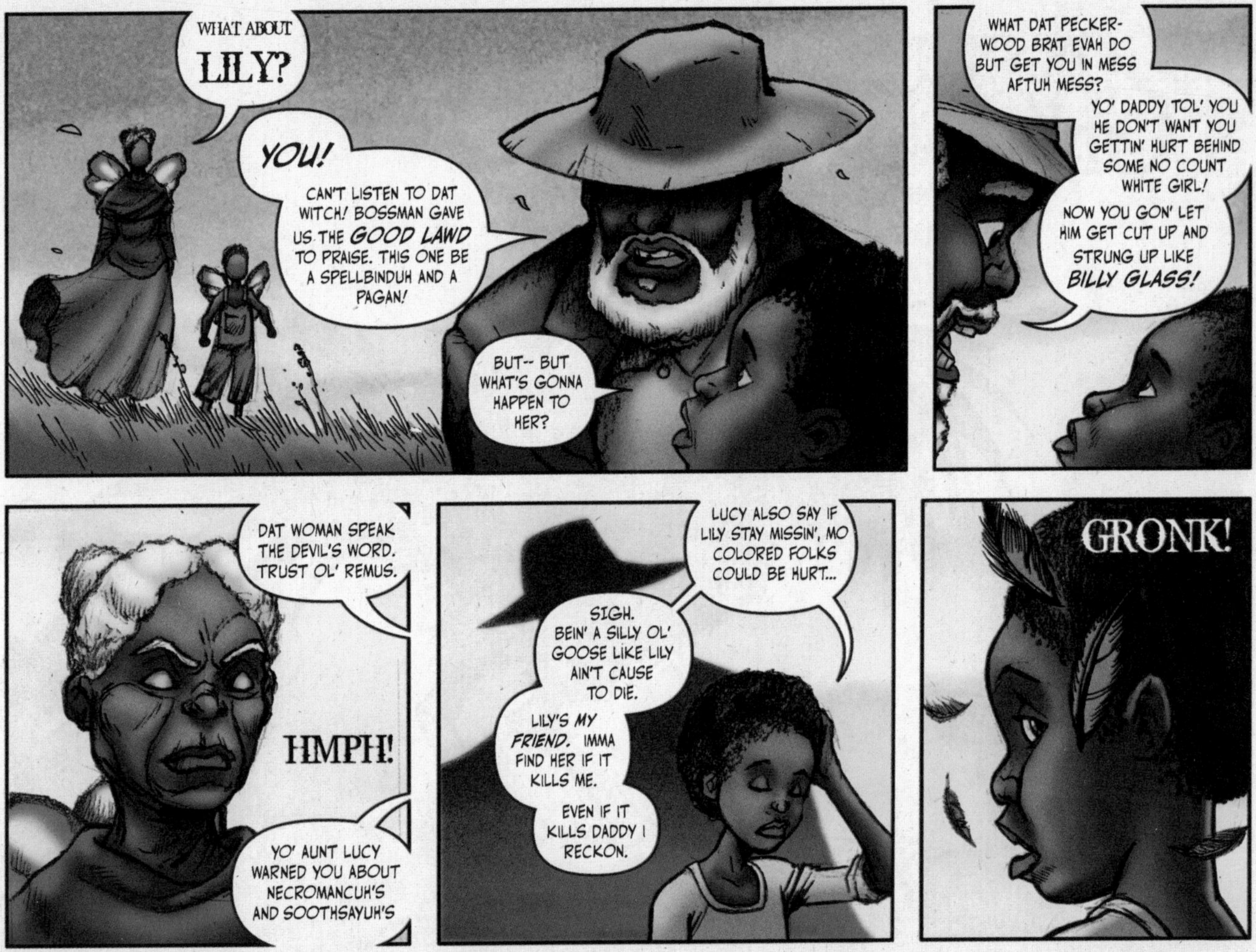
WHAT ABOUT LILY?
YOU!
CAN'T LISTEN TO DAT WITCH! BOSSMAN GAVE US THE GOOD LAWD TO PRAISE. THIS ONE BE A SPELLBINDUH AND A PAGAN!
BUT-- BUT WHAT'S GONNA HAPPEN TO HER?
WHAT DAT PECKER-WOOD BRAT EVAH DO BUT GET YOU IN MESS AFTUH MESS?
YO' DADDY TOL' YOU HE DON'T WANT YOU GETTIN' HURT BEHIND SOME NO COUNT WHITE GIRL!
NOW YOU GON' LET HIM GET CUT UP AND STRUNG UP LIKE BILLY GLASS!
DAT WOMAN SPEAK THE DEVIL'S WORD. TRUST OL' REMUS.
HMPH!
YO' AUNT LUCY WARNED YOU ABOUT NECROMANCUH'S AND SOOTHSAYUH'S
LUCY ALSO SAY IF LILY STAY MISSIN', MO COLORED FOLKS COULD BE HURT...
SIGH. BEIN' A SILLY OL' GOOSE LIKE LILY AIN'T CAUSE TO DIE.
LILY'S MY FRIEND. IMMA FIND HER IF IT KILLS ME.
EVEN IF IT KILLS DADDY I RECKON.
GRONK!

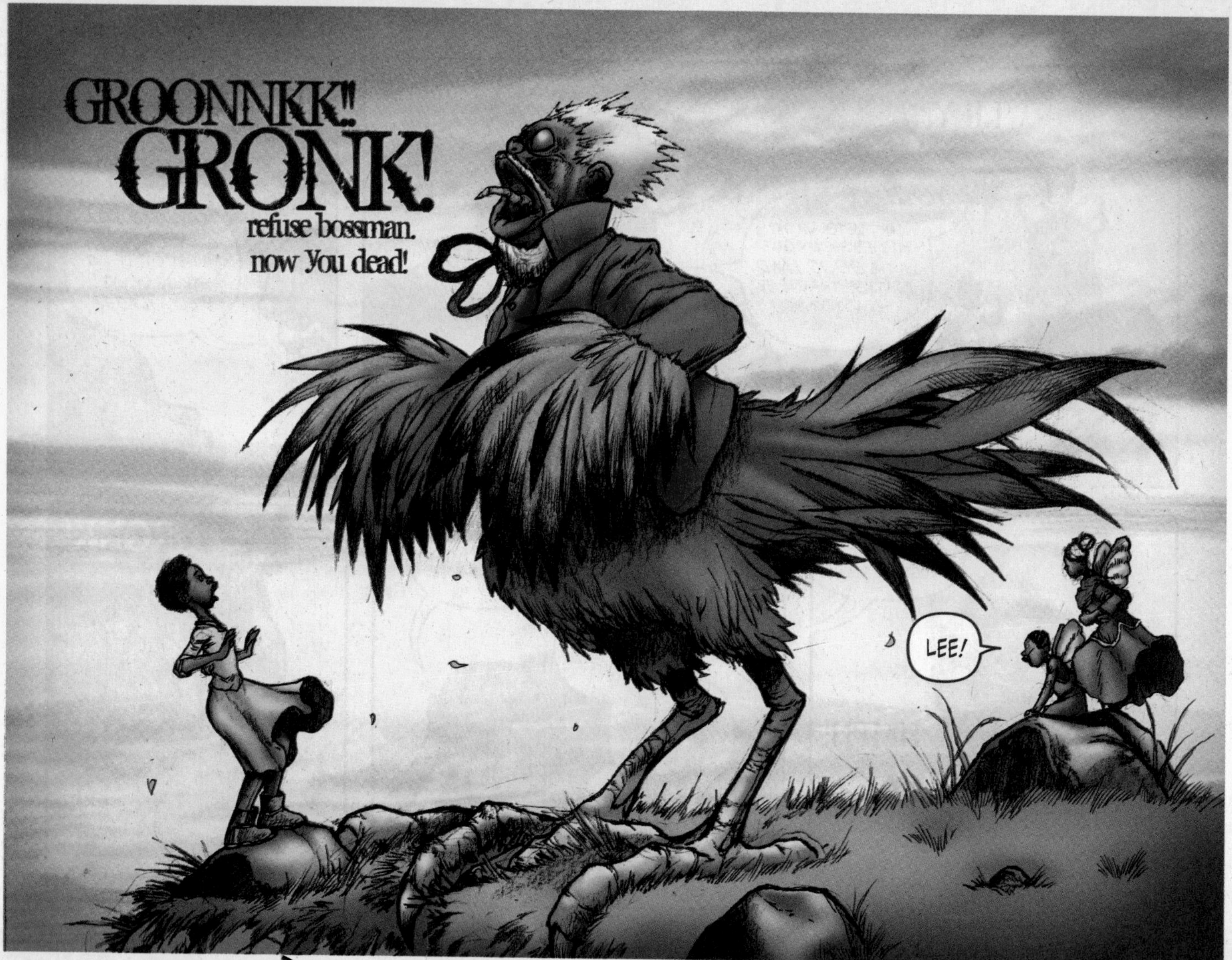
GROONNKK!!
GRONK!
refuse bossman.
now You dead!
LEE!

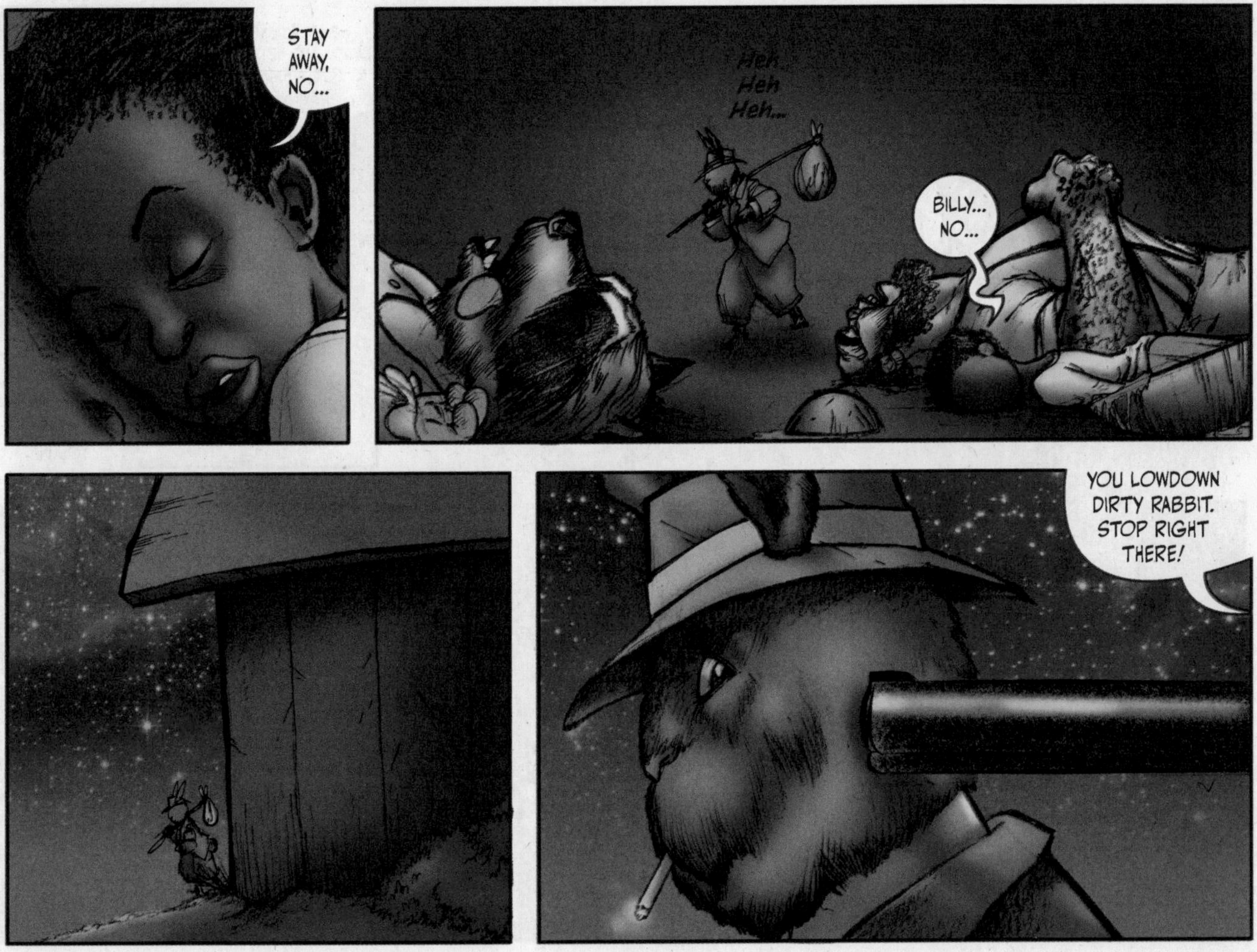
STAY AWAY, NO...
Heh Heh Heh...
BILLY... NO...
YOU LOWDOWN DIRTY RABBIT. STOP RIGHT THERE!

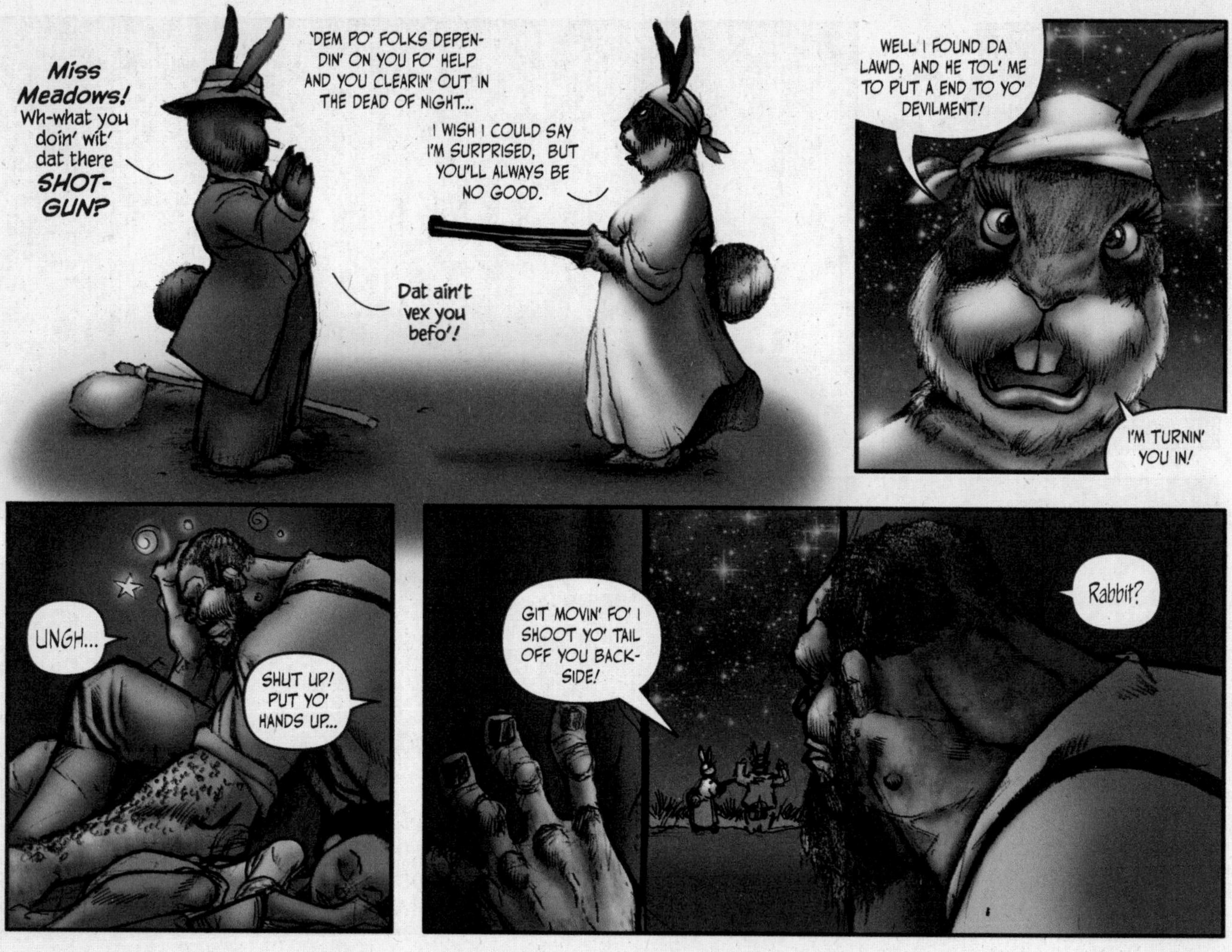
Miss Meadows! Wh-what you doin' wit' dat there SHOT-GUN?
'DEM PO' FOLKS DEPEN-DIN' ON YOU FO' HELP AND YOU CLEARIN' OUT IN THE DEAD OF NIGHT...
I WISH I COULD SAY I'M SURPRISED, BUT YOU'LL ALWAYS BE NO GOOD.
Dat ain't vex you befo'!
WELL I FOUND DA LAWD, AND HE TOL' ME TO PUT A END TO YO' DEVILMENT!
I'M TURNIN' YOU IN!
UNGH...
SHUT UP! PUT YO' HANDS UP...
GIT MOVIN' FO' I SHOOT YO' TAIL OFF YOU BACK-SIDE!
Rabbit?

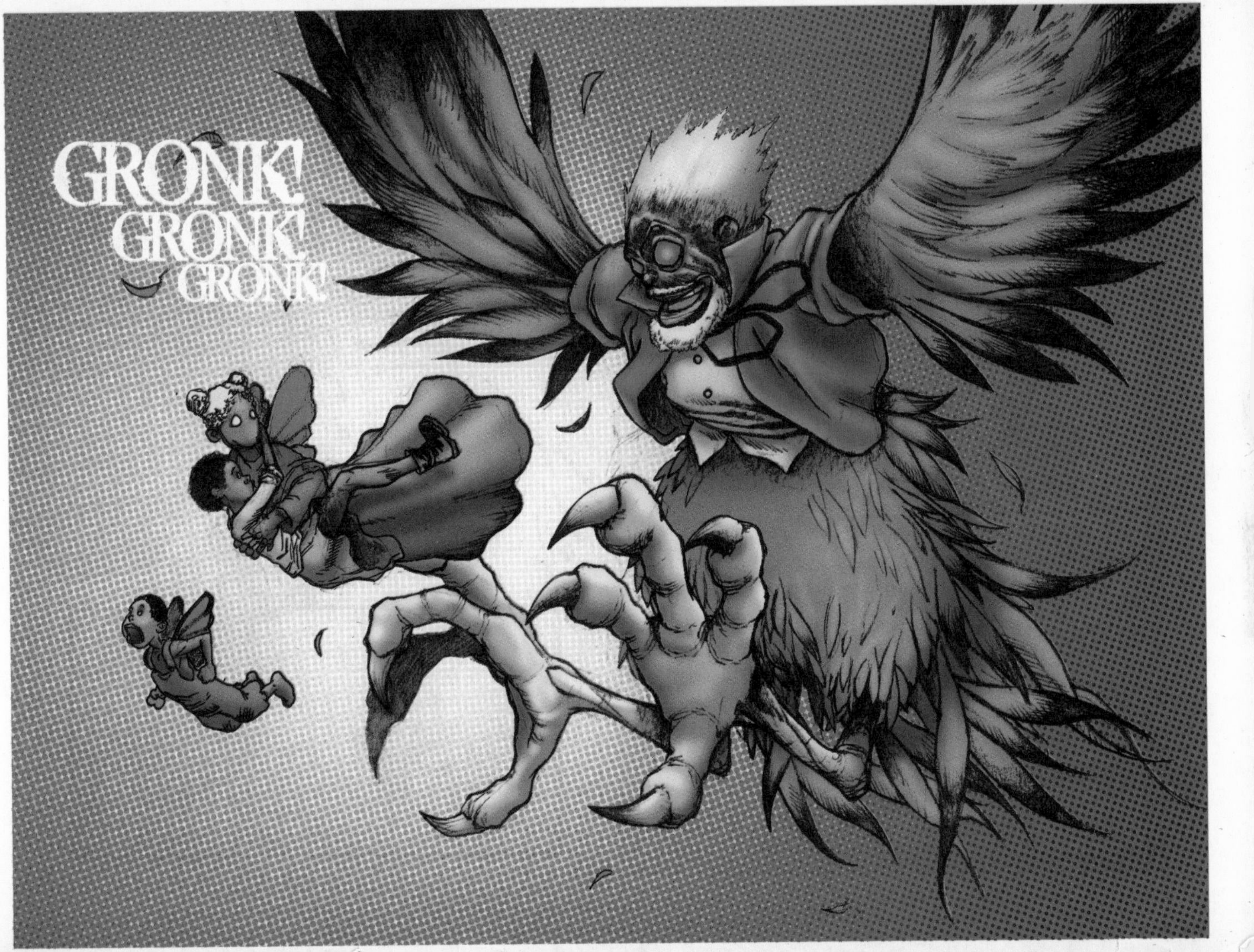
GRONK!
GRONK!
GRONK!

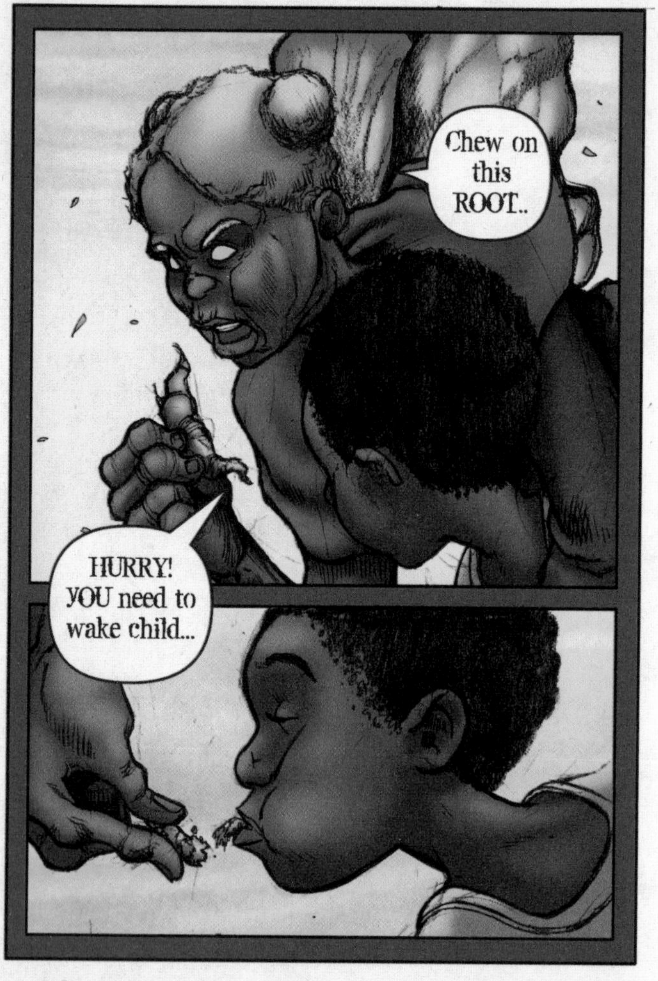
Chew on this ROOT..
HURRY! YOU need to wake child...

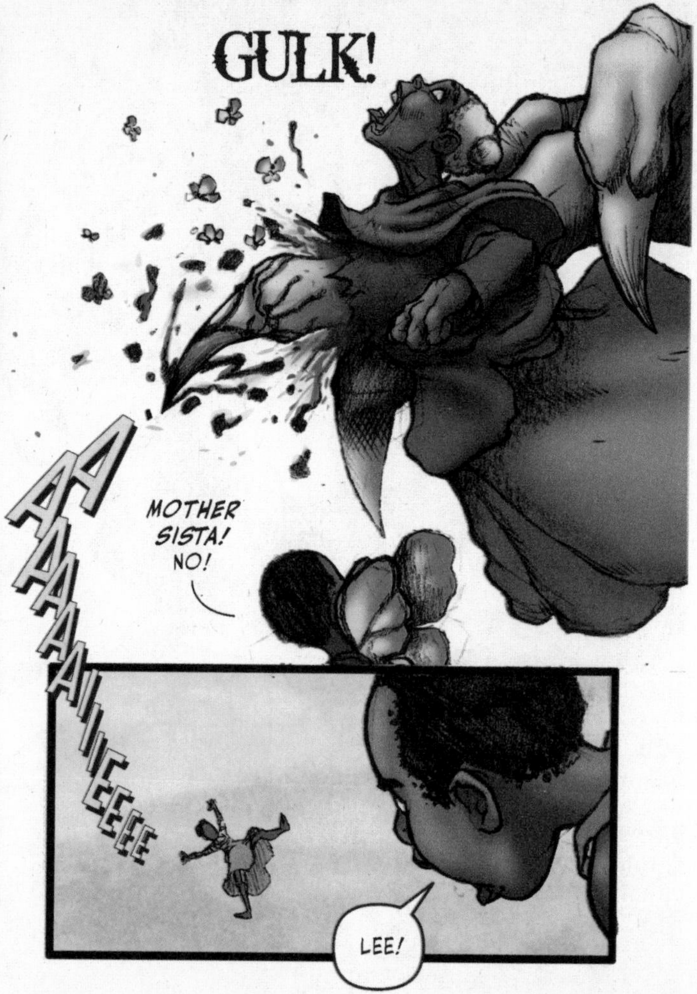
GULK!
AAAAAAIIIIEEEEE
MOTHER SISTA! NO!
LEE!

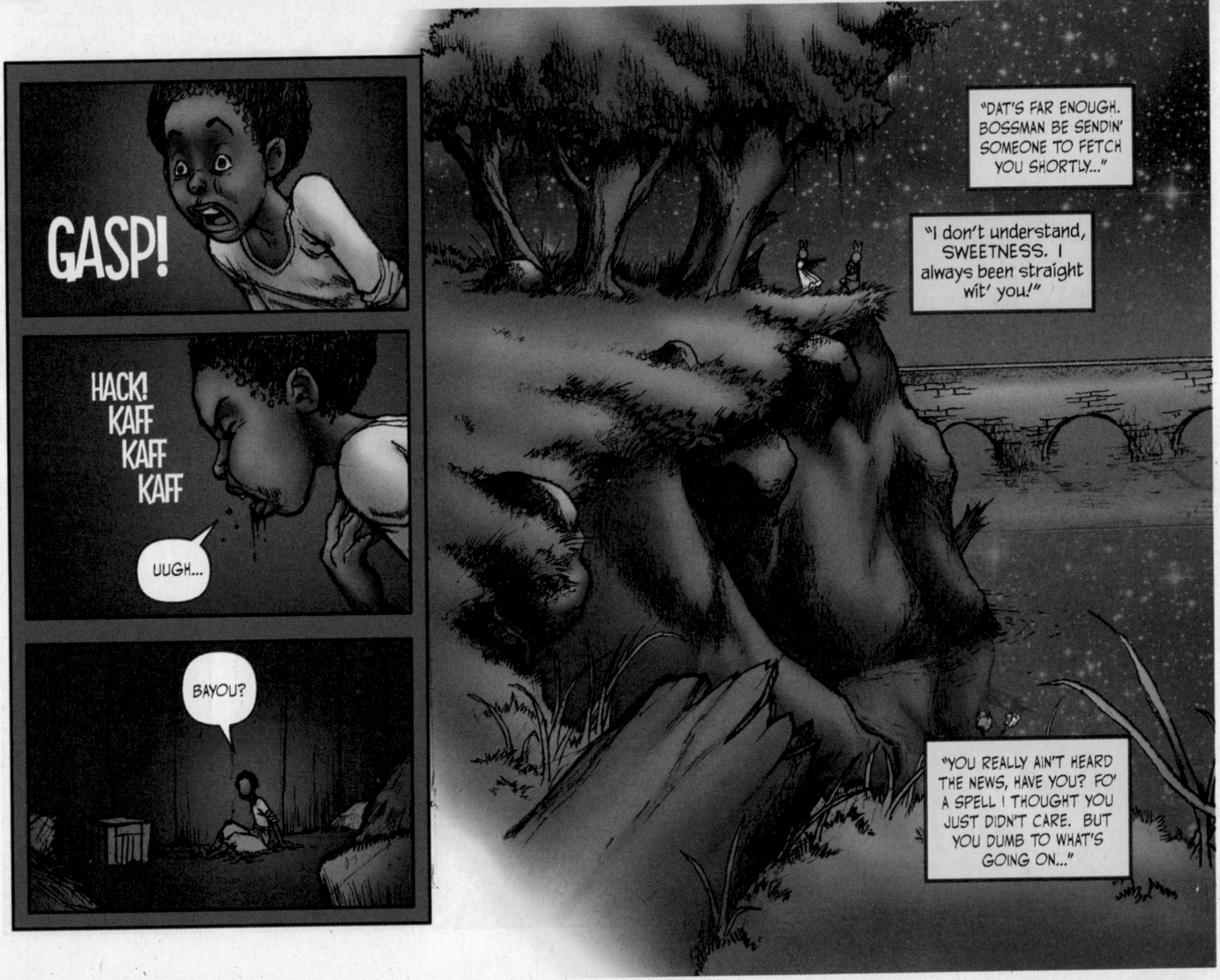
GASP!
HACK! KAFF KAFF KAFF
UUGH...
BAYOU?
"DAT'S FAR ENOUGH. BOSSMAN BE SENDIN' SOMEONE TO FETCH YOU SHORTLY..."
"I don't understand, SWEETNESS. I always been straight wit' you!"
"YOU REALLY AIN'T HEARD THE NEWS, HAVE YOU? FO' A SPELL I THOUGHT YOU JUST DIDN'T CARE. BUT YOU DUMB TO WHAT'S GOING ON..."

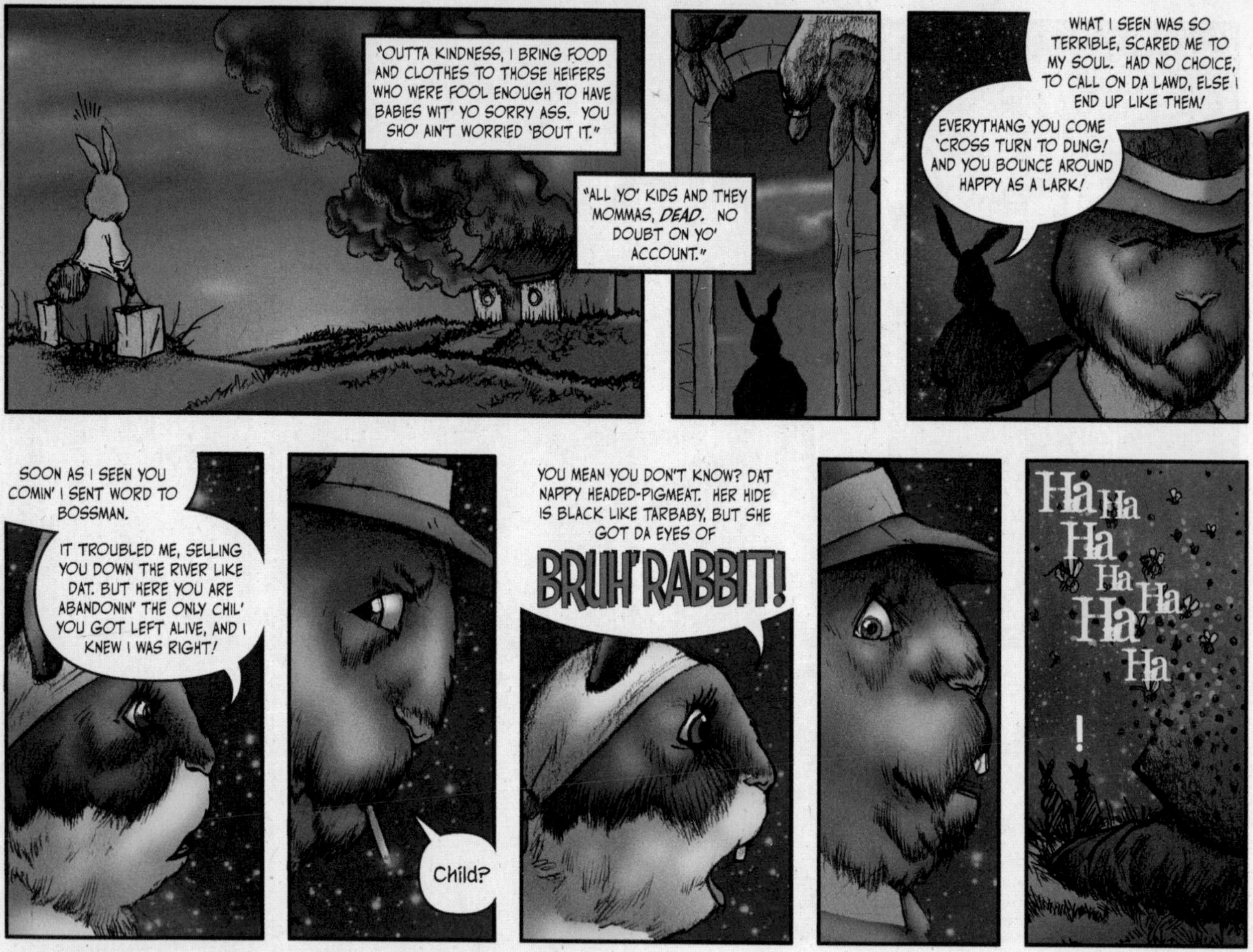
"OUTTA KINDNESS, I BRING FOOD AND CLOTHES TO THOSE HEIFERS WHO WERE FOOL ENOUGH TO HAVE BABIES WIT' YO SORRY ASS. YOU SHO' AIN'T WORRIED 'BOUT IT."
"ALL YO' KIDS AND THEY MOMMAS, *DEAD.* NO DOUBT ON YO' ACCOUNT."
WHAT I SEEN WAS SO TERRIBLE, SCARED ME TO MY SOUL. HAD NO CHOICE, TO CALL ON DA LAWD, ELSE I END UP LIKE THEM!
EVERYTHANG YOU COME 'CROSS TURN TO DUNG! AND YOU BOUNCE AROUND HAPPY AS A LARK!
SOON AS I SEEN YOU COMIN' I SENT WORD TO BOSSMAN.
IT TROUBLED ME, SELLING YOU DOWN THE RIVER LIKE DAT. BUT HERE YOU ARE ABANDONIN' THE ONLY CHIL' YOU GOT LEFT ALIVE, AND I KNEW I WAS RIGHT!
Child?
YOU MEAN YOU DON'T KNOW? DAT NAPPY HEADED-PIGMEAT. HER HIDE IS BLACK LIKE TARBABY, BUT SHE GOT DA EYES OF
BRUH'RABBIT!
Ha Ha Ha Ha Ha Ha Ha Ha
!

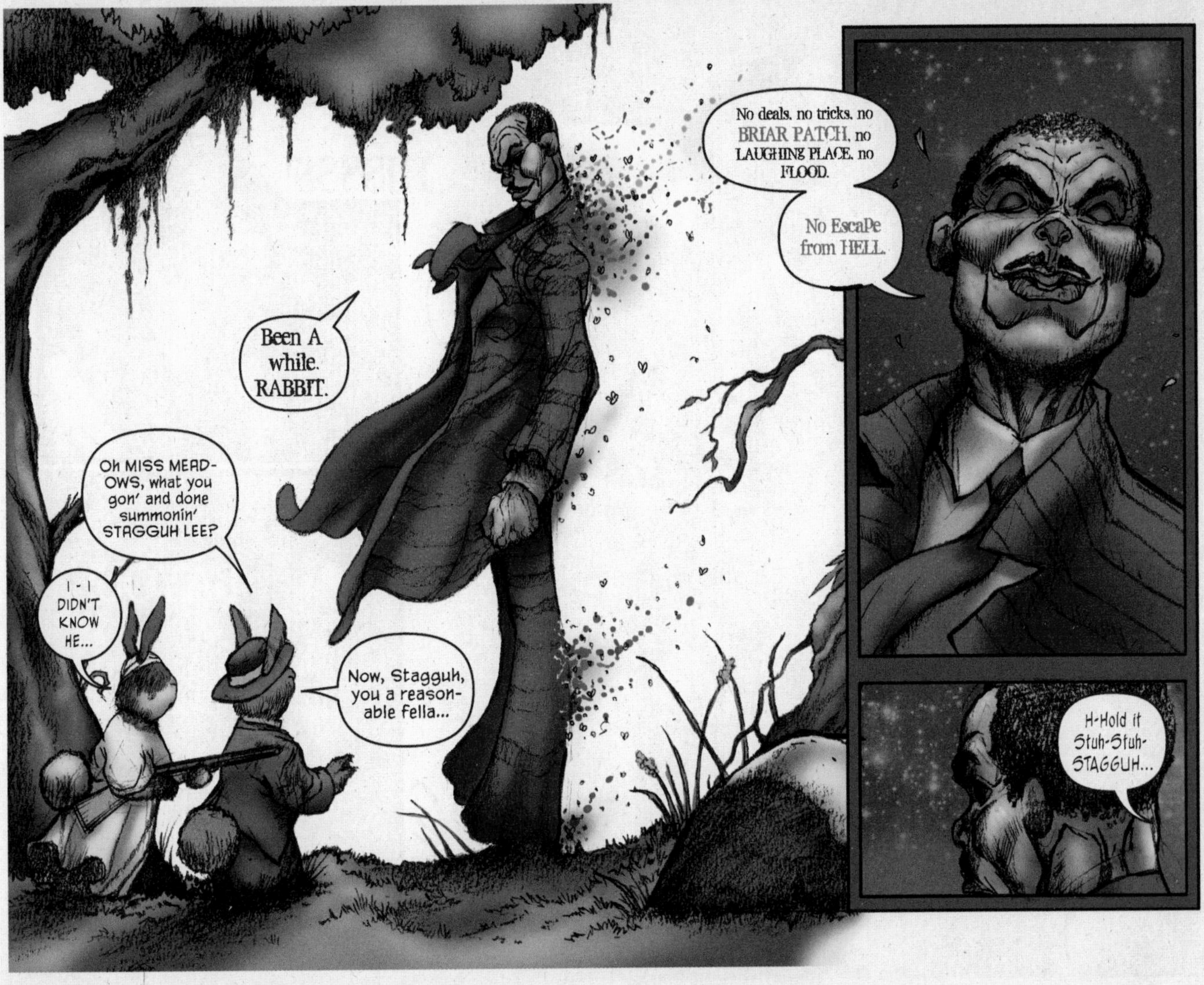
Oh MISS MEADOWS, what you gon' and done summonin' STAGGUH LEE?
I - I DIDN'T KNOW HE...
Now, Stagguh, you a reasonable fella...
Been A while. RABBIT.
No deals, no tricks, no BRIAR PATCH, no LAUGHING PLACE, no FLOOD.
No EscaPe from HELL.
H-Hold it Stuh-Stuh-STAGGUH...

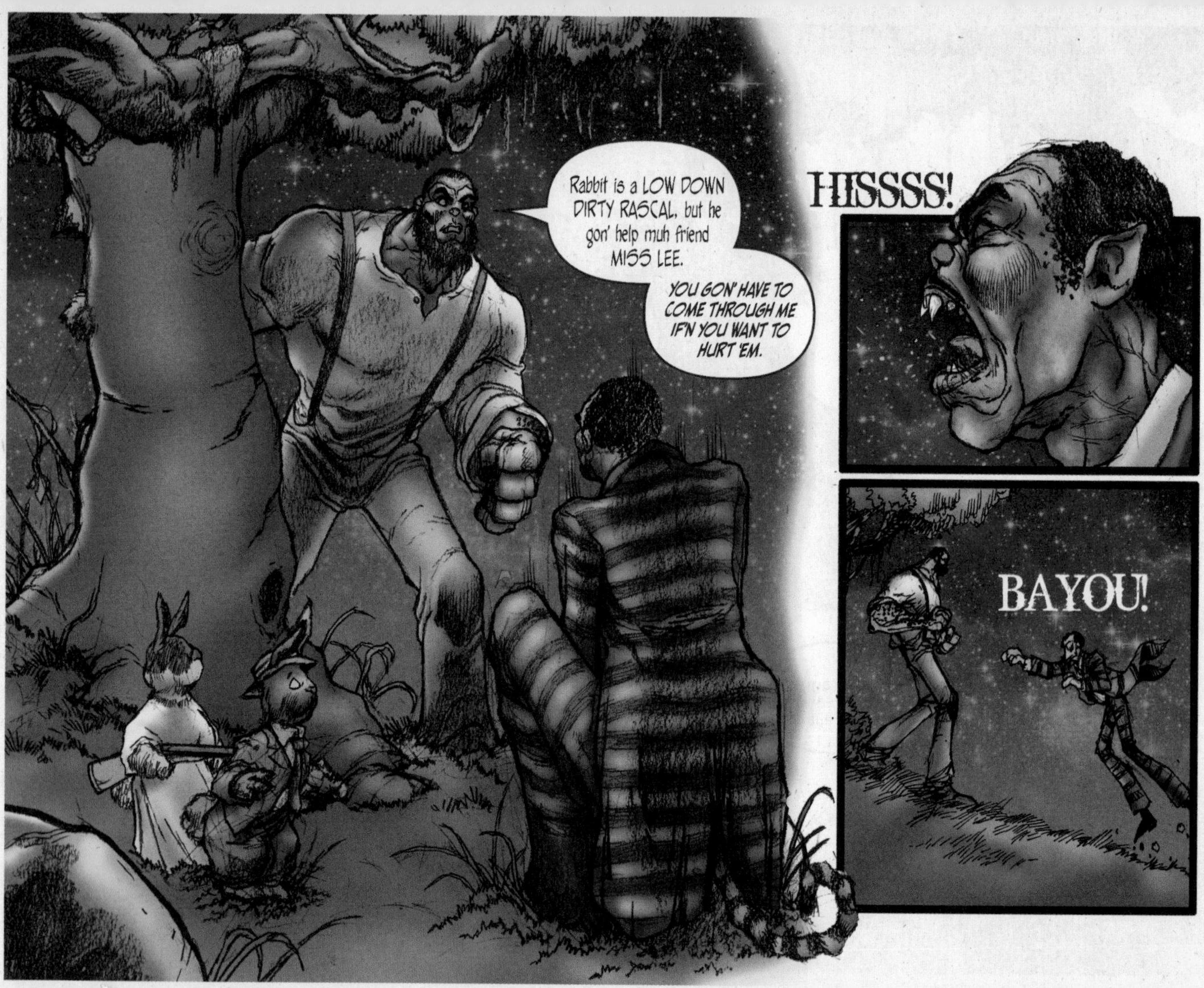
Rabbit is a LOW DOWN DIRTY RASCAL, but he gon' help muh friend MISS LEE.
YOU GON' HAVE TO COME THROUGH ME IF'N YOU WANT TO HURT 'EM.
HISSSS!
BAYOU!

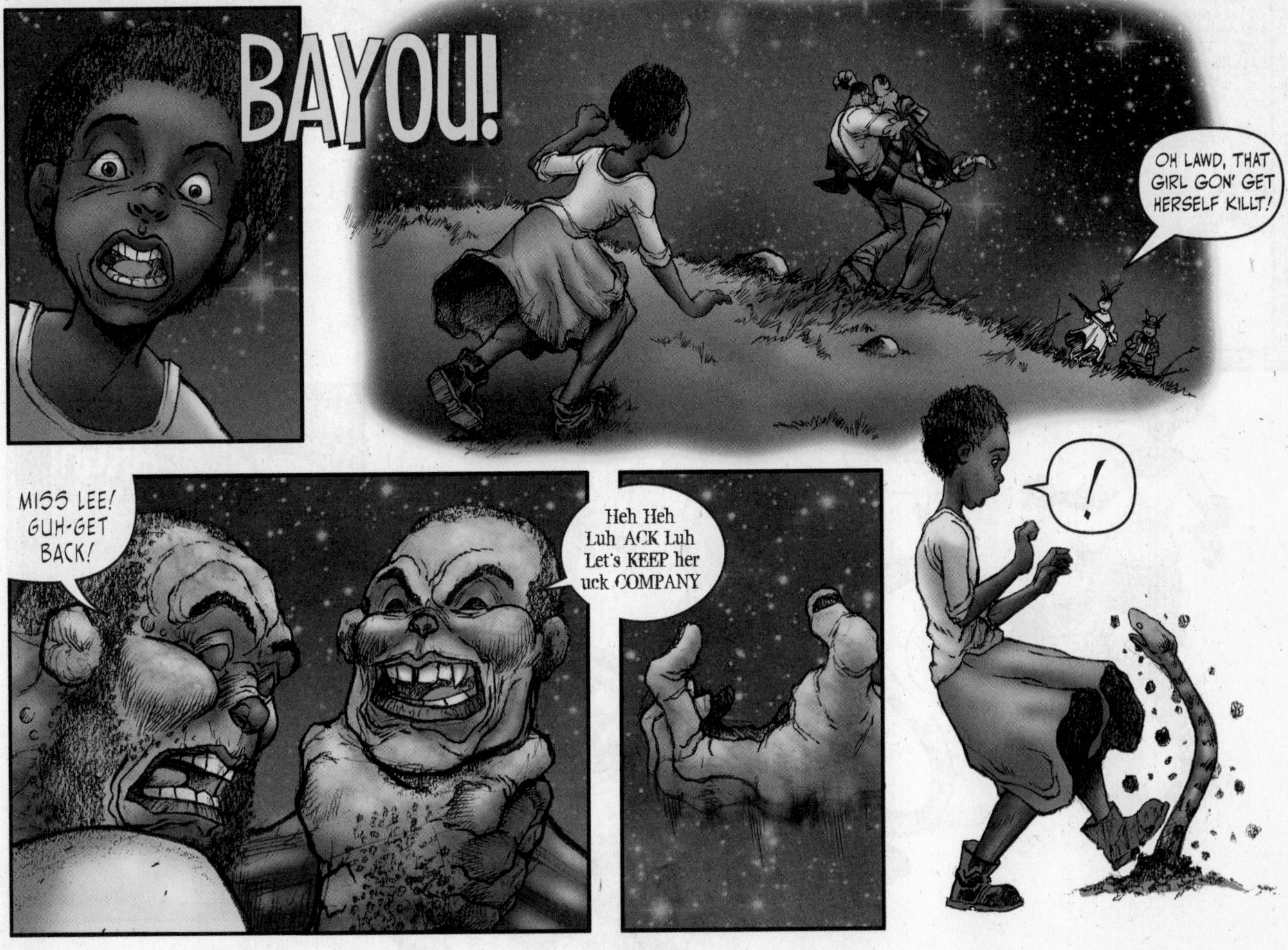
BAYOU!
OH LAWD, THAT GIRL GON' GET HERSELF KILLT!
MISS LEE! GUH-GET BACK!
Heh Heh Luh ACK Luh Let's KEEP her uck COMPANY
!

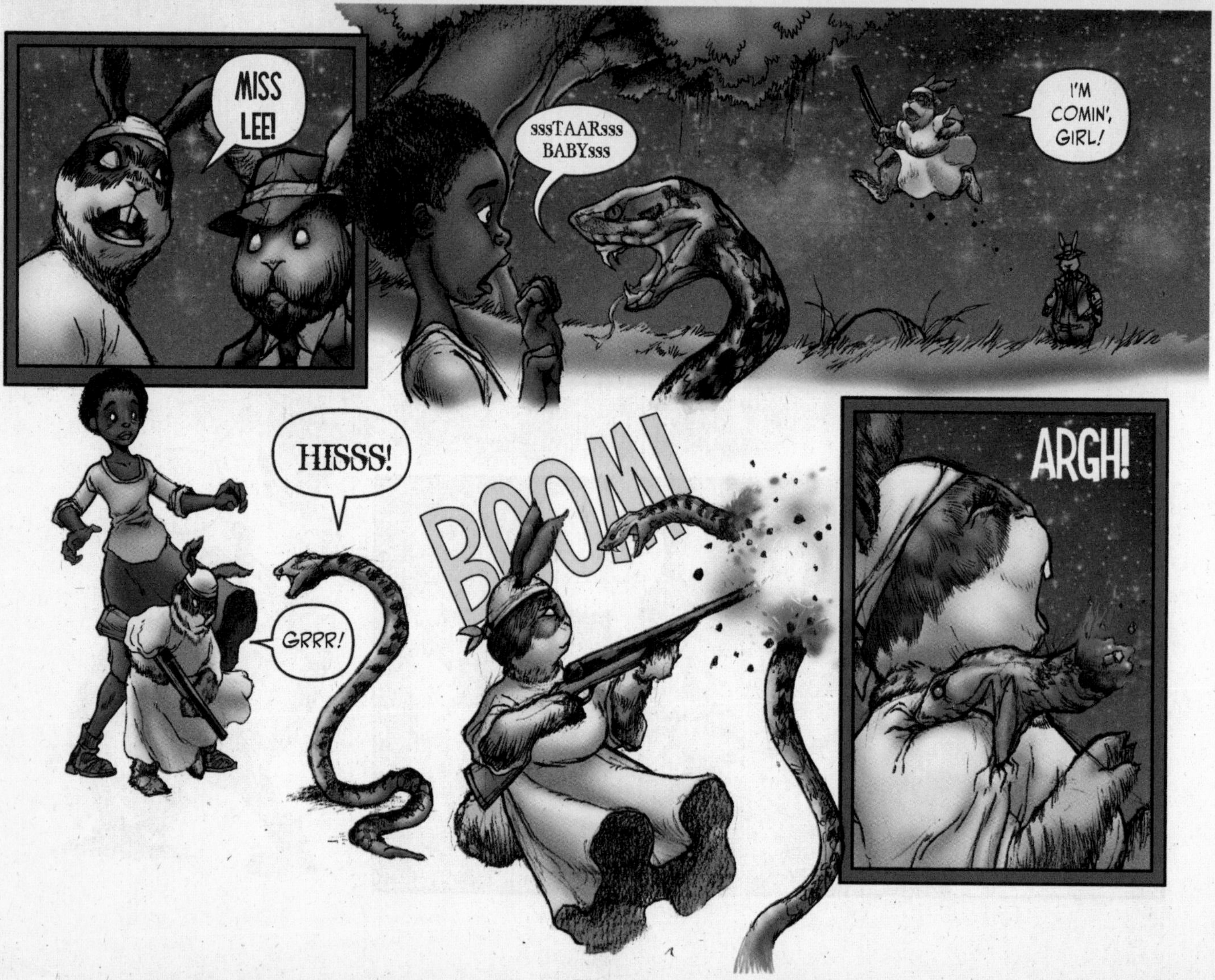
MISS LEE!
sssTAARsss BABYsss
I'M COMIN', GIRL!
HISSS!
GRRR!
BOOM!
ARGH!

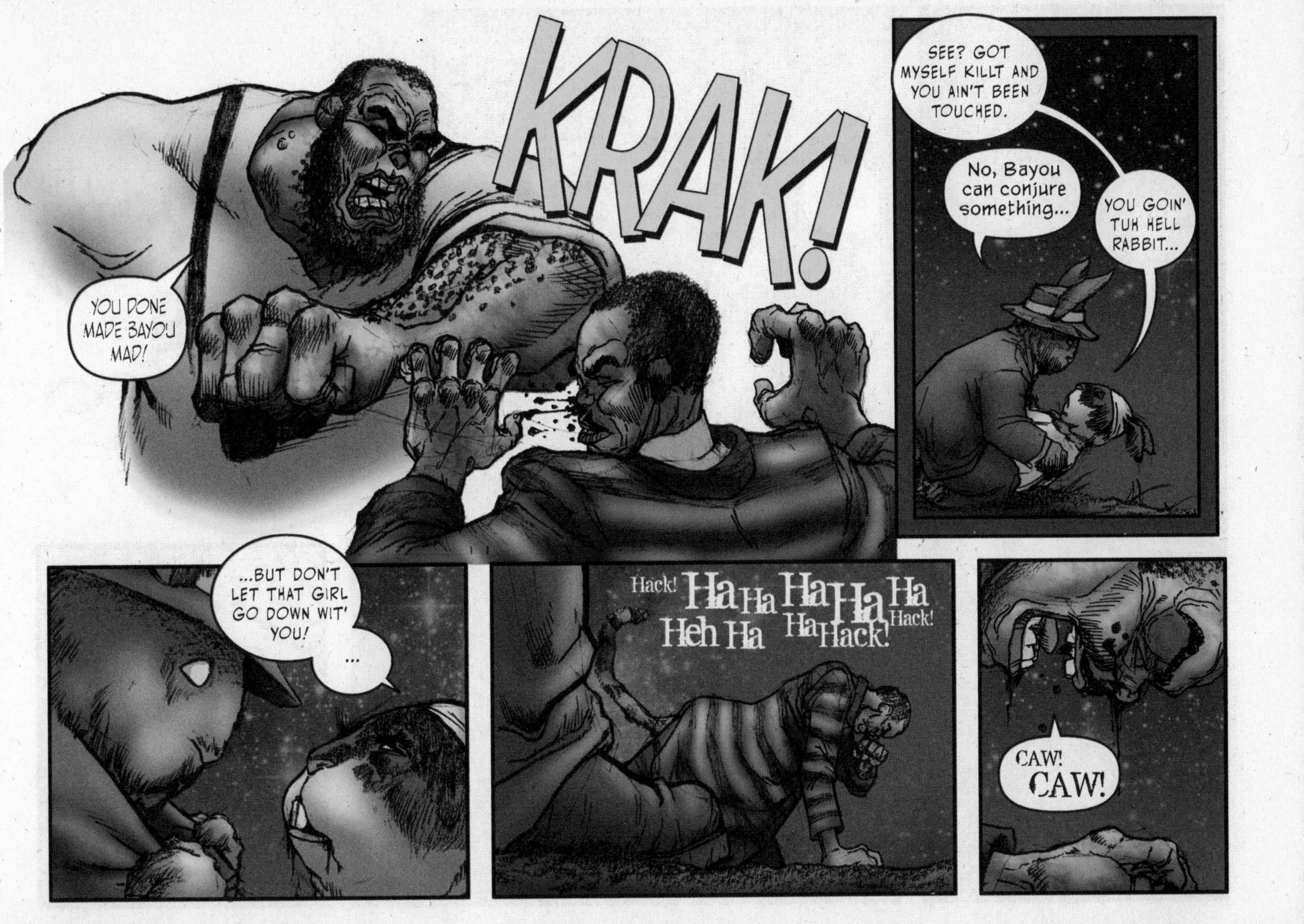
KRAK!
YOU DONE MADE BAYOU MAD!
SEE? GOT MYSELF KILLT AND YOU AIN'T BEEN TOUCHED.
No, Bayou can conjure something...
YOU GOIN' TUH HELL RABBIT...
...BUT DON'T LET THAT GIRL GO DOWN WIT' YOU!
...
Hack! Ha Ha Ha Ha Ha Heh Ha Ha Hack! Hack!
CAW! CAW!

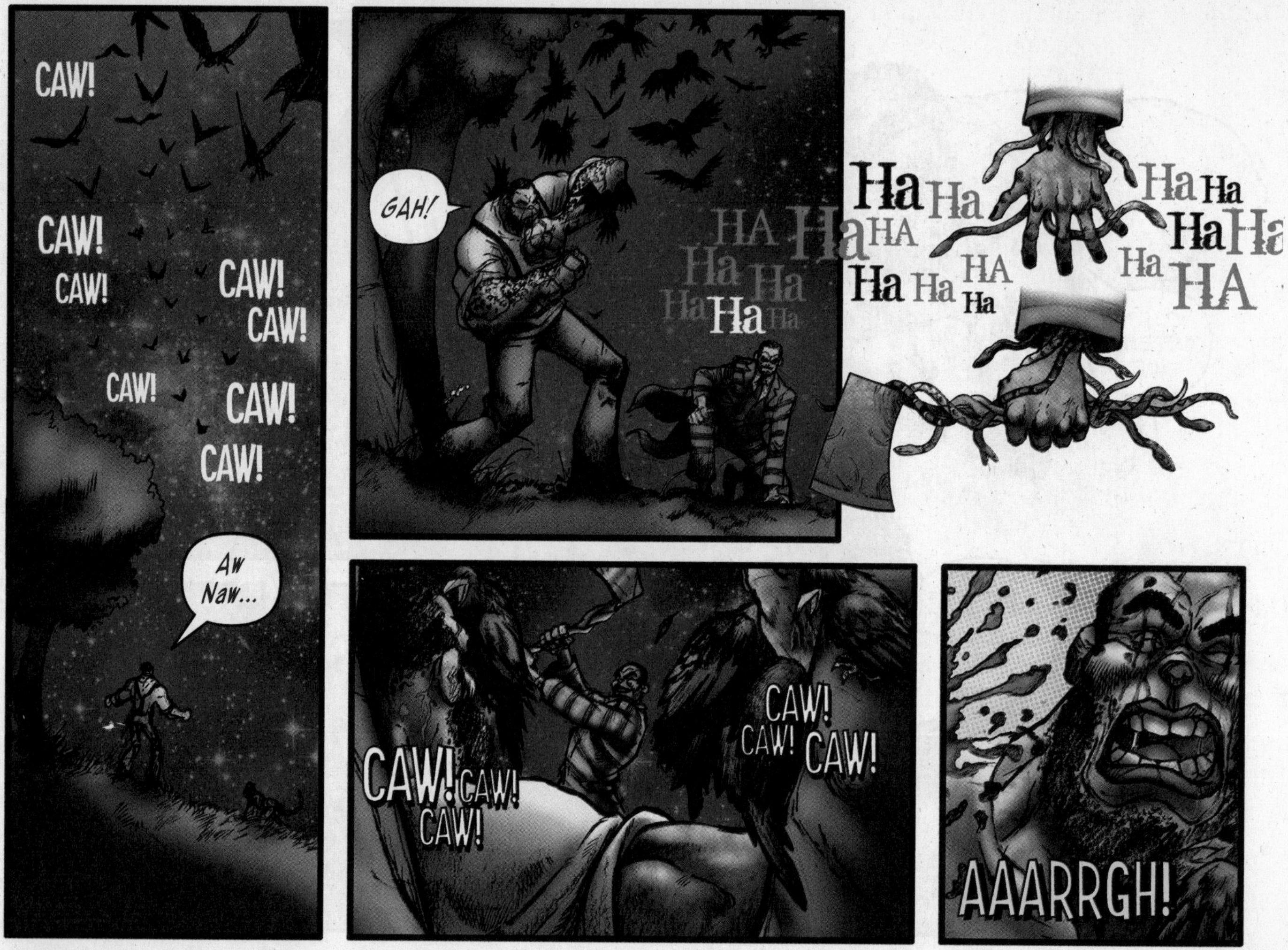
CAW!
CAW!
CAW!
CAW!
CAW!
CAW!
CAW!
CAW!
Aw Naw...
GAH!
HA Ha HA
Ha Ha
Ha Ha Ha
Ha Ha Ha Ha Ha Ha Ha Ha Ha Ha Ha HA Ha HA
CAW! CAW! CAW!
CAW! CAW! CAW!
AAARRGH!

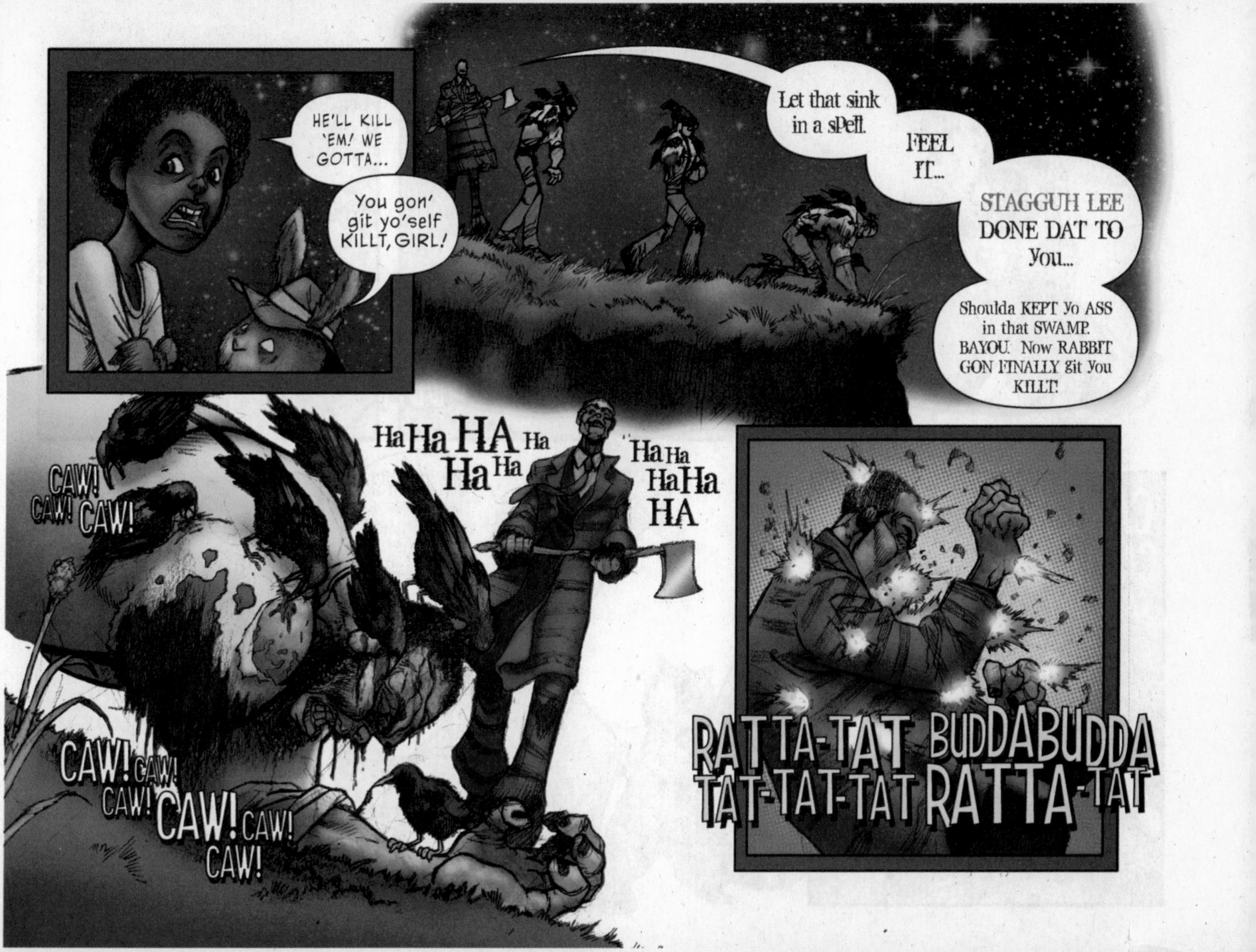
HE'LL KILL 'EM! WE GOTTA...
You gon' git yo'self KILLT, GIRL!
Let that sink in a spell.
FEEL IT...
STAGGUH LEE DONE DAT TO You...
Shoulda KEPT Yo ASS in that SWAMP. BAYOU. Now RABBIT GON FINALLY git You KILLT!
CAW! CAW! CAW!
Ha Ha HA Ha Ha Ha
Ha Ha Ha Ha HA
CAW! CAW! CAW! CAW! CAW! CAW!
RATTA-TAT BUDDABUDDA TAT-TAT-TAT RATTA-TAT

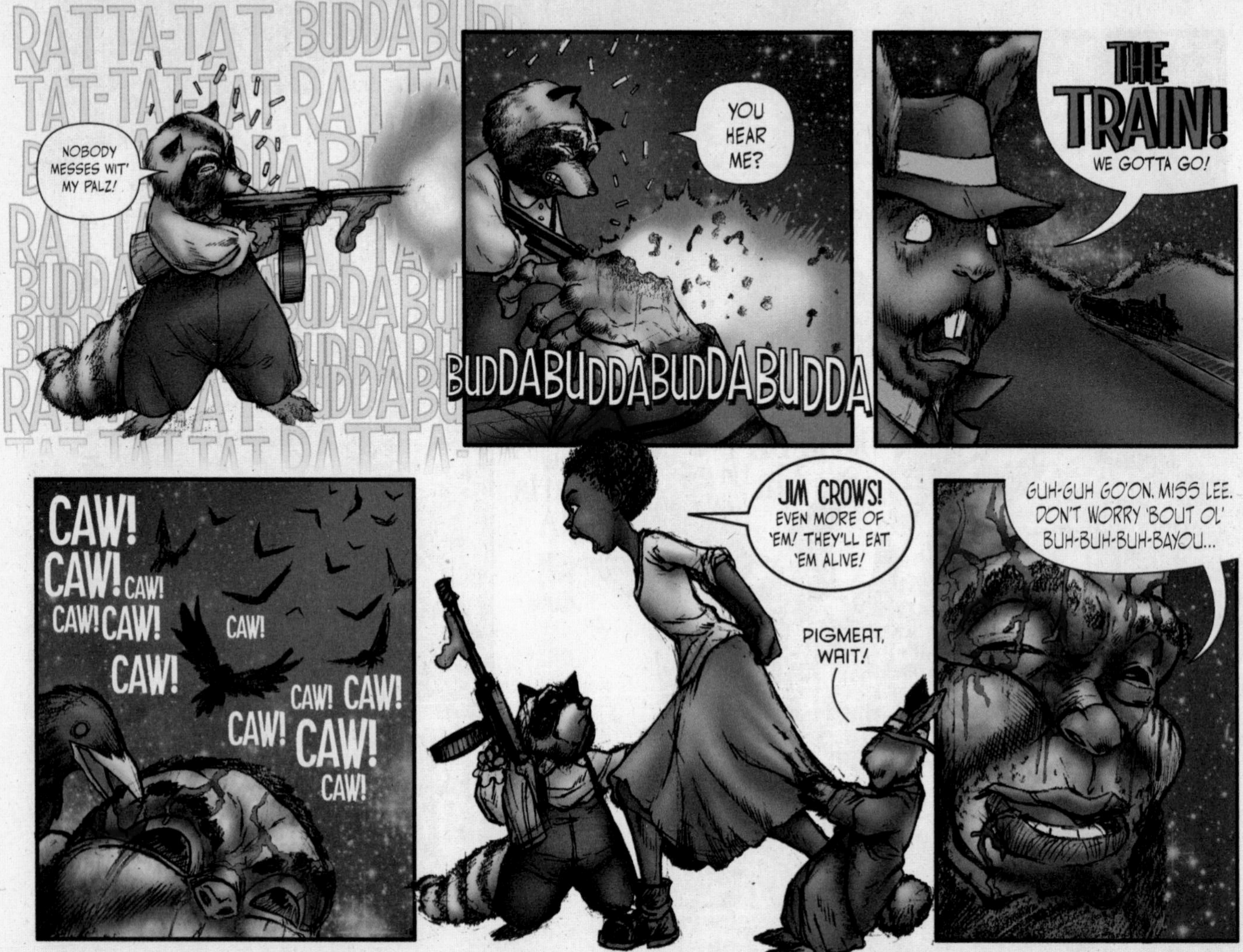

RATTA-TAT
TAT-TAT-TAT
NOBODY MESSES WIT' MY PALZ!
YOU HEAR ME?
BUDDABUDDABUDDABUDDA
THE TRAIN!
WE GOTTA GO!
CAW! CAW! CAW! CAW! CAW! CAW! CAW!
CAW! CAW! CAW! CAW! CAW!
JIM CROWS! EVEN MORE OF 'EM! THEY'LL EAT 'EM ALIVE!
PIGMEAT, WAIT!
GUH-GUH GO'ON, MISS LEE. DON'T WORRY 'BOUT OL' BUH-BUH-BUH-BAYOU...

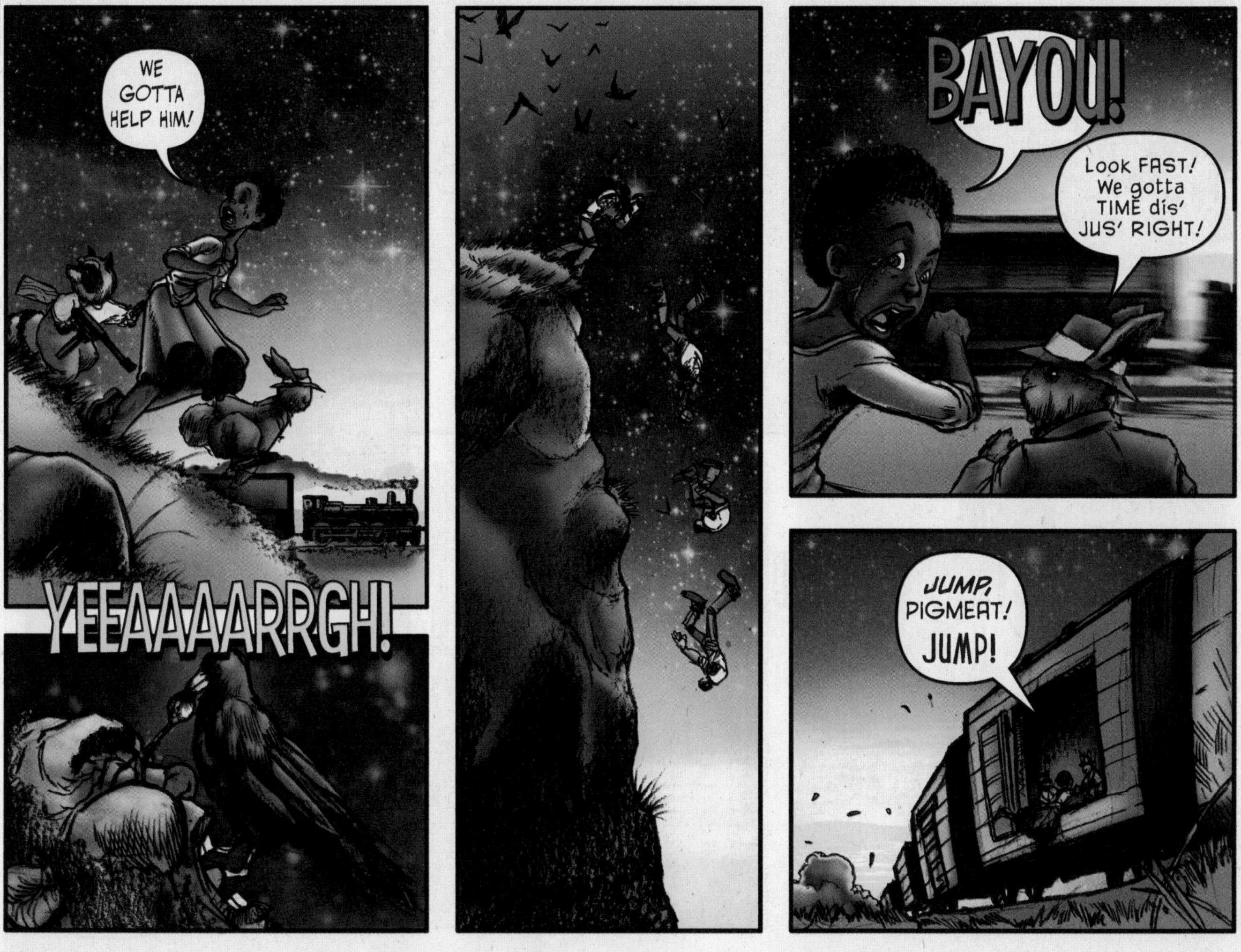
WE GOTTA HELP HIM!
YEEAAAAARRGH!
BAYOU!
Look FAST! We gotta TIME dis' JUS' RIGHT!
JUMP, PIGMEAT! JUMP!

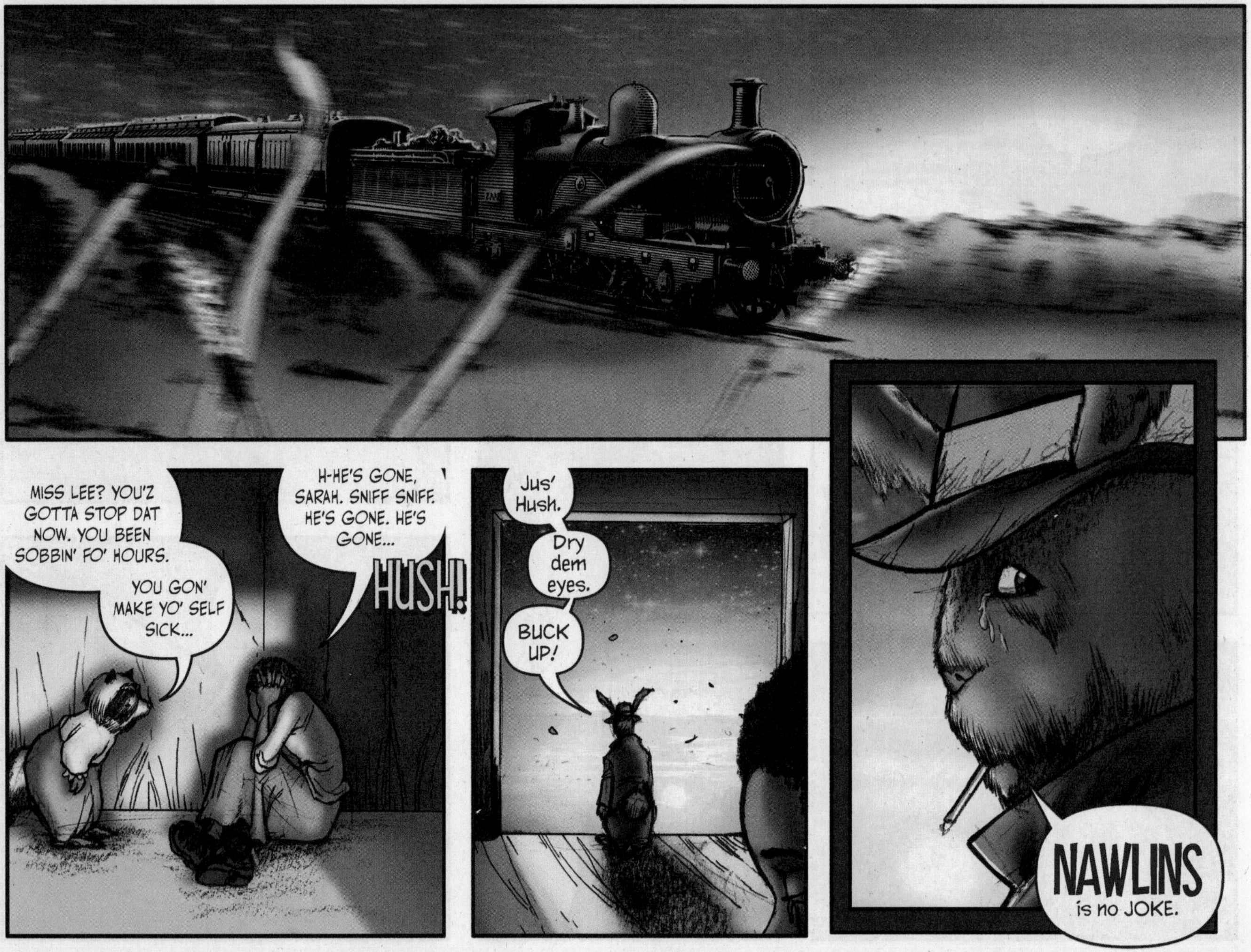
MISS LEE? YOU'Z GOTTA STOP DAT NOW. YOU BEEN SOBBIN' FO' HOURS.
YOU GON' MAKE YO' SELF SICK...
H-HE'S GONE, SARAH. SNIFF SNIFF. HE'S GONE. HE'S GONE...
HUSH!
Jus' Hush.
Dry dem eyes.
BUCK UP!
NAWLINS is no JOKE.

Jeremy Love with his brothers, Robert and Maurice, founded Gettosake Entertainment, home to self-published creations Chocolate Thunder and Fierce. In BAYOU, Love weaves an epic and haunting fantasy set in the Reconstruction-era South.

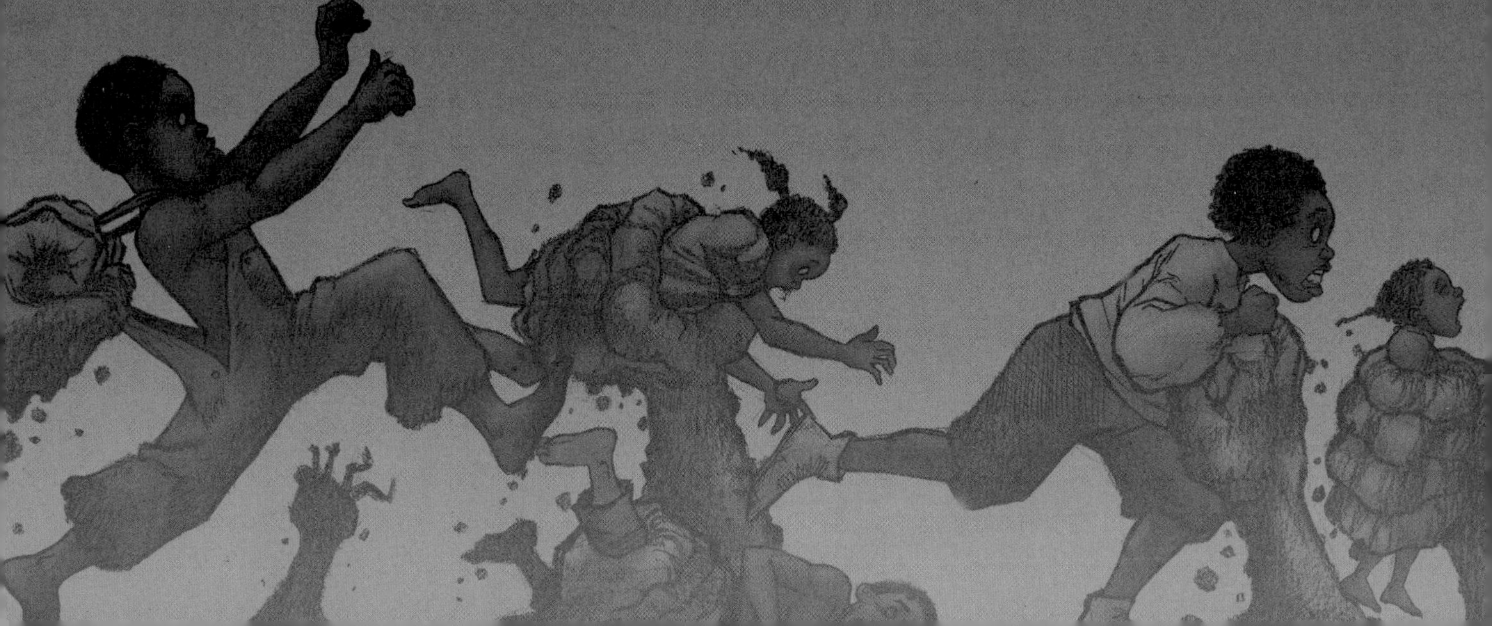

BAYOU

By Jeremy Love

Winner of a record-breaking five Glyph Awards, BAYOU is a critically acclaimed masterpiece.

Eisner-nominated for best digital comic and named great graphic novel for teens by the American Library Association.

IN STORES NOW